DEI 2.0

DEI 2.0

A Toolkit for Building
Your Own Online Diversity Course

Marlo Goldstein Hode, PhD

and

Darvelle Hutchins, PhD

UNIVERSITY OF MISSOURI PRESS

COLUMBIA

Library of Congress Cataloging-in-Publication Data

Names: Goldstein Hode, Marlo, author. | Hutchins, Darvelle, author.
Title: DEI 2.0 : a toolkit for building your own online diversity course /
    Marlo Goldstein Hode and Darvelle Hutchins.
Other titles: Toolkit for building your own online diversity course
Description: Columbia : University of Missouri Press, 2022. | Includes
    bibliographical references.
Identifiers: LCCN 2022013685 | ISBN 9780826222565 (spiral bound)
Subjects: LCSH: College personnel management--Web-based instruction--United
    States. | Diversity in the workplace--Web-based instruction--United
    States | Transformative learning. | Instructional systems--Design.
Classification: LCC LB2331.68 .G65 2022 | DDC 371.3--dc23/eng/20220521
LC record available at https://lccn.loc.gov/2022013685

Typefaces: Aktiv Grotesque and Minion

CONTENTS

Part 3
The Diversity 101 Curriculum

PREFACE

A Few Words from Dr. Marlo Goldstein Hode

Developing the curriculum and the online course presented in this book was a learning journey that started in 2012, when I was a doctoral student at the University of Missouri–Columbia. Because of my extensive background in professional development topics such as intercultural communication and conflict management, I was granted an assistantship in the diversity office. As the only trainer in the office, my ambitious charge was to provide DEI (diversity, equity, and inclusion) professional development for the university's faculty and staff. Given the limited time I had to deliver in-person training, and the limited time that faculty and staff have to participate in meaningful professional development programs, I thought that online learning might be an effective way to reach more people. Surely, I thought, I would be able to find an engaging "off-the-shelf" online DEI course that I might implement at our university. However, after reviewing several products on the market at the time, I realized that existing online training products were highly priced, geared toward the corporate environment, and lacked interactive, thought-provoking activities. That is when I decided to create my own online DEI course, entitled Diversity 101 to align with commonly understood higher education vernacular.

In order to create a curriculum based on best practices, my first step was to conduct a review of the research on DEI training. Doing so revealed that DEI is a broad training topic that one can approach in a variety of ways—not all of which are constructive. In fact, some research suggested that this type of training can evoke strong negative reactions by dominant-group members, a backlash against diversity initiatives, and result in damaged intergroup relations (Curry-Stevens, 2007). For example, training that focuses on raising awareness about specific identity groups runs the risk of reducing individuals to simplified or stereotypical identity characteristics, a phenomenon that only serves to perpetuate stereotypes and ignore intersecting social identities. Additionally, some diversity training is based on implicit assumptions about the way people function rather than social theories of human behavior or psychology.

In order to avoid these pitfalls, the Diversity 101 curriculum provided in this book is based on social science theories and research. It is designed to help participants develop cultural competence, which starts with the fostering of a greater awareness of one's own identity, culture, implicit biases, and privilege. In this learning process, participants engage in activities and discussions that help them gain new perspectives and increase their capacity to empathize (Goldstein Hode, Behm-Morawitz, & Hays, 2017; Hutchins & Goldstein Hode, 2021). As their sense of understanding and self-efficacy related to DEI grows, participants are more motivated to take action toward creating a more inclusive and equitable campus.

Because the course proved so successful with faculty and staff, it was later transformed into a credit-bearing course for upper-level Communication students. Although the core of the curriculum remained the same, the student version was enhanced with additional required readings, assignments, and a final project to provide the academic rigor necessary for a credit-bearing course. To help facilitate the course, I enlisted the help of Dr. Darvelle Hutchins, my coauthor, who was a PhD student at the time. We were thrilled to see students grappling with new concepts, engaging in meaningful dialogue, and applying what they had learned along the way to their final projects. With each successive semester that we offer the course, we learned new lessons, which we applied by continuing to revise and improve the assignments and rubrics.

Given our success with, and the increasing demand for, the course we developed, we are excited to offer this book as a way to give educators and practitioners at other colleges and universities the necessary tools to develop, facilitate, and evaluate an effective DEI course for faculty, staff, and students. Although off-the-shelf products have improved since 2012, we believe that a customized, in-house course experience may help participants connect better with each other and the content.

We have made many additions and improvements to the course over the years as we respond to an ever-changing landscape in the social justice world. Online pedagogy, technology, and available resources have also evolved in ways that allow for more types of engagement and a wealth of rich content.

> **To reflect the changes and improvements we've made along the way, the name of our book is DEI 2.0. However, we decided to keep the original name of the course and the curriculum, Diversity 101, because it clearly signifies what it is: a foundational DEI course for the higher education context.**

A Few Words from Dr. Darvelle Hutchins

Although I have worked alongside diverse populations for many years, lived in urban/metropolitan cities, and attended public, private, and technical college and university campuses, I think the genesis of my work in diversity, equity, inclusion, and belonging began with my graduate student experience at Marquette University in the year of 2015. I was teaching a communication seminar when a Black female student approached me to ask whether I felt a sense of belonging at Marquette's predominately White campus. With few faculty members, staff, and students who visibly looked like me (Black, male, 6-foot-3), her question got me thinking—so much so that I spent my graduate communication studies degree program taking courses on identity, identification, organizational communication, and organizational rhetoric. For my master's thesis project, I explored how institutions of higher education rhetorically communicate their valuation of and commitment to diversity and inclusion, and whether they aligned in actual practice in the lived experiences of Black faculty members. I continued to explore my interest in DEI in my doctoral program at the University of Missouri–Columbia (Mizzou), where I met Dr. Marlo Goldstein Hode.

After receiving acceptance into the Organizational Communication PhD program at Mizzou, a rare opportunity came available where the University's diversity office was looking for a graduate researcher to analyze and report data to support the implementation of the Inclusive Excellence framework across the University of Missouri System and to help create materials to assist academic and functional units in creating their Inclusive Excellence plans and setting action priorities around diversity, inclusion, and equity. Through my experience in this role, I solidified my foundational knowledge and skills related to key DEI concepts, the inclusive excellence framework, and learning how to create a space for difficult conversations. I had the opportunity to apply this knowledge and skill set in the teaching of the upper-level communication course that Dr. Goldstein Hode designed based on the Diversity 101 curriculum presented in this book. Dr. Goldstein Hode and I continued to collaborate in making course improvements and in conducting research on the impact of the course on participants' transformative learning. The culmination of our journey together is this book.

If someone had asked me back in 2015 where I saw myself professionally in the next five or ten years, I am sure that writing a book on diversity was not within my purview. But the reality is that although I had worked in human resources for several years, I was already doing DEI-focused work. I did not realize it at the time, but my conception of diversity work was narrow (limited to race and visible differences) and conflated with affirmative action goals. Further, I knew the unfortunate truth that many organizations regarded diversity and inclusion as window dressing and were not genuinely interested in the inclusion and belonging of all organizational members. This way of thinking was living and breathing in my experience as a diversity strategist at a telecommunication company in the midwestern United States where women's voices were silenced by men who often led and controlled the discourse in corporate meetings. In this workplace, minoritized employees were privy to conversations that reproduced stereotypes of their identities. The company was silent about social issues that impacted its underrepresented employees, and leaders failed to be transparent with employees about its diversity efforts. This type of experience and the challenges we face in our work every day kept me thinking about how to best design a facilitator guide that supports transformative diversity work. All this to say, I am honored to serve as coauthor of this timely resource so early in my career in the field of diversity.

In my work, I create space for productive dialogue on issues related to equity, inclusion, and intersectional diverse identities. I also research, design, implement, and coordinate DEI learning opportunities to increase cultural competence for faculty, staff, and students. The curricular framework presented within this book has been instrumental to my success in these endeavors. I am confident that you too will find value in this comprehensive facilitation guide, and I look forward to hearing about your successes and challenges in engaging in this meaningful work.

DEI Terminology

Words have power to include or exclude people, and therefore we should be intentional about our word choice. It is also true that the language of diversity is always evolving, and one size does not fit all. Because this book is designed to be an entry point into diversity, equity, and inclusion (DEI) education, we do not use some of the more popularized terminology used in social justice and antiracist circles. For example, in this book, we use the term *People of Color* (or POC) as an umbrella term to refer to people from various racial and ethnic backgrounds. The term *POC* emphasizes the common experience of racism experienced by racial and ethnic groups who are not White. However, the term *BIPOC* (Black, Indigenous, and People of Color) has become more widely used in social justice circles in order to highlight the specific racism and historic oppression experienced by Black and Indigenous communities. It is important to use this terminology particularly within the context of teaching and learning about Whiteness, White supremacy, and systemic racism. However, these topics are beyond the scope of our introductory curriculum, and so we use the more mainstream term *People of Color*.

We also use the term *minority/minorities*, rather than the term *minoritized*, which has become more popularized, particularly in higher education. The term *minoritized* is used to highlight the social construction of race that subordinates people who are not identified as White. To teach with this term entails providing an understanding of socialization and the social construction of race, gender, and other subordinated groups. Again, our choice was to use terminology that is more familiar to more people. However, if you feel comfortable and your course participants seem ready, we encourage you to take this approach.

Defining (or Not Defining) Diversity

There is no universal concept of *diversity*. Typically each organization defines it in its own way or neglects to define it at all (Point & Singh, 2003). Thus, it is a term that has become infused with various and contested meanings, each one connected to a particular set of statements, policies, and practices intended to increase, embrace, celebrate, or simply tolerate diversity. The ambiguous, amorphous nature of the term allows it take on different meanings with different effects. On the one hand, the term *diversity* can be a vehicle for action and accountability when it is constructed as a universal benefit (e.g., "Diversity is important for education") and integrated into institutional goals (e.g., in a mission statement, strategic plan, inclusive excellence plan, etc.). Simultaneously, diversity can "be defined in ways that reproduce rather than challenge social privilege" (Ahmed, 2007, p. 240) by concealing systemic inequities and privilege through feel-good-everybody-wins definitions of the term.

Often, the definition of diversity is constructed as either *all-inclusive* (everybody is diverse in some way) or *exclusive* to certain (previously excluded) groups. The all-inclusive approach postulates that differences such as race, class, gender, sexual orientation, disability, religion, education, age, political beliefs, and intellectual ideas are all aspects of diversity and therefore all individuals can be considered as *equally unique* (Kersten, 2000). While the idea of all-inclusive diversity has a certain appeal, this apolitical framing of it fails to promote an understanding or acknowledgment of the socially and historically constructed, hierarchically arranged nature of different identities; nor does it address the differentials of power and privilege ascribed to different identity categories (Hu-DeHart, 2000). In effect, by including everyone under the feel-good umbrella of diversity, structural inequalities, racism, sexism, discrimination, and harassment become decoupled from the understanding and agenda of diversity.

On the other side of this dichotomy, diversity is often defined as a quality attributed exclusively to certain "others," those who are different from the dominant norm and who have been historically marginalized and excluded in organizations and institutions. This *exclusive* conceptualization of diverse groups is also problematic. Although it acknowledges historically discriminated and marginalized groups, it may actually serve to perpetuate and foster that marginalization by constructing diverse individuals as *outsiders* in need of special consideration, while those with dominant identities are constructed as the "norm" or the "standard" by which the "outsiders" are judged (Iverson, 2012).

While neither the *all-inclusive* nor the *exclusive* model of diversity is ideal, we do not propose a solution to this tension; rather, we resist the temptation to offer a simple, either-or definition. Instead, in this book we help participants grapple with the complexity of the term and learn how to deploy it strategically and contextually.

Why This Book?

We decided to write this book after having received numerous inquiries from colleagues at different colleges and universities around the nation, all of whom were eagerly—in some cases desperately—searching for a premade course or substantial help with creating online diversity modules or courses, just as we had been a few years earlier. At the time, our diversity office's website promoting Diversity 101 was one of the first results to show up in a keyword search for "online diversity course higher education." In other words, there was not a whole lot else out there. Although off-the-shelf products have evolved and improved over the past few years, we continue to maintain that the best learning product is one that is made in-house and customized to the institution or organization in question. While we do not contend that our course is the best diversity education program available, our research and experience working with more than 1,000 individuals who have completed it indicate that it can be effective for a wide range of participants.

While there are many people who prefer face-to-face learning environments, we contend that the online environment can be perhaps an even more effective way to facilitate cognitive, affective, and behavioral learning of faculty, staff, and students. This is because, as will be discussed in the introduction, the online format has some distinct advantages over a face-to-face setting when it comes to facilitating learning about some of the challenging, even potentially upsetting, topics and concepts that a course in diversity comprises. Engaging in asynchronous online communication gives participants the time necessary for critical reflection and to formulate meaningful, well-thought-out responses to discussion prompts and peers' comments. This reflective aspect of the online environment is one reason that it can be conducive to *transformative learning*.

Transformative learning is a framework for designing and facilitating a self-reflective process through which adults can experience a change in deeply held beliefs based on problematic frames of reference for understanding the world and social relations (Curry-Stevens, 2007). In our current sociopolitical context, it is more critical than ever that our institutions of higher education provide this type of professional development opportunity so that we can effectively and collectively address the long-standing issues of systemic racism and inequality as they play out in the small daily interactions, practices, and unspoken norms on our campuses.

Our hope is that this book will serve as an encouraging and practical resource to help you lead and guide this important transformational process. To this end, we provide you with clear instructions and abundant resources to build your own engaging and transformative online DEI course tailored for faculty, staff, or students at your institution or organization. In addition to this facilitator's guide, we have created an accompanying participant workbook that provides those enrolled in the course with useful worksheets, summaries of course content, and additional resources to further their learning. You will also have access to online (and downloadable) PDFs of course documents that you can save and adjust to your needs. Together, these resources provide a complete, yet customizable, DEI course. We wish you the best of luck and thank you for taking on this important work in your institution!

Preface References

Ahmed, S. (2007). The language of diversity. *Ethnic and Racial Studies*, 30(2), 235–256.

Curry-Stevens, A. (2007). New forms of transformative education pedagogy for the privileged. *Journal of Transformative Education*, 5(1), 33–58. https://doi.org/10.1177/1541344607299394

Goldstein Hode, M., Behm-Morawitz, E., & Hays, A. (2017). Testing the effectiveness of an online diversity course for faculty and staff. *Journal of Diversity in Higher Education*. https://doi.org/10.1037/dhe0000063

Hu-DeHart, E. (2000). The diversity project: Institutionalizing multiculturalism or managing differences. *Academe*, 86(5), 39–42.

Hutchins, D., & Goldstein Hode, M. (2021). Exploring faculty and staff development of cultural competence through communicative learning in an online diversity course. *Journal of Diversity in Higher Education*, 14(4), 468–479. https://doi.org/10.1037/dhe0000162

Iverson, S. V. (2012). Constructing outsiders: The discursive framing of access in university diversity policies. *The Review of Higher Education*, 35(2), 149–177.

Kersten, A. (2000). Diversity management: Dialogue, dialectics and diversion. *Journal of Organizational Change Management*, 13(3), 235–248.

Point, S., & Singh, V. (2003). Defining and dimensionalising diversity: Evidence from corporate websites across Europe. *European Management Journal*, 21(6), 750–76.

INTRODUCTION

It is not our differences that divide us. It is our inability to recognize, accept, and celebrate those differences.

—Audre Lorde

People tend to have a lot of preconceived ideas about diversity training based on either their own experiences or things they have heard others say. Frankly, not all these preconceived ideas are positive. The television show *The Office* produced a widely popular episode called "Diversity Day" that exemplifies a nightmare scenario of a workplace diversity training exercise. The oblivious office manager, played by Steve Carell, facilitates an activity in which the participants are given an index card with one racial or ethnic identity group written on it. Without looking at what identity group their index card bears, they are instructed to place it on their forehead, then mingle around the room and treat people according to the stereotypes of the group written on the index card on their respective foreheads. The idea is that participants are supposed to guess what identity group is written on their index card based on the stereotypical things that people say to them. As painfully hilarious as this episode is, it also exemplifies some of the worst practices of diversity training: reinforcing stereotypes, reducing individuals to a single identity, causing extreme discomfort, and focusing on minorities.

People also have preconceived ideas about online learning, both positive and negative. Some people view online courses as a necessary, but deficient, substitute for face-to-face environments; some people prefer the online environment because it allows them to participate more passively; and still others have not had any experience taking an online course and fear it will be difficult to figure out and navigate. In general, people do not associate online learning with personal growth and transformation.

While it may seem that these preconceived ideas about both diversity training and online learning may work against the possible effectiveness of Diversity 101, it has been our experience that these negative expectations actually work *in favor* of the course. The initial modules gently disrupt participants' previously existing expectations about diversity training and online learning while at the same time creating a sense of safety. This builds the foundation for transformative learning, as will be discussed in the next section.

Transformative Learning Online

The Diversity 101 course design and curriculum were developed based on the tenets of transformative learning theory. The goal of transformative learning is "to understand why we see the world the way we do and to shake off the constraints of the limiting perspectives we carry with us into the learning experience" (Palloff & Pratt, 2007, p. 187). In other words, transformative learning is intended to *transform* the way that participants view themselves in relation to other individuals in organizations and large social systems. The Diversity 101 curriculum draws on relevant theories from intercultural communication, conflict resolution, organizational communication, sociology, and psychology to provide learners with the opportunity to critically examine their own perspectives and develop new ways of thinking about themselves and the world around them.

The online environment offers some distinct advantages over face-to-face environments for creating and fostering positive interactive learning communities—the foundation of transformative learning processes (Palloff & Pratt, 2007). Difficult and uncomfortable discussions about identity, racism, bias, and privilege ideally should begin after the participants have had the time to build a sense of trust and connection with one another, which requires a significant amount of time and sustained engagement. Since it is typically difficult for faculty and staff to commit to the time needed to do this type of work in a face-to-face environment, the online platform provides a convenient way for them to first get to know each other, then engage with and reflect on the content before participating in online discussions about these challenging topics.

Although research suggests that intergroup contact is an important way to build trust among members of different identity groups (Paluck, 2006; Pettigrew & Tropp, 2006; Tajfel, 1978), it can be very difficult to create safe, equitable, and sustainable face-to-face engagement opportunities for all participants. When, for example, a group of participants includes just a few people of color among a larger number of White people, the people of color may not feel comfortable to speak freely about their views and experiences. Likewise, White participants may not feel comfortable raising their questions or concerns for fear of offending or inviting blame (Case, 2007). The disembodied nature of online learning, in which our physical identities are not always visually present, can help mitigate some of these issues. This freedom from focus on our physical attributes helps to build a sense of community and safety and enables participants to engage more freely with each other over issues of diversity and inclusion. Moreover, online discussions can help promote more equality in participation by avoiding the dominance of certain voices and per-spectives, as often occurs in face-to-face settings.

In addition to mitigating some of the issues that can arise face-to-face, the online platform is conducive to promoting two of the key elements of transformative learn-ing: reflection and collaborative learning (Merryfield, 2001; Palloff & Pratt, 2007; Shea et al., 2005). The online format gives participants the time to reflect before responding—which is often not the case in an in-person setting—and therefore they may respond more thoughtfully to discussion prompts or peers' posts. Some online platforms also provide an option for participants to keep course-related journals in which they can confidentially share with the course facilitator their honest reflections on the course and the discussions, another tool for promoting meaningful reflection. Collaborative learning occurs through the dialogic process of reading and responding to other participants' discussion board posts.

Although transformative learning is essentially a peer-to-peer process, the fa-cilitator of the online diversity course plays both a central and sidelined position. In a more traditional instructional setting, the instructor is typically situated as an expert on the subject matter who helps students gain knowledge. In contrast, facil-itators of this diversity course should consider themselves as a learner engaged in the process along with the other participants. Everyone is an expert on their own lives, so each individual has important and valuable contributions to make. Thus, the learning community is a collaboration between facilitator and participants, one in which all parties are accountable and responsible (Hord, 2009). The role of the fa-cilitator is to help participants explore and question their own assumptions, beliefs, and points of view, as well as to generate and integrate alternative perspectives and new frames of reference. We also recognize that students in a credit-bearing course need more direct instruction and detailed feedback than participants in a professional development program, so in the section of this book focused on stu-dents, we refer to the role of *instructor* rather than facilitator, although guidance, tips, and examples of transformative facilitation provided in this book apply to both facilitators and instructors.

Diversity 101 Is for Everyone

Diversity 101 is designed as a voluntary, non-credit-bearing course for faculty and staff, who usually do not have a lot of extra time for professional development. Therefore, the required content and tasks are designed to provide meaningful, yet manageable (timewise), learning opportunities without extensive reading or writing assignments. Additional resources are provided each week to meet the needs of those who want to explore the module topics more deeply.

The Diversity 101 curriculum is designed to *meet learners where they are in their journey*. In other words, it is built on the assumption that those taking the course have varying levels of experience with and exposure to diversity and inclusion topics. It is accessible enough for people who are new to the topic, yet the approach is novel enough that even people who have considered these issues for some time will gain new insights, tools, and ways to think about them. The curriculum is also appropriate for people from any identity group, because it is based on the idea that each of us is a member of multiple identity groups; therefore, all participants have the opportunity to build self-awareness around dominant and nondominant aspects of our multifaceted identities. Finally, although the curriculum is designed for faculty and staff, the content and the activities are appropriate for students as well.

Although the course is called Diversity 101, it is appropriate for people at varying levels of preexisting knowledge about diversity and inclusion. For those who are new to the concepts, it's a great way to be introduced to them. For those who are already quite familiar with the topics, it's a good way to see and hear other perspectives as well as interact with colleagues from all over the University.

—Past participant

Book Content: Overview

Part 1 of the book provides the "Nuts and Bolts" to help you build your course and develop your skills as an online facilitator for a professional development course for faculty and staff or an instructor for a credit-bearing version of the course. The chapter on "Building and Facilitating Diversity 101" provides tips for creating video lectures, discusses the importance of finding your voice, and explains the different ways to maintain your online presence. The tips and practices in this chapter apply to any facilitating context (faculty, staff, and students).

While the curriculum is mostly the same for the faculty/staff course and the student course, there are additional considerations and issues when facilitating this course for students as a credit-bearing course, such as online classroom management, grading, attending to teacher-student power dynamics, and additional coursework to lend academic rigor to the core curriculum. We outline these differences in "Guidance for a Credit-Bearing Course" in part 2 and provide ample additional resources to support in the online resources.

After addressing the *how* of building and facilitating the course in part 1, part 2 delves into the *what*. The Diversity 101 curriculum offered in this book consists of nine modules structured developmentally so that each successive module builds on the previous ones in order of increasing challenge. The first three modules of the course are designed to ease the participants into the course with foundational, thought-provoking, and nonthreatening concepts such as understanding of diversity, inclusion, and identity. Building on this foundation, the following three modules introduce the challenging topics of unconscious bias, microaggressions, and privilege. The last three modules are designed to move from awareness to action by providing concepts, tools, and frameworks to enable participants to apply their learning to their organizational contexts.

Because the modules are designed to guide participants through a developmental process of learning, it is not recommended that you change the order in which we have presented them. However, the modules are designed to be relatively short, so you have flexibility in terms of how much content you cover at a time. As will be discussed in the chapter "Guidance for a Credit-Bearing Course," you can adapt the curriculum for use in a full-semester or an intensive online 8-week course. The table below provides a visual overview of the course modules, followed by a detailed description.

Curriculum Overview

Curriculum Part 1: Building a Foundation

Module 1: Growing a Learning Community

Module 2: Introduction to Diversity

Module 3: Diversity at the Interpersonal Level

Curriculum Part 2: Obstacles to Inclusion

Module 4: Introduction to Unconscious Bias

Module 5: Introduction to Microaggressions

Module 6: Introduction to Privilege

Curriculum Part 3: From Awareness to Action

Module 7: Inclusive Excellence

Module 8: Inclusion in Action

Module 9: Looking Back and Moving Forward

The first module, "Growing a Learning Community," sets the tone and expectations for participation in a peer-learning environment, as well as gives participants a safe and fun way to start to get to know one another. Module 2, "Introduction to

Diversity," takes a novel approach to introducing the concept of *diversity* by exploring the myriad meanings that the word invokes in organizational contexts. To help participants move beyond the idea that diversity is simply about "doing the right thing" in regard to people who are "different," this module provides a holistic, multilevel framework for understanding the importance of diversity in all of our lives. Module 3, "Diversity at the Interpersonal Level," engages participants in an identity mapping activity to highlight the complex, multilayered nature of our identities and the importance of digging below the surface level of people's identities. This module also helps raise participants' awareness about how they define and view their own identities and how that in turn influences how they relate to others.

Because these initial modules are typically not what participants expect from an online "diversity" course, the critical reflection and self-awareness provoked by the content can trigger the process of *transformative learning*. Transformative learning processes begin with a *disorienting dilemma*, a situation in which people have an experience that does not fit their expectation and causes a shift in thinking or perspective (Mezirow, 1997). These modules also serve to enhance participants' intrinsic motivation (affective learning) to work toward helping to create a more inclusive campus environment, which helps the participant confront the challenges of the next set of modules.

The next part of the curriculum, "Obstacles to Inclusion" (Modules 4, 5, and 6), is designed to build participants' empathy and understanding of the lived experiences of people who are different from themselves, as well as the underlying structures and power dynamic that reinforce inequality and oppression. Module 4, "Introduction to Unconscious Bias," provides a research-based and accessible overview of unconscious bias—something all of us have—and some ways to mitigate its influence on our decision-making processes. Module 5, "Introduction to Microaggressions," takes a nuanced and balanced approach to introducing this somewhat controversial concept and its potentially harmful effects. Module 6, "Introduction to Privilege," is perhaps the most difficult for participants to grapple with because it challenges their understanding of their place in the world in terms of dominant and nondominant aspects of their identity that they may not have previously considered. This module presents an intersectional approach to the concept of privilege, one that focuses on race, gender, social class, sexual orientation, gender identity, physical ability, and religion. This approach allows all participants to explore those aspects of their identity that afford or deny them unseen and unearned privileges. The content in this part of the module provides the basis for real transformative learning, as participants try to develop new ways to understand themselves, their thoughts, their behaviors, and the ways in which society treats them and others.

Typically, participants are motivated to make changes after these three challenging modules. Therefore, the final part of the curriculum, "From Awareness to Action" (Modules 7, 8, and 9), provides frameworks, tools, and concepts to help people formulate concrete plans for next steps and applying what they have learned. Module 7 introduces an "Inclusive Excellence" framework to help participants conceptualize how DEI needs to be integrated into all aspects of an academic instiution's functioning. By completing hands-on activities, participants begin to look at their environment through a lens of inclusion, which will inform their action-planning in the next module. Module 8, "Inclusion in Action," helps develop participants' sense of self-efficacy and motivation to take actions toward creating a more inclusive campus culture. The final module, "Looking Back and Moving Forward," does not introduce new content but rather provides a thoughtful course wrap-up and reflection. It gives participants the opportunity to reflect on their learning journey through the course, as well as share their hopes and appreciation for their fellow peer learners.

How to Use This Book

This book is meant to provide you with everything you need to build and facilitate an online course based on the Diversity 101 curriculum. The Participant Workbook, PowerPoint slides, activity sheets, and additional resources can be downloaded by visiting www.dei360consulting.com and use the code deitoolkit .

Building the course involves designing the online space for the modules in your Learning Management System (LMS) and creating the content. Developing a consistent structure helps course participants know what is expected of them in each module. The structure of the modules in this guide consists of a module overview, content videos, activities, discussion forums, and suggestions for taking action to apply module concepts. To help you design these elements, each module chapter in this book includes:

Background Information. Each module chapter begins with the rationale and the theoretical concepts presented in the module it comprises. This background information is not part of the online course; it is provided so that you have firm grounding in the curriculum design.

Module Overview. The module overview is what course-takers would see at the beginning of each module to orient them to the material. The overview starts with a set of *essential questions* (McTighe & Wiggins, 2013) to activate prior knowledge, stimulate thought, and spark more questions. In addition to the essential questions, you should provide a list of the tasks and assignments that the participants need to complete, along with the due dates.

Video Scripts. This book provides *scripts* for video lectures using narrated PowerPoint presentations. The scripts for the video mini-lectures can be used verbatim, but we recommend that facilitators revise and fine-tune the scripts to better reflect their own voice and the particular context in which they are facilitating.

PowerPoint Slides. In order to make it convenient for you to customize this course, you will have online access to PowerPoint slides to accompany the lecture provided for each module, as well as activity worksheets for participants. The PowerPoint templates will need to be branded with your campus logo. To download the PowerPoints, visit www.dei360consulting.com and use the code deitoolkit.

Engagement Activities. Most of the modules include activities that participants complete on their own, then discuss with the group in the discussion board. Relevant worksheets are provided in the participant workbook and online.

Facilitator Notes. Facilitator notes include things like special instructions, additional background information, and other tips that will help you facilitate that particular activity or discussion.

Discussion Forum Content. The discussion forums are the heart and soul of the course, where participants share, discuss, and question. This book provides suggested discussion prompts along with actual examples of participants' responses. The discussion questions should be revised so that they are appropriate to your context.

Facilitator Feedback to Course Takers. Thoughtful facilitator feedback to the discussion board participation can help push participant thinking about challenging, and sometimes emotional, topics a little further. Examples of facilitator feedback developed and refined over several years of facilitating this course are provided to help you construct your own feedback to participants' discussions.

Participant Workbook

You are provided online access to download a Participant Workbook, which contains module summaries, activity and worksheets, and reflection questions. This resource will not only be useful as participants engage in the course, but it is also a resource that is useful to go back to over and over again as they continue to learn, grow, and change their perspectives. You can provide printouts for your participants or provide them with the link to download or print themselves.

Customizing the Course for Your Context

The best DEI course is one that reflects your institution. There are various ways that you can customize this course to your organization context:

- **PowerPoint slide decks.** This facilitator guide provides access to professionally designed slide decks that align with the sample scripts in this book. There are placeholders in the first and last slide of each deck for you to add your school or department logo. The photos are all licensed and available for your use.
- **Course name.** You can choose a course name that reflects the focus of your course. For example, if you are in a medical context, you may want to name your course "DEI in Healthcare." If you are working with faculty and staff, you may want to name your course something like "Diversity & Inclusion in the Academic Workplace."
- **Course length.** Although this course was originally designed to complete over the course of a 15-week semester, we suggest you plan a timeframe that works with your academic calendar and culture. We have found success in dividing the course into three mini-courses of three modules each with a week or two break in between. We have also facilitated it in an intensive 9-week summer course.
- **Options for discussions.** The examples in this book are from asynchronous online discussions. However, if your participants have interest and availability, you can also hold the module discussions in person or on a video conferencing platform. Many participants prefer to have face-to-face discussions, but it is challenging to find times that work for everyone.
- **Offer certificates or digital badges.** After taking this course, several past participants have commented that it should be required of everyone who works at the institution. Although I agree that everyone should engage with these topics, I have found that "requiring" this type of learning can actually work against the goals. Instead, using incentives such as certificates or digital badges can be more motivating and conducive to learning than required participation. Furthermore, digital badges can be added to email signatures and social media platforms, thus promoting the program and contributing to a culture that acknowledges and celebrates DEI professional development efforts.

INTRODUCTION REFERENCES

Case, K. A. (2007). Raising white privilege awareness and reducing racial prejudice: Assessing diversity course effectiveness. *Teaching of Psychology, 34*(4), 231–235.

Hord, S. M. (2009). Professional learning communities. *Journal of Staff Development, 30*(1), 40–43.

McTighe, J., & Wiggins, G. P. (2013). *Essential questions: Opening doors to student understanding.* ASCD.

Merryfield, M. M. (2001). The paradoxes of teaching a multicultural education course online. *Journal of Teacher Education, 52*(4), 283–299.

Mezirow, J. (1997). Transformative learning: Theory to practice. *New Directions for Adult and Continuing Education, 1997*(74), 5–12.

Palloff, R. M., & Pratt, K. (2007). *Building online learning communities: Effective strategies for the virtual classroom* (2nd ed.). John Wiley & Sons.

Paluck, E. L. (2006). Diversity training and intergroup contact: A call to action research. *Journal of Social Issues, 62*(3), 577–595.

Pettigrew, T. F., & Tropp, L. R. (2006). A meta-analytic test of intergroup contact theory. *Journal of Personality and Social Psychology, 90*(5), 751.

Shea, P., Li, C. S., Swan, K., & Pickett, A. (2005). Developing learning community in online asynchronous college courses: The role of teaching presence. *Journal of Asynchronous Learning Networks, 9*(4), 59–82.

Tajfel, H. (1978). Social categorization, social identity and social comparison. In H. Tajfel (Ed.), *Differentiation between social groups: Studies in the social psychology of intergroup relations* (pp. 61–76). Academic Press.

PART 1

Nuts and Bolts

BUILDING AND FACILITATING DIVERSITY 101

Although this book provides you with a curriculum and content, building an online course still takes a lot of work. This chapter describes the *nuts and bolts* that you will need to develop or find to construct your version of Diversity 101 in an online course environment. You will use many of these same tools for building the credit-bearing course for students, which is discussed in part 2.

Tools of the Trade

Video Lectures

The core of the this course are the facilitator-narrated video lectures. These video lectures provide the food for thought and fodder for discussion. In this book, we provide sample scripts for each module that you may replicate or adjust to create your own narrated presentations. In what follows, you are provided with some additional guidance, tips, considerations, and resources for creating video lectures using PowerPoint presentations.

Add Visual Images

The PowerPoint templates provided with this book include images and graphics that you are free to use. You may also want to add your own visual images to customize the visuals to your organizational context. One of the first places you should check for images to use is your institution's marketing and communications office. The more your presentation reflects the people, places, and branding of your campus or organization, the more relevant the content in the course feels to the participant. You should also check with your institution's instructional technology department to see what licensing agreements they have that might grant you access to images, graphics, and videos. Additionally, the internet is replete with images available under Creative Common Licensing. Whatever you do, do not risk infringing on third-party copyrighted material.

Design for Accessibility

It is much easier to design for accessibility up front than to go back and redo your content. Designing for accessibility means making sure your video content is accessible to people with hearing or visual impairments, disabilities, or restrictions. Fortunately, many of the best practices for making PowerPoint presentations also apply to designing for accessibility, such as considerations of font size, color schema, slide titles, etc. If your institution does not have an in-house resource for helping to ensure online accessibility, you should consult Microsoft Office Accessibility Center, which provides comprehensive how-to guides for PowerPoint and other Microsoft Office applications.

Decide Whether to Do Scripted or Extemporaneous Lecture Recording

Some people have a talent for recording their lectures as they speak extemporaneously, but for others, reading a script with an animated voice works better. Whichever method works best for you, it is helpful to plan out what you want to say, at least in an outline form if not fully written out. In this book, we provide you with scripted lectures, which you are welcome to use as is or as a starting point for developing your own lectures that sound more like your own voice. There is, however, one distinct benefit of using scripted lectures: it makes creating closed captioning a whole lot easier. Scripted lectures can be converted into transcript files and easily uploaded to create closed captioning for your videos. Closed captioning is not only an important accessibility feature but also helpful for visual learners, ESL (English as a Second Language) participants, and those who may be less familiar with some of the terminology. Luckily, YouTube also has a feature for creating closed captions without uploading a file.

Recording PowerPoint Lectures

There are multiple ways to record your PowerPoint lecture, a few suggestions are offered here. The easiest way is to contact your instructional technology department (if you have one) and ask for professional help. If you are on your own, you have at least four options. First, you can simply use the *Record Slide Show* function. This will allow you to record your voice, animations, slide timings, and laser pointer. You can then upload your presentation to the online platform, and it will start automatically when participants open it. You can also convert your PowerPoint presentation into a video by using the *Save As* function and select a video file format that can be streamed over the internet. (PowerPoint 2010 saves as a Windows Media File [.wmv]; later versions also allow you to save as an MPEG-4 [.mp4] file.) A third way requires purchasing and learning to use a video editing software program, such as Camtasia. Camtasia is fairly inexpensive and easy to learn. It allows for direct recording from PowerPoint with its add-in plug-in. Camtasia also makes it easy to edit your videos, add animations, and upload files for closed captioning. Finally, you can also use Zoom to record your lectures while you share your screen.

Make It Real with Digital Media

In addition to your own recorded videos, you can make the course content come alive through a carefully curated set of digital media resources. There are examples provided in the companion website (www.dei360consulting.com), but in order to be as current and relevant as possible, you should search for ways to connect the content to your current context and the broader social context. NOTE: Copyright law typically allows for fair use of copyright material in the context of nonprofit educational institutions. This fair use stipulation does not apply to for-profit institutions. Check with your institution about how to obtain permissions to use copyrighted material.

Assessing the Effectiveness of Diversity 101 on Participant Learning

It is important to utilize some method of assessment or evaluation of participant learning, not only to better gauge the participants' respective levels of understanding and learning but also to build credibility and accountability for your diversity education efforts. Over the past few years, there has been growing criticism of diversity training. For example, the cover story of the July–August 2016 issue of *Harvard Business Review* was entitled *Why Diversity Programs Fail* (Dobbin & Kalev, 2016). Looking at data from Fortune 500 companies, the article argued that mandated diversity trainings had no impact on the level of demographic diversity of the companies. This analysis assumes that the purpose of diversity training is merely to increase the demographic diversity of a company, which is not an appropriate measure for training effectiveness. Hiring and retention are a subset of diversity-related topics. The approach discussed in the article seems to be based on a compliance perspective rather than a professional development one. Unfortunately, in discussions of diversity training, it seems that people often fail to come to a shared understanding of what they are talking about. Therefore, it is important to identify specific goals and learning objectives of the diversity training initiative and to ensure that effectiveness is measured in alignment with them. There are many ways to conceptualize and evaluate the impact of a course on participant learning. In the remainder of this chapter, we describe what you should try to assess in terms of effectiveness and why.

The overarching goal of Diversity 101, and other diversity-related professional development program, is to increase participants' cultural competence in order to enhance their capacity to create and foster inclusive working and learning environments with people from different cultural (broadly defined) backgrounds (Martin & Vaughn, 2010). Cultural competence refers to "a set of cognitive, affective, and behavioral skills and characteristics that support effective and appropriate interaction in a variety of cultural contexts" (Bennett, 1998, p. 97). The Diversity 101 curriculum features targeted activities designed for cognitive, affective, and behavioral learning.

Cognitive learning involves the internalization and integration of knowledge and critical thinking around a particular topic (Krathwohl et al., 1964). The Diversity 101 curriculum provides foundational knowledge of concepts such as identity, unconscious bias, and privilege that help participants gain increased self-awareness and engage in critical self-reflection. This type of knowledge facilitates the development of key cultural competence skills such as perspective-taking. *Affective learning* refers to changes in attitudes, emotions, and feelings. Diversity 101 affective goals include increased self-awareness, openness to learning, and empathy toward and curiosity about people with different backgrounds. *Behavioral learning* refers to desired changes in behavior. The behavioral learning goals in Diversity 101 are focused on changes in interpersonal behaviors as well as making changes in job-related practices.

For Diversity 101, we developed a pre/post-course survey instrument to measure changes as a result of participating in the course. The surveys include some questions from previously validated instruments, but most of the questions are directly connected to course content. There were also several open-ended qualitative questions on the post-course survey to gain a deeper understanding of participants' perceptions of the course, their participation, and their learning. A copy of the surveys is provided in the online supplemental resources. Early results were published in the *Journal of Diversity in Higher Education* (Goldstein Hode et al., 2017), and you can see more recent unpublished quantitative results in Table 1. Although participant learning was impacted by variables such as comfort level with online courses and previous exposure to diversity, overall, the results show that participants did "move" in the right direction in terms of the intended learning outcomes of Diversity 101. Although it is good to see the numbers, the participant responses to discussion board prompts tend to be more interesting and reflective of their learning processes. Examples are shared throughout this book.

Table 1. Pre/Post Test Analysis of Diversity

		Pre		Post	Diff	
		Count	Mean	Mean	Mean	Sig
Measure	Knowledge	103	3.555	4.379	.823	**,++
	Self-Efficacy	103	3.780	4.285	.505	**,++
	Openness to Learning	103	3.905	4.403	.498	**,++
	Awareness of Privilege	103	3.784	4.166	.383	**,++
	Meaning of Diversity	103	3.579	3.909	.330	**,++
	Sensitivity	103	3.859	4.112	.252	**,++
	Awareness of Bias	103	3.819	4.014	.194	**,++
	Value of Diversity	103	4.788	4.909	.120	**,++

Notes: ** Significant at the .01 level, * Significant at the .05 level by Paired Sample T-test

++ Significant at the .01 level, * Significant at the .05 level by Wilcoxon Signed Rank Test

Facilitating Diversity 101

The role of the facilitator is the most critical aspect to fostering an online environment that promotes transformative learning (Andresen, 2009; Palloff & Pratt, 2007; Shea et al., 2005). In contrast to face-to-face learning wherein the instructor often talks more than do the students, online instructors should take a backseat in the discussions and instead focus on setting a good tone, modeling an authentic online presence, and asking thought-provoking discussion questions (Boettcher & Conrad, 2021). In other words, the instructor's function in an online environment, especially one focused on transformative learning, should be to create a learning community that promotes active learning, a sense of trust, and the foundation for authentic dialogue: all key elements to the transformative learning process. Throughout the course, the facilitator wears different hats: cheerleader, coach, provocateur, mediator, and guide. In this chapter, we discuss the various tasks the facilitator should do prior to, during, and at the conclusion of the course.

Find Your Voice

In order to be effective in the role of online facilitator, you will need to model an authentic and honest online presence (Gurley, 2018; Shea et al., 2005). As you read through the lecture scripts and facilitator feedback to participant online discussions provided throughout this book, think about your own tone and style. Encouraging participants to share, reflect, and engage with one another requires that facilitators communicate with a voice that is genuine, vulnerable, and caring. Therefore, it is important that you speak and write in ways that are natural rather than academic. In other words, the principal goal here is to put participants at ease and model a genuine form of communication that will encourage participants to contribute to the discussions in a natural, authentic way. Formal academic writing is not conducive to this goal.

Setting the Tone before the Course Begins

The facilitator should begin the work of building an online community from the very first communication to the participants. Since many people have preconceived ideas, fears, or concerns about both online learning and diversity training, it is helpful to send an email to the participants a week or so before the start of the course to set the right tone and put the participants at ease (Boettcher & Conrad, 2021). In this initial communication, the facilitator should express enthusiasm to motivate the participants, address some commonly held fears and concerns about the topic, as well as about online courses, and begin to shape realistic but positive expectations for participation in a peer-centered learning community. Here is an example of a welcome letter to new participants.

Greetings, Diversity 101 Participants!

[Show enthusiasm and excitement about the cohort] As you'll soon learn from the introductions, we have a very interesting and varied group of people here! Bringing people together from all across campus is to me one of the most beneficial aspects of Diversity 101, so I am very excited about facilitating this learning process and engaging with you over the next few weeks!

[Set expectations, put people at ease] In terms of setting expectations, please note that this course is intentionally designed to start off slow and ease everyone into the online structure and group dynamic. Each week's content builds on the previous week, and thus the course gets a bit more challenging as we go along.

For those of you who are eager to dive right into the tough stuff, please be patient with the process . . . we'll get there. And for those of you who are nervous about the tough stuff, please don't worry . . . we'll ease in slowly. And for some of you, none of this will be tough stuff, but perhaps just a reminder/refresher . . . but also a unique opportunity to engage and build community with colleagues from across campus around these important issues.

[Establish role as facilitator/co-learner] My job as your facilitator is to keep everybody on track, to provide some additional insights and questions, and to help make sure that you get what you need out of this course. I am also a co-learner because you all bring unique knowledge, experience, and insights from your own lived experiences. Thank you for this opportunity, and I look forward to learning with you!

Creating and Cultivating Online Community

A primary role of the facilitator is to create and cultivate a sense of community among the participants (Conrad & Donaldson, 2012). The first critical step toward creating and maintaining a space for thoughtful, honest discussions is to provide guidelines and community norms for online participation, as will be discussed in "Module 1: Building a Learning Community." These guidelines are essential for creating an online space where people feel safe enough to share their thoughts openly and respectfully. The facilitator continues to foster this sense of a learning community by providing thoughtful discussion questions or prompts likely to provoke meaningful discussion. (Sample discussion questions are provided throughout each chapter.) Finally, the facilitator continues to support the learning community by acting as a cheerleader and motivator for the discussion by consistently expressing gratitude and encouragement to the participants in order to tap into and nurture their intrinsic motivation, as well as to empower and encourage participants to be accountable for their own learning and that of the others in the group. Throughout this book, we provide examples of providing this type of feedback.

Discussion Forum Participation

Research on online pedagogy suggests that the more that facilitators/instructors intervene in online discussions, the less likely the participants are to feel responsible to step up (Andresen, 2009; Boettcher & Conrad, 2021; Stavredes, 2011). For this reason, it is recommended that facilitators minimally engage in the online discussions, yet still maintain an online presence (Boettcher & Conrad, 2021). A general rule of thumb is to refrain from responding until each participant has posted their responses to the discussion questions and at least a few have responded to their peers' posts. In some discussions, you may want to offer a few comments to individual students (but avoid responding to the same people every time) that prompt further thinking, ask for clarification, and/or offer a different perspective (Stavredes, 2011). The strategy that we use (and is modeled in this book) is to write one discussion feedback post for all the participants to see that summarizes some of the major themes that came out in the discussions, provides further insights, and includes some additional resources (i.e., videos, articles, blogs) to explore the topic further. This facilitator guide provides example facilitator feedback for each module.

Many participants appreciate the asynchronous online discussions because it gives them time to reflect and to carefully choose their words in reply to discussion questions or to other participants' posts. However, it is also true that many participants would like opportunities to engage in face-to-face discussions. Ideally, you can offer both by scheduling in-person or video discussions after participants have engaged in the module content and online discussion. This way, they come to the face-to-face discussion after some deeper reflection and understanding of what their co-learners think about the module concepts.

Sometimes You Have to Step In

If a participant unintentionally says something offensive about a group of people or toward another participant, the facilitator should intervene. The best approach to any given situation is trying to figure a way to turn it into a learning opportunity for all participants, while at the same time maintaining a delicate balance between acknowledging the impact of the words on the receiver(s) yet not vilifying the offending party. Here are some tips:

- Hold off for a little while and see if one of the other participants chimes in first. This gives participants an opportunity to practice stepping up. The feedback may also seem less threatening if it comes from a fellow peer learner than the facilitator.
- Thank the offending party for the learning opportunity raised by the situation and acknowledge the importance of learning to approach these situations.

- Remind everyone of the community norms and guidelines that were discussed in the course orientation module, particularly the guideline that asks participants to assume good intentions of each other.
- Don't assume that everyone in the group understands why something was offensive. Take the time to explicitly name it and explain it.
- Focus on the problematic nature of what was said, not on the person who said it, nor on the person to whom it was directed.

In addition to a public intervention, the facilitator should follow up privately with all parties involved. For example, in a past cohort, an older woman used an outdated, and no longer acceptable, term to refer to people of Asian descent. She was clearly not aware of the change in terminology. So, on the discussion board, I thanked her for the learning opportunity presented to the group and explained the new terminology and why it had evolved. Later, in a private email, I wrote:

I wanted to thank you again for providing that learning opportunity for the group. I know it can be uncomfortable when we learn that language or terms that we thought were okay to say are offensive to some groups of people, especially when you had no intention to offend. Unfortunately, this discomfort is part of our learning process. And we have to be willing to make mistakes, learn, and move on if we are ever going to get better at this. Please do let me know if you have any questions or concerns about my response to your post. Thanks again!

Maintain Facilitator Presence by Introducing and Concluding Each Module

Although facilitator presence should be somewhat minimal in the online discussion space, there are other avenues of communication that help facilitators maintain online presence and give participants the sense that the facilitator is present and taking care of the group. One way that facilitators maintain an online presence is by sending emails or posting announcements that introduce the upcoming module and wrap up the previous one (Boettcher & Conrad, 2021). These messages can serve several purposes: provide encouragement and gratitude for the previous discussion, help to bridge one module to the next, provide reminders about upcoming tasks, and set expectations for the upcoming module. Below is an example email closing out one module and introducing the next one.

Congratulations on Completing Module 1

Thank you again for a thought-provoking discussion about diversity and inclusion in your work areas! You've really highlighted some of the great things already going on in your areas, as well as identified some areas for improvement. It seems like everyone got some new ideas and/or food for thought.

Before you move on to the next module, please take the next day or so to revisit the discussion board, being mindful to respond to people who reply to your posts if warranted and reply to those who have not yet had any feedback/reply.

The next module is the most content-dense module so far, so please check the module overview and allow yourself enough time to complete each section. The content addresses some challenging topics that create obstacles to inclusion on our campus and in the workplace. People who encounter some of these concepts for the first time often have a very emotional reaction (guilt, shame, anger, defensiveness). So, if these concepts are new to you, please don't worry . . . you are not alone with whatever you may be feeling. Frankly, this material should make us all feel a little uncomfortable . . . and this is a good thing, because it means that we are in the zone of learning and increasing self-awareness (which is often uncomfortable).

Once again, many thanks to all of you for your willingness to contribute your time and energy to this learning process!

Solicit Feedback

Every few modules, it is helpful to ask participants for feedback to gauge how they are doing with the course content and discussions. It is helpful to let them choose between providing feedback in an anonymous survey and/or a journal entry or in a private communication between the participant and the facilitator. The journal entries can serve as a proxy for one-on-one meetings, a forum in which the participant can raise any personal questions or areas of concern. Writing in journals also is a reflective practice that can further facilitate transformative learning. Participants should be encouraged to use the space as they see fit: to ask questions; process thoughts; express frustrations/confusions; and/or just check in about how they are feeling about the course. Empathetic and encouraging facilitator responses to participant journal entries are critical factors in building participants' sense of comfort and safety in the course.

Part 1 References

Andresen, M. A. (2009). Asynchronous discussion forums: Success factors, outcomes, assessments, and limitations. *Journal of Educational Technology & Society, 12*(1), 249–257.

Bennett, M. J. (1998). *Basic concepts of intercultural communication: Selected readings.* Intercultural Press.

Boettcher, J. V., & Conrad, R. M. (2021). *The online teaching survival guide: Simple and practical pedagogical tips.* John Wiley & Sons.

Conrad, R. M., & Donaldson, J. A. (2012). *Continuing to engage the online learner: More activities and resources for creative instruction* (Vol. 35). John Wiley & Sons.

Dobbin, F., & Kalev, A. (2016, July-August). Why diversity programs fail. *Harvard Business Review.* https://hbr.org/2016/07/why-diversity-programs-fail

Goldstein Hode, M., Behm-Morawitz, E., & Hays, A. (2018). Testing the effectiveness of an online diversity course for faculty and staff. *Journal of Diversity in Higher Education, 11*(3), 347–365. https://doi.org/10.1037/dhe0000063

Gurley, L. E. (2018). Educators' Preparation to Teach, Perceived Teaching Presence, and Perceived Teaching Presence Behaviors in Blended and Online Learning Environments. *Online Learning, 22*(2), 197–220.

Krathwohl, D. R., Bloom, B. S., & Masia, B. B. (1964). *Taxonomy of educational objectives: The classification of educational goals Handbook II.* David McKay.

Martin, M., & Vaughn, B. (2010, October 25). Cultural competence: The nuts & bolts of diversity and inclusion. *Diversity Officer Magazine.* http://diversityofficermagazine.com/cultural-competence/cultural-competence-the-nuts-bolts-of-diversity-inclusion/

Palloff, R. M., & Pratt, K. (2007). *Building online learning communities: Effective strategies for the virtual classroom* (2nd ed.). John Wiley & Sons.

Shea, P., Li, C. S., Swan, K., & Pickett, A. (2005). Developing learning community in online asynchronous college courses: The role of teaching presence. *Journal of Asynchronous Learning Networks, 9*(4), 59–82.

Stavredes, T. (2011). *Effective online teaching: Foundations and strategies for student success.* John Wiley & Sons.

PART 2

Guidance for a Credit-Bearing Course

While there are many similarities in how to approach Diversity 101 as a professional development course for faculty and staff as compared to a credit-bearing course for students, there are also some important differences in the way the course is facilitated, structured, and designed. For example, in a credit-bearing course for students, the facilitator's role is a dual one of both facilitator and instructor. In other words, as a facilitator, you introduce and close modules with thoughtful insights, manage online discussions, and provide effective feedback. As an instructor, you must also provide expertise, evaluate student work, and help students meet their particular learning goals. Moreover, a credit-bearing course for students must be academically rigorous enough to ensure that students meet a certain standard of academic performance and are able to achieve desired learning outcomes. Academic rigor entails required reading and assignments, includes formative and summative assessments, and has a clearly defined evaluation and grading schema. So, while the Diversity 101 curriculum is just as appropriate for students as it is for faculty and staff, there are additional considerations and elements needed for an effective, inclusive, online credit-bearing course for students.

In this chapter, we draw upon our years of experience teaching this course to students, as well as best practices in online pedagogy in general. We start by discussing how to start your course in a way that helps your students begin to build a sense of online community as well as helps them understand how to succeed in the course. Then, we will discuss the various types of assignments and assessments the course includes, as well as how to grade them. We conclude this chapter by providing tips and insights on how to support your students' achievement of learning outcomes through your online presence or your communication within and outside of a diversity course.

Starting Off on the Right Foot

Creating an inclusive online environment means making an intentional and ongoing effort to ensure that all students feel like they belong and can thrive in the learning environment. As was mentioned, this work should start even before your course begins. We provide considerable detail as to how to create an inclusive course syllabus and how to develop an effective online orientation, both of which are key elements to starting your course off on the right foot!

An Inclusive Course Syllabus

One step you can take right at the beginning of your course is to set the tone for diversity and inclusion through your syllabus. A course syllabus is a comprehensive guide that outlines what students need to know in order to be successful in a course, including policies, rules, required texts, and a schedule of assignments. Although there is no correct way to create a course syllabus, one that is detailed and user-friendly can greatly support your students' learning, particularly in an online environment (Boettcher & Conrad, 2021). In this section, we will walk you through key areas of a good online syllabus, one that will help support student learning. The great news is that once you have developed this detailed document, it is just a matter of updating it for future courses. Below we provide a description of key components to include in an inclusive syllabus. You can also find examples of each item in the annotated Example Syllabus available for download and customization at www.dei360consulting.com.

Contact Information

In order to make it easy for students to find the information when they need it, be sure to provide your contact information at the top of your syllabus. It is also important to provide more than one way in which students can reach you, including email, phone, and a chat platform such as Slack or WhatsApp. If you feel comfortable, you can provide your students with your cell phone number so that they may text or call you. The more avenues of communication you provide, the more likely your students will be to reach out to you when they need help.

Personal Pronouns and Salutations

We suggest that you include your pronouns in your syllabus and signature line as a way to acknowledge and normalize nonbinary gender identities and to ensure students are aware of your gender identity so they may address you correctly. It is equally important that you specify how you prefer students to address you in the course (i.e., do you prefer a first-name basis, such as Jane, or should students address you as Dr., Ms., or Mrs. Doe?). Your decision on how students should address you may vary depending on whether your class consists of undergraduates, graduate students, or colleagues and other adult learners. An example of how to include your full contact information is provided in the annotated Example Syllabus available in the online resources.

Virtual Office Hours

It is extremely important to offer virtual office hours to support your online students. The first step in doing so is to find a reliable communication platform that is easily accessible to your students. Some popular platforms for video conferencing include Skype and Zoom, but not all students will or will always have access to adequate internet speeds for video calls, so you should offer the option to meet over the phone as well.

To help meet the various needs of your students, we recommend that instructors offer drop-in hours at set times each week; require at least one scheduled one-on-one meeting with each student toward the beginning of the semester; and offer open-group office hours for students who want extra support on a particular assignment. As with any face-to-face or online course, a supportive instructor will understand that not every student can attend the scheduled office hours and will therefore be flexible in an effort to support students around their schedules. Office hours and availability should be included in the course syllabus.

Course Rationale and Learning Objectives

Provide a course rationale that clearly articulates how the learning outcomes will help students develop cultural competence skills that are critical for success in today's diverse workplace, as well as society in general. This clarity will ensure students understand what they will learn in the course and why it is relevant to their lives.

Course Expectations

Course expectations typically include assignment and project deadlines, required technology, and guidance for communicating with peers and the instructor. You should also provide an approximation of how much time student learners are expected to devote to your course each week to help ensure that they set aside enough time to complete assignments. It is not only vital to communicate your expectations in the course syllabus, but it is also helpful to reference these expectations throughout the course.

Online "Netiquette"

In order to foster a healthy and engaged online learning environment, the instructor should provide a basic set of online "netiquette" rules in the course syllabus.

"Netiquette" refers to a specific set of rules that apply to communication in an online environment. In addition to these basic netiquette rules, instructors should engage the students in establishing community norms and guidelines for their particular learning community. This will be discussed further in the orientation module. Instructors should include reminders of the netiquette and community norms and guidelines with the instructions for each discussion forum.

Required Readings

The curriculum offered in this book was designed for a communication course; therefore, many of the scholarly articles required are from the field of communication or related disciplines. Instructors will need to customize the required reading list to their academic discipline. That said, our course also includes a great deal of freely available multimedia content such as videos, podcasts, blogs, and online magazines. Using a variety of free online multimedia resources to support the learning objectives helps ensure not only that students will find the content relevant but also that students with fewer economic resources are not unduly burdened by having to purchase books and materials.

Course Policies

The course policies section is one of the most crucial sections in the syllabus. It is the place to which students will turn when deciding whether or not to submit an assignment late, what to do if they disagree with a grade, how to seek assistance for an accommodation related to disabilities, and how to request an accommodation for religious holidays. In addition to ensuring that your syllabus is aligned with your department's required policies, such as that for academic integrity and accommodations, you should also consider policies that foster inclusion, such as for preferred names and civil discourse. Providing accurate and complete policy information is important, so you may want to ask a colleague, department chair, or one of the staff at your campus center for teaching and learning to review your policy statements to ensure that they are in accordance.

Attendance

Unlike tracking attendance in traditional college classes in which students gather at a specific time and location, keeping track of attendance in an online class presents a more complex task. Nonetheless, students in an online class can demonstrate attendance in a variety of ways, such as by completing the weekly course assignments, posting to discussion forums, and responding to and interacting regularly with their peers in online discussions. Some institutions have an online attendance policy that requires reporting for the purposes of financial aid requirements. If your organization does not already have an online attendance policy in place, it is then up to you as the course instructor to decide what constitutes being "present" in your online class. For example, you can require that students log in at least two times per week. Your Learning Management System (LMS) likely provides a way to track student activity, so you can identify who has not been present. No matter what you determine as the best way to track attendance and levels of participation, we encourage you to reach out to inactive students within the first week of the course to make sure they understand the requirements. It is not uncommon that some students will unenroll or withdraw themselves from the course after realizing the amount of time and attention required to succeed.

Late Work

It is almost inevitable that one or even all of your students will submit a late assignment at least once during the course. The reasons that students submit late work can range from them not feeling up to completing a required task to more extenuating life circumstances, such as technology issues, serious illness, death of a family member, or other events beyond one's control. You will want to have a statement written in your syllabus that addresses how students should communicate with you in such instances and the types of documentation you may require for a grade exception. On one hand, instructors should be understanding of and try to accommodate extenuating circumstances; on the other hand, late submissions in this course can have a negative impact on the entire learning community, which is dependent on timely and thoughtful interactions among peers. Additionally, receiving late work creates a heavier workload for the course instructor, who now must grade past-due work while keeping on top of grading for the current module. Therefore, instructors should create a late policy that holds students accountable but is not so punitive that they cannot recover should they have a bad week. You might also consider offering extra-credit opportunities to help make up lost points for late work. Including a late-work penalty in the course syllabus and explaining the purpose behind it helps reduce late submissions.

Support Resources for Students

Including information in your syllabus that supports students from different identity groups communicates to them that you are aware and that you care. It is important to try to address the concerns of all students who may need additional support by providing them with relevant information and resources. For example:

- Students with disabilities (Americans with Disabilities Act [ADA] policy, location of disability services, invitation to speak to you about accommodations)
- Students who have mental health issues (location of online and on-campus mental health services, help line information)
- Students who celebrate non-Christian holidays (religious accommodations policy, not scheduling exams or presentations on major Muslim or Jewish holidays)
- Transgender students (preferred name policy, usage of preferred pronouns, locations of gender-neutral bathrooms)
- Students with financial challenges (designated workspaces on campus, food pantry or other assistance available on campus or in the community, open-source or other free resources, options to buy expensive equipment from previous students or financial assistance programs)
- First-generation college students (a list of resources on campus or online that help students navigate the financial and academic complexities of higher education)

Course Calendar

A detailed course calendar is a tool that students can use to keep on track with assignments as well as plan ahead. The calendar lists the variety of tasks that students must complete for each module, the approximate amount of time needed, and the points associated, if any. In the companion website (www.dei360consulting.com) we offer a template that you can customize.

Online Course Orientation for Students

The online course orientation sets the tone for the course and lets students know what is expected of them and what they can expect in a student-instructor relationship. Students who enroll in your online course may experience a mixture of emotions including curiosity, nervousness, fear, and even excitement. You can help reduce their anxiety by informing them up front about what they can expect and how you intend to support them throughout the course. As you will see in the next chapter, the professional development version of Diversity 101 includes an orientation module. Students need additional information and support, so here we provide you with a few ideas on how to get students set up for success in your course.

Instructor Video Introduction

One of the first things you'll want to do in your online learning space is create an introduction video. This helps students get to know you as a person and get a sense of your personality and your passion for teaching and your subject matter. Students will often engage and put more effort forth in courses in which they feel they know more about you as a person. Consider addressing the following questions in your introduction:

- What excites you about the course topics, including how they connect to real-world issues or events? What do you want students to get excited about?
- What inspired you to become an instructor in the area you are teaching? How did you overcome academic hurdles? What do you love about teaching?
- What do you enjoy doing outside of academia?
- Reassure students that you are there to help them and that they should not hesitate to reach out to you.

Videos can be very informal, simply using your webcam or smartphone. Make sure you choose a relatively quiet place with good lighting. If using your smartphone, consider using a tripod to keep a steady, centered frame. To make the video more personal, you may also want to record in a fun or relevant setting.

Video Course Overview and Navigation

Creating a video that walks students through the basics of the syllabus, explaining the course structure, and showing them how to navigate your course helps ensure them that they know how to access the course modules, check assignment due dates, submit assignments, email the instructor, and so forth. By taking the time to walk students through how to navigate the course, you can save yourself from having to respond to a flood of emails later.

Syllabus Quiz

Although it is the students' responsibility to remain informed about your plans, the reality is that not all students will take the time to read the syllabus in its entirety.

One way to ensure that they capture the most important information is to include a multiple-choice Syllabus Quiz as part of your online orientation to the course using your online learning platform.

Student Introductions

Creating intentional opportunities for students to get to know each other at the beginning of (and throughout) the course helps build trust and foster a sense of community (Conrad & Donaldson, 2012). These initial activities also provide a low-stakes opportunity to engage with the technology of the course, which is particularly helpful to students who are new to online learning. Introductions should serve as a fun and nonthreatening icebreaker to ease students into the course, the course technology, and the learning community. Effective introduction activities should require that students:

- Share something personal
- Read one another's entries
- Respond to one another's entries
- Find something in common with several others in the learning community
- Be imaginative or express genuine emotions or openness

Some good introduction discussion prompts include:

- What experience do you have with this course topic?
- How does this course topic relate to your career goals?
- If someone were to visit your town or your state for the first time, what are your top five recommendations of things to do, places to eat, or sights to visit?
- What was the best class (online or in person) that you have ever taken? Why did you like it so well? What was the worst class you have ever taken? Why was it so bad?
- What is your biggest fear or hope about engaging in an online class?

After posting an initial response to the prompt, ask students to find and reply to at least two or three students with whom they have something in common and two or three students who shared a perspective or experience different from their own. Instructors might also consider posting a brief hello or welcome message to each student, as they introduce themselves, as a way to let them know that you see and acknowledge them.

Creating Community Norms and Guidelines

Engaging students in a discussion about online communication norms and guidelines at the very beginning of a course is an essential step in fostering community and creating a productive learning environment (Boettcher & Conrad, 2021; Palloff & Pratt, 2007; Stavredes, 2011). While instructors should include general expectations for online communication in the syllabus by providing a set of netiquette guidelines, you should have students collaboratively create community norms and guidelines that are more personal and geared toward the specific online learning community they are creating. Involving students in these discussions raises their awareness and helps them better buy in to guidelines regarding online communication. See the online resources for an example activity for creating community norms and guidelines with your students.

Open-Discussion Forum

Without a doubt, students new to the course will have questions about you as an instructor, the syllabus, how to balance course work in light of other commitments, and so forth. We recommend that you create an open forum for questions and comments related to the course or related events in the community or the world. This could also be a space for students to share links to resources, stories, videos, or any other media that is relevant to the online learning community. Of course, it is important that you monitor how students use this space to make sure they are adhering to the netiquette guidelines and community norms and guidelines as written in your course syllabus.

Assignments, Assessments, and Grading

Many of the assignments in Diversity 101 require that students recall, reflect on, and share their personal lived experiences with the goal of providing culturally rich insights to all learners. In the previous section we discussed the importance of starting off on the right foot by building a sense of online community that allows for students to develop a level of openness necessary for them to feel comfortable with sharing their personal experiences with sensitive issues such as bias, microaggressions, and privilege. Although there is great educational value in sharing these stories, it is important to acknowledge the emotional work involved in asking students to recall and share their potentially oppressive histories. This understanding can create an additional challenge when grading this work. You might be wondering: "How do I grade a student's lived experience without invalidating the experience itself?" and

"How can I work to be mindful of and to reduce my own bias when grading the work of students whose lived realities I do not relate to?" These are critical questions that we need to keep in mind as we evaluate students' work in a diversity and inclusion course. Thus, in this section, we provide some guidance as we discuss the various types of assignments and assessments we use in Diversity 101, as well as how to grade them while being mindful of one's own positionality and bias.

Weekly Formative Assessments

Formative assessments hold students accountable for engaging with the course content and will give you a sense of how your students are doing with the material. In Diversity 101, students are assigned a variety of meaningful and impactful but low-stakes assessments (e.g., quizzes, role-play scenarios, reading summaries, informal discussions, and interactive activities). The low-stakes activities are assigned a low number of points for completion but are not evaluated using a rubric.

Summative Assessments

At the end of each module, students will engage in a Module Summary Discussion that requires them to synthesize, apply, and reflect on the required readings for that week as well as the other activities or assignments of that module. The expectation for these discussions is that students will draw upon (and cite) specific information from the readings and consider how, going forward, their enhanced or even new understanding of the issues covered might prompt them to change certain thought patterns or behaviors in real life. Students are provided with a grading rubric so that the expectations for their participation in the discussion forum are very clear. The rubric includes expectations not only of responding to the proposed discussion forum questions but also of replying thoughtfully to peers. The most productive online interactions are those that allow students the necessary time and space to reflect on their discussion post as well as those of their fellow learners. For this reason, you are encouraged to require that students post their initial response and their responses to their peers on different days. You can download and customize an example discussion forum rubric in the online companion site (www.dei360consulting.com, access code **deitoolkit**).

Group Assignment

The student version of Diversity 101 includes a module on organizational change. The purpose of this module is to familiarize students with strategies that can be applied to enhance workplace diversity and inclusion. In order to provide students with a meaningful way to engage with the organizational strategies provided in the module, we developed a group assignment that is simple on the surface but more challenging in the execution. Each team works together to create a set of ideas, practices, frameworks, and initiatives that promote and foster diversity and inclusion in organizations. The purpose of this assignment is two-fold. First, it gives students an opportunity to engage, and perhaps even struggle, in the process of working as part of a structured team. Second, the final products of each team are collected to create a toolbox of resources that all students can use in their individual final projects. This structured process gives each participant an opportunity to choose what role they would like to play in the group as it works through a suggested step-by-step process in the execution of the assignment. A detailed description of the assignment and the suggested instructions to the students can be found in the online resources.

Final Project: Real-World Application

The purpose of the final project in Diversity 101 is for students to develop their ability to improve workplace cultures and productivity through the practical application of course concepts to the organization of their choice. Students are encouraged to choose a company or organization that is related to their career and/or educational goals. Their task is to create a proposal for customized diversity initiative in the form of a presentation directed toward the leaders of the company, organization, or educational institution of which they are currently a part or hope to attend in the future. This diversity initiative should address business concerns such as corporate culture, recruitment of new employees, client relations, or productivity. Although the final product of the project is not due until the end of the course, smaller developmental assignments are due throughout the course to help keep students on track and give them opportunities to apply course-related concepts to their specific organizational context. Through each step of this project process, students practice and develop important career and life skills such as collaboration, giving and implementing feedback, and creativity.

A detailed description of the project, instructions to students, and the grading rubrics are provided in the online companion site. Here, we want to provide some additional insights based on our experiences facilitating this process over the years.

Help Students Narrow the Scope of the Project Site

Students tend to be excited about the opportunity to choose an organization they are interested in as their project site. That said, we often have to convince students to narrow the scope of their organizational site of interest. Focusing on a very large or complex organization can make the final project unmanageable and leave the student feeling overworked and defeated. For instance, when students have chosen the National Football League (NFL) as their organization, we encourage them to either focus on a particular team or on one department or area of the organizations (such as outreach, communications, or marketing).

Changing the Project Site

The project is designed to engage students in finding information about their project site early in the course. If they realize that they are having trouble finding information at the early stages, they still have time to change their organization of focus, which we encourage them to do. We have, however, had students who were so eager to focus on a particular organization that they put off the request to change until it finally became apparent to them that they would not be able to collect as much information as necessary. We discourage last-minute changes because assignments were meant to provide the foundation for the final project. That said, we listen to the student's reasons and plans for project execution and help them decide if it is best for them to stay with the original idea or do the extra work to do the last-minute change.

Provide Examples of Past Work and Resources

Students are most effective when they are provided with an explanation and example of what is expected of them for a particular assignment. Thus, we include an example of a prior students' work (with their permission of course) to demonstrate what a well-developed final project should look like. Once you have one group of students through the course, be sure to ask for permission to share successful projects with future cohorts.

Supporting Your Students through Your Online Presence

One of the most important online teaching practices for connecting with students and facilitating their success in an online course is the instructor's online presence. Online presence refers to students viewing you as a real person who cares about them as individuals, who cares about their learning, and who has the expertise to help them continue to learn and grow. In an online course, the instructor can create a sense of belonging that fosters a welcoming, caring, and supportive learning environment through different methods of clear and frequent communication within and outside of the course Learning Management System (LMS). Frequent communication invites students to model like behavior, which is key to building an effective online community and reducing possible anxieties and a sense of isolation related to online learning. Thus, in what follows, we discuss the different opportunities that you as an instructor of Diversity 101 might take in order to show participants your humanity and create an authentic online presence.

Weekly Announcements

Weekly announcements are one of the primary strategies for maintaining your online presence. You should start each week or each module with an opening announcement to introduce the new module, explaining how it builds upon or connects to the previous module(s), highlighting deadlines and assignments, and expressing your enthusiasm and encouragement. Similarly, at the end of the module you should send a closing announcement that summarizes or provides general feedback on the module discussions, adds additional insights about the real-world application of course concepts, shares additional resources, and sets the tone for the next module. These announcements are also a great way to provide group feedback on assignments, such as the group project. If you notice that a large percentage of those enrolled in the course have fallen behind on weekly formative assessment activities, you might wish to send "friendly reminders," announcements to remind them of deadlines. These reminder announcements of weekly deadlines are particularly helpful to those students who are used to or expecting a self-paced course, which does not have weekly deadlines.

Email

In order to address personal matters or issues relating to their progress in the course, encourage students to email you if they are unable to meet with you during office hours or about urgent matters. While you are encouraged to support your students, doing so should never be at the expense of your personal well-being (e.g., feeling obligated to respond to a student's email at 11 p.m. with a question about an assignment due before midnight). To prevent this from happening, you may find it useful to identify specific hours in your syllabus for responding to student emails as well as set expectations for how fast you will reply (e.g., within 24 hours) and provide an option for urgent issues (e.g., write "time sensitive" in the subject line). We typically urge students to email us for personal matters such as the need for accommodation, to communicate personal circumstances that can hinder their progress and success in the course, and to provide feedback and/or concerns related to the course.

Answering Questions

If students email you with general questions related to the course, you can ask them also to post the question in the Q&A open discussion forum, which gives other students a chance to reply or at least to benefit from your response to the question. Additionally, if a student asks a question that has already been covered within the LMS, in your response, you should refer the student to the course syllabus, course announcements, or wherever the information has been covered. Taking this approach can encourage students to review the course materials instead of reaching out to you. The deterrence will hopefully reduce email overload and allow you the time and space to respond to individual student issues or concerns.

Inactivity the First Week

You should email students who are inactive for the first week of the course to express your concern and to let them know that they run the risk of being dropped from the course. If they do not respond with an explanation of extenuating circumstances that allow for accommodation, you should indeed drop them.

Similarly, students who enroll late may not fully understand the importance of online engagement and deadlines. You should email those students to formulate a plan and timeline to ensure they are caught up in the class. Since a lot of community building and foundation work is done within the first week, we typically do not allow students to enroll later than that unless they demonstrate a clear understanding of the importance of making up the work and have a plan to do so as quickly as possible.

Virtual Office Hours

Virtual office hours typically occur through a video conferencing platform (i.e., Skype or Zoom) or other flexible formats (i.e., email, online chat, telephone) during a time determined by the instructor. Virtual office hours are beneficial for student learning and engagement because they allow for increased student-faculty contact and provide a virtual space for students to get answers to questions related to the course content. Unfortunately, many students do not understand the purpose and value of attending the office hours, so by the time they finally decide to make use of them, it is almost always too late. For this reason, it is important to explain the purpose of virtual office hours up front and throughout the course. You might also require that students meet with you at least once at the beginning of the course to help them establish a level of comfort with you and a better understanding of the usefulness of office hours. Increasing students' use of virtual office hours can help them succeed in your course as well as decrease their need to email you with questions or concerns. Finally, as mentioned in an earlier section, instructors should be open to meeting with students outside of their scheduled office hours in light of other commitments students may have at that time.

Feedback on Assignments

Constructive feedback is essential to student success in any course, but it is particularly important in online courses in which students do not receive the informal feedback that they may have gotten in a face-to-face class setting. Therefore, in the online setting, students necessarily rely more on the instructor's written or video feedback on assignments in order to gauge what they are doing correctly and incorrectly. Feedback should be given in a timely manner and comments should tie the feedback to the grading rubric for that particular assignment. Below are some tips for providing effective feedback for Diversity 101 assignments.

TIP: Provide Group Feedback on Module Activities

Most modules in the Diversity 101 course involve formative assessments such as interactive or reflective activities that require students to post responses to a discussion forum. These activities are low-stakes or simply graded for completion. Instructors should provide feedback to the class as a whole by summarizing the discussion, correcting any misconceptions, and pointing out a few particular posts that make a relevant point. Doing so communicates to students that you are following the discussion and that everyone's participation matters.

TIP: Provide Detailed Feedback on First and Second Summary Discussion Forums

The Summary Discussion forum is the summative assessment for most modules. As previously discussed, student participation in these discussions is guided by a detailed rubric intended to inform them about how to successfully complete the assignment. Early in the course, however, students may not understand how to meet the criteria or how you will evaluate their work in relation to the rubric. Therefore, providing detailed feedback on the first Summary Discussion helps them better understand how to meet your expectations. Detailed feedback on the second Summary Discussion, in turn, lets them know if they have successfully followed your comments from the previous assignment. After that, your feedback can focus more on responses to the substance of what they post than on the specific criteria outlined in the rubric such as number and style of citations, copy editing, and answering all of the questions. The rubric we use in Diversity 101 also includes expectations for replying to peers' posts, including number and quality of replies. When student responses fail to meet these expectations, your feedback will let them know how they can better contribute to the online learning environment.

TIP: Provide Additional Support for Academic Writing and Citation Issues

The Diversity 101 rubric includes expectations for writing and citations, but not all students are equipped to meet these requirements. Our academic discipline uses APA style citations, a style with which some undergraduate students tend to struggle. It is therefore helpful to provide at least one group office hour focused on answering questions and providing guidance on using APA. It is also important to share (and sometimes direct students to use) any available online tutorial resources.

Managing Hot Moments

Due to the nature of the content of Diversity 101, the nature of online (mis)communication, and the fact that students will be sharing their personal experiences (and thus making themselves vulnerable), it is possible that what we call "hot moments" will occur in the online discussions. Sometimes the hot moment may be a misunderstanding or a sharp difference of perspectives. You can intervene by asking questions in the discussion forum that will help the students clarify their meaning and understand one another better. And there are times when you simply must step in, such as when a student makes an offensive comment or joke based on race, gender, disability, religious background, or sexual orientation. Such remarks may not always be intentional, but if left unaddressed they can create a hostile or unwelcoming environment for all students, not just those students targeted by the comments. Below are some basic guidelines for addressing these touchy situations.

Addressing Unintentionally Offensive Comments

If the behavior involves something unintentionally offensive, such as the use of out-of-date terminology that some identity groups find offensive, you should first reach out to the offending student and explain that although they might not have meant any offense (or even have been aware that their terminology was no longer considered acceptable), their comments could have had a negative impact. Let them know that you are going to post a response on the discussion board in case other students might also need the information. Then post to the discussion board without mentioning the offending student by name but rather focusing on what was said, with the corrected information. For example,

Incident: A student posts a comment about "the Indians" who were protesting the Dakota Access Pipeline.

Instructor Response to Student via Email: *Hi Sally! Thank you for your discussion post about the protests over the Dakota Access Pipeline. In addition to raising an important topic, you have unintentionally provided an additional learning opportunity for the class by using the word "Indian." Although this label is still used in many places and may be preferred by some people who identify with indigenous communities, the more widely preferred term is "Native American." This raises an important topic about preferred labels and changing terminology that is important for everyone to consider, so I am going to address it on the discussion board. I think everyone will really benefit from this discussion, so thank you again. Please let me know if you have any questions or concerns.*

Instructor Response to Group Discussion Board: *Hi all! I wanted to take this opportunity to discuss an important issue under the broad topic of "inclusive language." At the heart of it, inclusive language is about using terminology (or labels) preferred by the people about whom you are writing. This is one way to show respect for people who are different from you in terms of race, ethnicity, gender, nationality, etc. This isn't always easy because preferred terminology often evolves and changes. For example, while the term "Indian" was widely used for centuries and it is still used by government agencies and within those communities, today it is more appropriate to use the term "Native American." That said, not every person of Native American decent is going to prefer that term either, so there is no hard-and-fast rule. I've attached a few resources in our additional resources section for those who want to explore more. I'll continue to post information as opportunities arise!*

Addressing Intentionally Offensive Comments

If the behavior involves direct attacks or intentionally offensive language, remove the post immediately. To make sure that students who saw the offending post know that you are handling the situation, you can post a comment referring to the community norms or netiquette guidelines and any other campus policies that might apply. Then reach out to the individual student who made the offensive comment and give them the opportunity to discuss the behavior. It is important to remember how little we may know about some students, their troubles, or their mental health. In the best case, these students might just need some additional support. In the worst case, they could be a danger to themselves or others. To address the offensive behavior, you should have a meeting or phone call with the student. In most cases, your basic goals for this conversation will be to help the student understand the negative impact of their behavior, to understand more clearly what may have led to this behavior, and to provide both support and consequences. Below are some prompts to help you think through how to approach this conversation. It may be helpful for you to script out what you would like to say ahead of time. Even if you do not follow the script, thinking out the words you would like to use can help you in the heat of the moment.

1. **Describe the situation in objective terms.** It is also helpful to refer to any policies or course norms that were violated.
    We need to talk about what happened this week on the discussion board. As you know, the use of racial slurs is completely prohibited in our learning community as well as by the student code of conduct.

2. **Describe the student's previous behaviors, both positive and negative.** This gives context to the incident and lets the student know that you do not only see their negative behavior.
    Although you have made some important contributions to our discussions, I've also spoken to you a few times about how your tone and use of sarcasm can sometimes be off-putting. Your use of racial slurs is an escalation of inappropriate behavior and crosses a line.

3. **Describe the impact of the behavior on you and/or the other students in the course.** It is important that the student understands the impact of their behavior in real practical terms, rather than emotional terms, which the student may simply deny or dismiss. In other words, rather than telling them that

they hurt someone's feelings, tell them that they had a negative impact on their educational experience.

This language is hurtful to your peers and destructive to our learning process. Just like you, everyone is paying money and investing time to be here, so everyone has the right to a respectful learning environment.

4. **Describe the options the student has or the actions you will take in response.** Depending on how severe the incident was, it may be possible to bring the student back into the community, if they are willing to take responsibility for their actions. Severe incidents likely violate student conduct policies and may need to be referred to the appropriate office. Discuss the issue with the chair of your department to find out the appropriate processes.

   I would like to work with you to remain in the course, but we will need to do some work to repair the impact of your behavior on our learning community. Please let me know if you are willing to discuss this further. In either case, I will be notifying your academic advisor so she can follow up with you and see if there are other support resources that might be helpful to you.

If the student persists in the disruptive behavior and/or reacts negatively to your attempts to have a discussion, contact their academic advisor to seek input and support. You might also consider other mental health or safety resources available at your institution.

Students with Real-Life Situations

While enrolled in your course, students may experience physical and mental illness, new job assignments/promotion, death of a family member, and so forth. First and foremost, you will want to express empathy and support for whatever it is that they are going through. You should also be as flexible as possible as you work with the student to determine the appropriate course of action moving forward. This may depend on how far along the student has progressed in the course as well as their capacity to do the work moving forward. It is important to help students be realistic about what they will be able to do given their current situation.

Part 2 References

Boettcher, J. V., & Conrad, R. M. (2021). *The online teaching survival guide: Simple and practical pedagogical tips*. John Wiley & Sons.

Conrad, R. M., & Donaldson, J. A. (2012). *Continuing to engage the online learner: More activities and resources for creative instruction* (Vol. 35). John Wiley & Sons.

Palloff, R. M., & Pratt, K. (2007). *Building online learning communities: Effective strategies for the virtual classroom* (2nd ed.). John Wiley & Sons.

Stavredes, T. (2011). *Effective online teaching: Foundations and strategies for student success*. John Wiley & Sons.

PART 3

The Diversity 101 Curriculum

Module 1

GROWING A LEARNING COMMUNITY

The first module is the participants' entry point into the learning environment, so it is important to set a collaborative and welcoming tone. While the student version of the orientation module described in the previous chapter focuses on community building and ensuring that students understand course expectations, the orientation module for faculty and staff focuses on preparing participants to be part of a learning community. A learning community, or community of practice, is a voluntary association among participants who share a common goal or interest as well as a sense of accountability and responsibility to each other and the learning process (Cox, 2004; Hord, 2009; Sherer et al., 2003). In this way, a learning community promotes more active learning, a sense of trust, and the foundation for authentic dialogue, all key elements to the transformative learning process. After being introduced to the concept of a learning community, the participants introduce themselves by answering discussion prompts. As you will see below, each of the discussion board prompts has a strategic purpose in terms of building a sense of community and entering the topic of diversity in a safe, fun, and comfortable way. The introductions not only give the participants the opportunity to get to know one another but they also give the facilitator a lot of useful information about where people are in terms of their starting points, their concerns, and their hopes.

The module overview below provides information about what participants will learn and the tasks they will need to accomplish. This module does not include any scripted videos, but you are encouraged to create your own introduction video to share with participants. You may also want to share your screen and walk the participants through the course site and highlight features such as module structure, how to reply to discussion posts, additional resources, and other relevant features. Module 1 typically does not require more than an hour to complete the required tasks.

Module 1 Overview: Sample Text

Growing a Learning Community

Community is about a sense of belonging. It involves a conscious commitment to uphold and contribute to the needs and interests of the group. In the context of this course, it is assumed that we have a shared interest in our own personal growth and learning, as well as a commitment to making our communities more inclusive, equitable, and enjoyable for all. By participating in this course, you are a member of a learning community committed to supporting each other's learning through active participation and thoughtful engagement.

Learning communities are like gardens. We must first prepare the soil before we start planting seeds of knowledge. That's what this module is about!

Essential Questions

In this module, we'll explore the following essential questions designed to build the foundation for this course:

- What is a learning community?
- What does it mean to be part of a learning community whose purpose it is to explore difficult issues in order to create more welcoming and inclusive campuses and society?
- Who are the members of our learning community?
- What are our responsibilities to each other to ensure this is a safe, supportive place for conversation and differences of perspective?

Activities

The activities in this module consist of watching the Instructor Introduction video, which also includes tips for participating in this course. Then, you will introduce yourself and meet your co-learners via online video introductions (with option for text if preferred). You will then be asked to review some suggested guidelines and community norms and provide your feedback.

The module concludes with suggested Action Item resources to help you implement these introductory (soil preparation) practices in your own work areas.

Videos

Instructor Introduction Video

Discussions

There are two discussions for this module:

- Introductions
- Community Norms and Guidelines

Readings, Handouts, and Additional Resources

See additional resources section for optional articles about learning communities.

Module 1 Activities

Discussion 1. Introductions

Module 1 includes two activities. The first is the introductions discussion forum, followed by a consideration of community norms and guidelines. These activities help the participants get comfortable with one another and with the structure of the course.

Discussion 1. Sample Text

Welcome to our online learning community! Let's learn about who is in the learning community. Please post your responses to the following prompts in the discussion forum. Then, read the responses of several of your peers. Reply to at least two people: one person with whom you have things in common and one person who has different experiences or interests.

Facilitator Note about Discussion Prompt #1: The first part of the introduction highlights some aspects of diversity that typically go unrecognized. The participants in this course may reflect diversity in terms of organizational tenure, organizational position or role, and area of expertise. Some participants have been at the university for decades, while others have been there for months. Some participants are faculty members, while others are staff or administrators. Participants come from a variety of departments and hold varying types of professional expertise. For example, a typical cohort has included a Dean from the Law School, a Human Resource Administrator, a Manager from Food Services, a Program Associate from Residential Life, a Department Chair from School of Medicine, a Health Educator, and an Advisor from International Programs. It is important to point out to participants how much this aspect of the group's diversity enriches the group's learning. Regardless of organizational rank, experience, or education, all participants are equal and valuable participants in the learning community.

Discussion Prompt #1: State your job, department, and how long you've been at the university.

Facilitator Note about Discussion Prompt #2: Asking participants to share their preferred name and pronouns is in and of itself a practice of inclusion. For a variety of reasons, participants may prefer to be called by a name that is different from how it appears on the class roster. As for personal pronouns, participants who do not work in student affairs or are not acquainted with social justice trends may be unaware of the practice of sharing one's pronouns. Nonetheless, it is important to introduce the concept in the beginning of the course in order to reassure all involved that the online community is a safe place, particularly since there may also be participants who do not identify within the gender binary.

Discussion Prompt #2: What name and pronouns do you use? People's pronouns are typically him/his, her/hers, or them/theirs (gender neutral pronouns for those who do not identify as a binary gender, i.e., male or female). If this is a new concept/practice for you, don't worry...we'll go into more in later in the course when we talk about inclusive language and inclusive practices. For the moment, just go with it and trust that the purpose is to build a safe and inclusive community, where we don't make assumptions about each other and we are all valued and seen.

Facilitator Note about Discussion Prompt #3: This question provides participants who are new to the online course platform with the opportunity to express any fears or concerns they have (which is often met with supportive remarks by peer learners in response). It also gives the facilitator some important information in terms of how much additional explanation/encouragement some participants may need for engaging on the platform.

Discussion Prompt #3: What is your experience/comfort level with online classes?

Facilitator Note about Discussion Prompt #4: Giving people a chance to share why they are taking the course helps everyone understand each other's starting points and intentions. Participants come to the course for different reasons, with different levels of awareness or experiences, and with different learning needs. Stating one's intentions of up front helps to situate people and avoid the formation of assumptions.

Discussion Prompt #4: What are your reasons for taking this course?

Facilitator Note about Discussion Prompt #5: This simple icebreaker question is an almost fool-proof way to start the course off on the right foot. The premise is simple. People enjoy talking about what they enjoy doing and they enjoy connecting around shared interests, as well as learning about new things they might enjoy doing. It is clear that this activity achieves its purpose when participants respond to each other's posts (i.e., "I love that place too!" or "I never heard of that place, but I can't wait to check it out!"). In addition to putting people at ease, this activity provides a simple demonstration of the value of diversity, as I explain in my follow-up to the introductions.

Discussion Prompt #5: If you were asked to give recommendations to a person visiting [your town] or [your state] for the very first time, what are five things that you would recommend that they do, see, and/or eat?

Discussion 1. Conclusion: Sample Text

Thank you for the great introductions thus far! I love starting the course with the introduction question about what people recommend for fun and enjoyment. I learn about someplace new and interesting every time...even after facilitating this course so many times! More importantly, as you may have noticed already, our introduction discussion is a perfect demonstration of diversity at its best. I always see many shared interests among individuals who might also be very different from each other (in various ways), as well as many people getting new and interesting ideas from this diversity of perspectives/experiences. As you will see in our upcoming discussions, you have so much to learn from the variety of perspectives and experiences that you each bring to the conversation.

Discussion 2. Community Norms and Guidelines

Having participants actively engage with the Community Norms and Guidelines provides a layer of accountability that you may refer back to later if needed. For example, if participants are not posting discussions on time, the facilitator might say, "As we agreed to in the community norms and guidelines, it is important to respect the deadlines so that we can move forward in the discussion as a group." It also gives participants the opportunity to consider their role and responsibility in the course and reflect on the importance of intentional communication in other contexts.

Discussion 2. Sample Text

The success of this course depends on thoughtful participation in our online discussions. These discussions are the way we will engage with each other, share experiences, challenge assumptions, and get to know each other as colleagues and as individuals. In order to have thoughtful and productive discussions, it is important that we have some shared understanding about how we will engage with each other. This is particularly important in an online environment, where there is lots of room for miscommunication and misunderstanding.

Below are some suggested norms and guidelines to help make this a productive and worthwhile experience for everyone. Please read and reflect on each of these suggestions. Consider what you agree with, what might be difficult for you, and what is missing. Post your reflections to the discussion forum.

Community Norms and Guidelines: Sample Text

Respect deadlines. In order to simulate a full group discussion on the discussion boards, it is imperative that you post no later than the weekly deadlines as listed in each module.

Demonstrate respect for differences. We all come to the table with differing experiences and viewpoints, which means that we have so much to learn from each other! In order to get the most out of this opportunity, it is important that we don't shy away from differences. Rather, we should show respect for differences by seeking to understand, asking questions, clarifying our understanding, and/or respectfully explaining our own perspective. This allows everybody to come away with a new way of seeing the issue.

Respect confidentiality. Some of the topics/issues we discuss may be sensitive and/or personal. While it is totally okay to talk about the things you are learning with your colleagues, please do not share what other participants post outside of this course without their explicit permission.

Assume good intentions. If someone says something that bothers you for any reason, assume that they did not mean to be offensive and ask them to clarify what they meant, then explain the impact it had on you. If someone tells you that something you wrote bothered them, assume that they are not attacking you but rather that they are sharing something that might be important for you to know.

Be generous. Your weekly posts are not simply requirements for participation; they are your contributions to group learning. So please be generous to your peers by being thoughtful, open, and honest.

Be inclusive. It's important to be intentional about making sure we "see" each other in an online community by making sure that everyone has at least one response and replying to people who ask us questions. If you are unsure who to respond to, try looking for posts that have not yet received a reply.

Be substantive. Your peers will get more out of a reply that goes beyond "I agree" or "I like your post." Explain why their post resonates with you. Conversely, try NOT to avoid responding to posts with which you disagree or that you do not understand. Ask questions, seek clarification, explain your differing view. This is how we all learn.

Be organized. Although this is a voluntary course, your timely participation is required to make it work. Past participants have suggested making reminders in your calendar to help keep up with posting deadlines. I highly recommend this strategy. However, I will send a "friendly reminder" as the deadline approaches. I will send another if you miss a deadline. If you get such messages from me, I hope you will forgive my "nagging" and remember that I'm just trying to keep us all moving along together so that we all get the most out of it. And if you need an extension, just let me know.

Be patient. Be patient with yourselves . . . expect some discomfort in this learning process. Be patient with each other . . . understand that we all come to this from different starting points and perspectives. Try to meet people where they are.

Discussion 2. Forum Prompts: Community Norms and Guidelines

1. Which guidelines stood out to you as particularly important for our group success? Why?
2. Are there any guidelines that you might have trouble with? If so, which ones and why?

3. Is there anything that you would like to add or take away from the guidelines?
4. Do you think these guidelines might be useful in other contexts? If so, where and why?

Examples of Participant Discussion Forum Posts

[Camille, 45 years old, African American, female staff member] I don't have any issues with these guidelines, nothing I would take away. But I'd like to add one, at least for myself. I'm reminded that there is a big difference between knowing the "correct" answer and internalizing it as a truth, a value, and in manifesting it in daily behavior. I think we need to commit to being honest with ourselves, to dig as deep as feels right to each of us. That takes courage, and that takes trust—hence, the importance of confidentiality. If I can't trust you to hear my fears and confusion without judgment, my growth through this course will be hindered, and I think yours will be, too. Similarly, I want to hear your honest thoughts and feedback, and I promise I will withhold judgment as well

[Tristan, 37 years old, White, female faculty member] Hi Camille, I honestly could not have said this better as you covered the confidentiality and trust factor perfectly, at least how I perceive it. This was actually a concern of mine expressed to the instructor prior to the course, so thank you for a well-said response.

[Olivia, 27 years old, bi-racial, female staff member] Camille, I love that you said this. It does take courage, and I'm right there with you that I want to hear honest thoughts and feedback so that I truly learn something.

The closing of the module should demonstrate enthusiasm, encourage ongoing participation, and include reminders of upcoming tasks. It also is an opportunity to encourage participants to put their learning into practice by taking some action based on a concept from the module. An example is provided for each module.

Module 1 Conclusion: Sample Text

Thank you for your participation in the orientation module! This is important work for building our learning community and for getting you ready to dive into the course content. I hope you are feeling a bit more comfortable with the online format and are now excited to move forward with your cohort of peer learners! The activities you engaged in can also be applied outside of the course site. Here are couple of ideas for you to take action:

Facilitate a community norms and guidelines activity. Next time you have a meeting or start a new discussion topic with your students, facilitate a discussion to create some community norms and guidelines for your team or your class.

Get to know your coworkers a little better. Based on our introductions activity, ask some of your coworkers what their top 5 recommendations are for fun and enjoyment either where they live now or where they are from. You might not only get some great ideas, but you learn a little bit more about people when they share what they enjoy.

Before you move forward to the next module, please make sure that you have read all of your peers' introductions, replied to several people, and commented on the Community Norms and Guidelines.

Having successfully completed the requirements of this module, most participants who had some trepidation about the course because of the content and/or the online platform will be feeling more at ease and more confident in regard to participating in the course. Those who were very eager to dive in may also have benefited from the reminder that it is important to do some work up front and be very intentional about moving forward.

Module 1 References

Cox, M. D. (2004). Introduction to faculty learning communities. *New Directions for Teaching and Learning, 2004*(97), 5–23.

Hord, S. M. (2009). Professional learning communities. *Journal of Staff Development, 30*(1), 40–43.

Sherer, P. D., Shea, T. P., & Kristensen, E. (2003). Online communities of practice: A catalyst for faculty development. *Innovative Higher Education, 27*(3), 183–194.

Module 2

INTRODUCTION TO DIVERSITY

We all should know that diversity makes for a rich tapestry, and we must understand that all the threads of the tapestry are equal in value no matter what their color.
—Maya Angelou

Inclusion is not a matter of political correctness. It is the key to growth.
—Jesse Jackson

As previously discussed, many participants come to a diversity training or course with preconceived notions about what diversity means and why it matters. The purpose of this module is to deepen their perspectives on the concept of diversity and increase their understanding and ability to articulate why diversity, equity, and inclusion (DEI) are important concepts for individuals, groups, organizations, and society.

Module 2 serves as a catalyst to transformative learning by encouraging participants to question some of their long-held assumptions about the meaning of the term *diversity* and to begin thinking about the concept in more nuanced and complex ways.

This course isn't just useful for the work environment, but in our everyday life. We are all unique individuals with different layers. Each of us is diverse in our own unique way, and for others to see our uniqueness is what life is all about. Take this course and learn about your own layers and the layers of others. You will come away viewing diversity in a whole new way.

–Sarah, 46-year-old, White, female staff member and past participant

---

Module 2 Overview: Sample Text

Introduction to Diversity

Most people come to a diversity training or course with preconceived notions about what diversity means and why it matters. The purpose of this module is to broaden your perspectives about the concept of diversity and increase your understanding and ability to articulate why diversity, equity, and inclusion (DEI) are important concepts for individuals, groups, organizations, and society.

Essential Questions
- What is diversity?
- Why is diversity important to where we work and live?
- What does diversity have to do with me?

In this module, you will watch two videos, do a "defining diversity" activity off-line with some people you know, then engage in conversation with your colleagues in this course about what you learned.

Videos

The content in this module is divided into two topics presented in short video mini-lectures:

Video Mini-Lecture #1: This part of the module explores four dominant approaches to diversity in the workplace and higher education: *Diversity as demographics* (recruiting, hiring, and promoting previously excluded groups), *diversity as cultural differences* (managing diversity), *diversity as good for business* (harnessing diversity for educational or business goals), and *diversity as social justice* (addressing discrimination, harassment, and exclusion). The purpose of explaining approaches to diversity rather than definitions of diversity is to provide a more complex understanding of how diversity relates to workplace practices so that we can be more precise with our usage of the term and its implied meanings.

Video Mini-Lecture #2: This part of the module is intended to build your capacity to articulate why diversity and inclusion are important, not just for some people but for everyone. This part of the module presents a multilevel model of the importance and impact of diversity that provides a framework for understanding the interrelated relationship between individuals, groups, organizations, institutions, society, and the global context.

Discussions

Please post your initial responses to the discussion prompts by _____ .
A synchronous dialogue will take place on _____ .

Additional Resources

The additional resources in this module include articles from magazines and academic journals to deepen your understanding of diversity and inclusion in the workplace.

What is diversity?

1. the condition of having or being composed of differing elements, *especially*: the inclusion of different types of people (such as people of different races or cultures) in a group or organization programs intended to promote *diversity* in schools

2. an instance of being composed of differing elements or qualities

Diversity. (n.d.). Retrieved September 29, 2021, from https://www.merriam-webster.com/dictionary/diversity

MODULE 2A.1

What Is Diversity?

It might seem like there is a straightforward or simple response to this question. And, in fact, the *Merriam-Webster Dictionary* offers two definitions of the word *diversity*. One is "the condition of having or being composed of differing elements," such as "the inclusion of different types of people in a group or organization." The second definition is "an instance of being composed of differing elements or qualities," such as a diversity of opinions. These definitions seem pretty straightforward, but when I started listening to how people use the word *diversity*, I'd hear things like . . .

Things people say about diversity...

"He just doesn't care about diversity." ●

"You just aren't diverse enough." ●

"I think diversity is really important." ●

"They need to hire more people who are diverse." ●

"We need to celebrate diversity." ●

"Diversity must be integrated into everything we do." ●

"She is really a believer [in diversity]." ●

MODULE 2A.2

Things People Say about Diversity . . .

"He just doesn't care about diversity." "You just aren't diverse enough." "We need to celebrate diversity." "They need to hire more people who are diverse." Based on these quotes, one might wonder what in the heck diversity is?! Is it a feeling? A value? A personal quality?

MODULE 2A.3

Talking about Diversity . . .

The different ways we talk about diversity has to do with the different things we do about diversity. There are four main approaches to diversity in organizational life. One common understanding of diversity is in terms of demographics. Diversity in terms of demographics is an important part of the conversation because women and minorities are underrepresented in many industries and at the upper levels of many organizations.

Another approach to diversity is in terms of managing differences. These differences involve culturally based values, assumptions, beliefs, and ways of communicating that can be beneficial to the workplace but also problematic if we do not have the awareness and skills to handle these differences effectively. From this perspective we talk about diversity as something that needs to be understood, managed, embraced, or celebrated.

Another approach to diversity is what is often referred to as "The Business Case." The business case doesn't view diversity as a problem to be managed but rather as benefit to be "harnessed" to achieve organizational goals. In the corporate world, that means the bottom line. In health care, government, non-profit, education, and other service industries, the business case for diversity is mission-driven and refers to the need to have a diverse employee and leadership base in order to provide better, more effective service to the communities they serve.

And finally, a fourth way we talk about diversity is in relation to equity and inclusion. When we talk about diversity from this perspective, we are focusing on aspects of our organizational structures and climate that create barriers for different groups of people. Of course, we have made, and continue to make, great strides in policies, laws, and practices that create more equitable opportunities for people of all backgrounds. But the fact remains that there is still more to do in making our workplaces inclusive and welcoming for individuals who do not fit the profile of the majority in terms of race, ethnicity, gender and gender identity, physical/mental ability, sexual orientation, and so on. From this perspective, diversity is viewed as a social and organizational justice issue.

You might be wondering how the simple word *diversity* came to mean so many different things. Let me take you through a brief history of the concept of workplace diversity that will help you understand where we are today.

The pre-diversity era

1960s – 1970s

- Civil Rights
- Affirmative Action
- Compliance
- Representation/Quotas
- Equity
- Anti-discrimination

Manuscripts and Archives Division, The New York Public Library. "New York University Weinstein Hall demonstration" *The New York Public Library Digital Collections*, 1970.

MODULE 2A.4

The Pre-Diversity Era

In the civil rights era of the 1960s and 1970s, diversity was not the buzzword that it is today. In fact, I'm not sure if people were really talking about diversity at all. At that time, people in organizations were talking about equal rights and representation of women and people of color, compliance with new rules around hiring and contracting, anti-discrimination policies, and so on. Thinking about these topics, you can see how the civil rights era set the foundation for some of the ways that we talk about diversity today . . . particularly when we focus on demographics and policies. But as we move forward, you'll see how diversity has come to mean so much more.

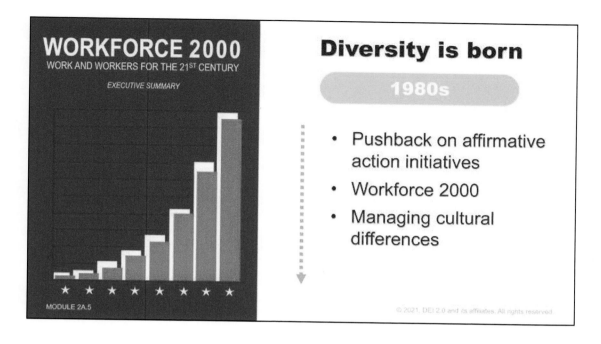

Diversity Is Born

In the 1980s there was a big cultural shift. The Reagan era marked the rise of neo-liberal politics and a big backlash against government intervention in businesses, such as policies requiring quotas for hiring women and people of color.

However, in the late 1980s, the Department of Labor issued a widely cited report called Workforce 2000, which talked about the need for businesses and other workplaces to respond to the fast-growing increase of women and minorities into the workforce. Basically, it said that the workforce was changing and that business as usual was no longer going to cut it. Companies were going to have to learn how to manage cultural differences in order to stay viable.

People who had been working in affirmative action or equal opportunity areas also realized that, in order to stay viable, they were going to have to change their tactics for working with companies. This period marked the rise of "diversity training" as consultants and practitioners tried to help companies face the challenges of their new diverse workforce.

At this time, diversity was often seen as a problem to be managed. It's also interesting to note that in these few decades, discussions around diversity almost exclusively centered on women and people of color. I think this may be why, even today, when people talk about diversity, they are often referring specifically to racial and gender diversity . . . even though we know that diversity is far broader than that.

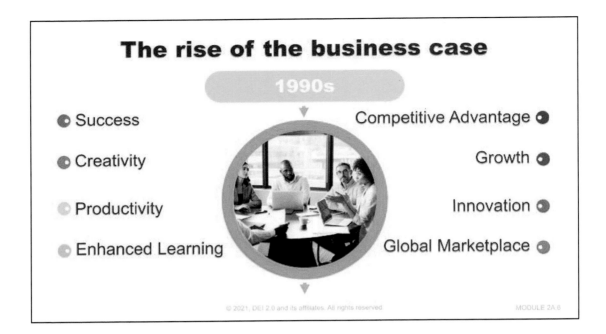

The rise of the business case

1990s

- Success
- Creativity
- Productivity
- Enhanced Learning

- Competitive Advantage
- Growth
- Innovation
- Global Marketplace

© 2021, DEI 2.0 and its affiliates. All rights reserved.

MODULE 2A.6

The Rise of the Business Case

The 1990s marked the rise of the internet, increased economic power of diverse U.S. markets, and a more competitive global economy. Savvy corporations understood that they needed a diverse and culturally competent workforce in order to meet the challenges and reap the benefits of these new markets. The business case is based on the idea that a diverse employee base can lead to a more productive workforce, a broader and happier customer base, and a competitive advantage in the global marketplace.

When we talk about diversity from the business case perspective, we use terms like *competitive advantage*, *productivity*, *growth*, and *creativity*. In contrast to the previous decades that focused on social justice and managing differences, the business case for diversity focuses on the benefits that are derived in an organization inclusive of people from a variety of backgrounds who bring their differing perspectives, experiences, and knowledge. There is a large body of research that shows that racial and gender diversity in organizations is correlated with higher financial returns and overall company performance.

Beyond Diversity to Inclusion

The 2000s marked another important shift in the way that we understand, talk about, and do things related to diversity. We didn't shift away from the word *diversity*, but we now talk about diversity in terms of *inclusion*.

Inclusion entails an expansive understanding of diversity beyond race, ethnicity, and gender. Inclusion considers all aspects of identity that make a difference in our daily lives, such as disability, religious affiliation, sexual orientation, gender identity, health status, socioeconomic status, and so on.

In practice, inclusion means that all members of an organization feel welcomed and valued for who they are and what they bring to the table. It means that policies and practices do not create obstacles to full participation and engagement in organizational life.

Put another way, diversity is about inviting a bunch of different people to the dinner table. Inclusion is making sure that everyone can participate in the making and eating of the food. This way, everyone gets what they need to thrive. Not only is an inclusive dinner more delicious than a dinner prepared for one set of tastes, it is also healthier and ensures an organization is fortified with ideas, knowledge, and talent from a wide range of perspectives, experiences, and backgrounds.

Understanding and acknowledging structural racism

REALITY   EQUALITY   EQUITY   LIBERATION

The difference between the terms equality, equity, and liberation, illustrated; © Interaction Institute for Social Change | Artist: Angus Maguire

Understanding and Acknowledging Structural Racism

The most recent shift in the way we understand and talk about issues related to diversity and inclusion is marked by terminology such as *structural racism*, *institutionalized racism*, *anti-racism*, and *White supremacy*. The issues highlighted in this terminology are not new. What is new is the growing awareness and willingness to name the problems that the civil rights era began to address.

The murder of George Floyd in May 2020 reignited the Black Lives Matter movement, which arose out of the protests in response to the killing of Michael Brown in 2014. The momentum of this new era of civil rights activism is changing the way our society and our institutions understand, talk about, and approach racial diversity, equity, and inclusion. We saw this shift most notably in President Biden's inaugural address when he repudiated White supremacy and vowed to fight systemic racism.

This important acknowledgement, explicitly naming the problem in a way that had not been done in recent history, sets the tone for our work moving forward.

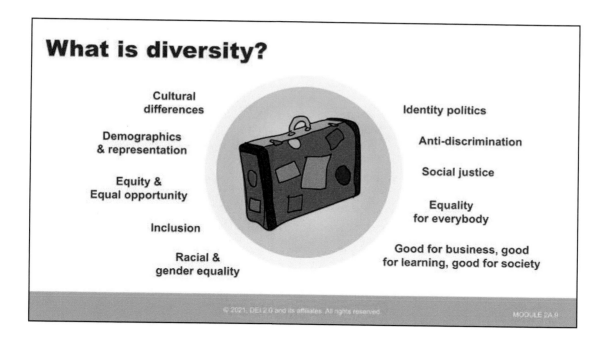

What is diversity?

Cultural differences

Demographics & representation

Equity & Equal opportunity

Inclusion

Racial & gender equality

Identity politics

Anti-discrimination

Social justice

Equality for everybody

Good for business, good for learning, good for society

MODULE 2A.9

What Is Diversity?

In the meantime, let's go back to the question. I think of diversity as a well-worn suitcase that we've been carrying down this road for many decades, adding new meanings as we go along. The new meanings do not erase or replace the previous meanings; they are all still relevant and important. Each of the meanings of diversity implies different strategies, policies, practices, and approaches, so clarity is important.

If we are not clear about what we mean, two people can be talking about diversity and think they are talking about the same thing, even if they are not. Another problem is that when a word becomes a stand-in for so many meanings, it almost ceases to have any meaning at all.

So perhaps we should think about being more precise with our usage of the word. For example, when we are talking about the need for more representation of people from different racial backgrounds, let's use the term *racial diversity*. Or when we are noting the lack of women in leadership positions, for example, we should say *gender diversity*. And when we want to talk about ensuring our plans, policies, and practices do not exclude people from various identity groups, let's use the word *inclusion* or *equity*.

I also encourage you to open dialogue and ask questions the next time someone says something like "We need to celebrate diversity" or "We need diversity training." Take a minute to dig a little deeper and ask, "What precisely do you mean by that?"

Module 2 Activity: Ask Around

Facilitator Note: This activity is impactful on two fronts. First, participants engage in interesting or meaningful conversations about diversity with people in their lives. Then, they come back to the course site to reflect on and share that experience with others.

Activity Instructions: Sample Text

Now that you've watched that video, aren't you curious about what people would say if you asked them to define diversity?

Go ahead and ask a few students, friends, and/or family members (ideally, ask a "diverse" sample of people in terms of age, gender, and/or race/ethnicity) what the word *diversity* means to them. Let them know it's for a class and that their identity will not be shared with your classmates.

Write a brief post on this discussion about that experience, reflecting on questions such as:

What do you learn by asking people to define diversity? Did all of them see it the same way? If not, how did their views differ? Did you have any good conversations based on asking this question?

Read and reply to at least two of your peers' posts.

Examples of Participant Discussion Forum Posts

The following example responses were taken from an undergraduate cohort:

[Savannah, an 18-year-old, Latina, female student] I was at a family gathering tonight and I was able to ask three generations on what they thought diversity meant. I asked my grandparents who range in age from 80 to 90, my parents who are in their 50s, and cousins/friends who are all in their 20s. My grandparents, all who are immigrants to this country, say that diversity is accepting differences and being treated equally. They all faced issues of discrimination and had to work extra hard to prove themselves to be successful, so that makes sense that is how they would define it. My parents are both working professionals, and they talked about it from the business perspective because it is part of their work life. They talked about the global world and said that to be successful you have to find a way to meet the needs of diverse customers. The people my age really talked about acceptance and inclusion and that it doesn't matter what one's race, gender, or sexual identity is but that we should be accepting of differences

[Jackie, 20-year-old, White, female student] After watching the video on diversity, even my own knowledge and thoughts about it had changed. I asked my parents, sisters, and friends. The ages of the participants differed from 19 to 58 including demographics, socioeconomic status and ethnicity taken into account. I learned that many people consider diversity to be differences in individuals and that we enrich the environment around us by celebrating these rather than looking at them in a negative way. I found that those who were closer in age had similar definitions and views. Contrary to my initial view, those I asked who are older (and perhaps wiser) considered diversity in settings such as school, jobs, public. But younger people considered it as inclusive to everyone. One of the best conversations I had on this was with my dad; he has worked for the same company for more years than I have been alive, and he has seen how things have changed over time, and although we will always have differences with people and in society, we have come a long way making diversity flourish in each way possible!

[Howard, a 19-year-old, African American, male student] From the people I asked about how they view the term diversity, the answers ranged everywhere from the rather succinct and basic view of diversity simply meaning many different people, ideas, etc., to it being approached from a professional standpoint, to it being tied directly into the idea of inclusiveness. There were many similarities in our views for some, but others either were much more general or far more detailed. I understand that diversity can mean very different things depending on the context, and thus different experiences affect how each person responds when asked to define diversity. Someone in the professional world, for example, will approach the question from an angle that may reflect certain diversity training from their job. I had an interesting conversation with someone who went into rather deep detail and reflected on the question from their experiences in the workplace, explaining the importance of tolerance, inclusion of others, and avoiding being narrow-minded.

Why should you care about diversity? I assume that you do indeed care because you are investing your time to learn more by taking this class. But how easy is it for you to answer this question?

When I hear people talk about diversity, it seems like there a lot of folks who feel like diversity has nothing to do with them. Some folks feel that diversity programming is a waste of time, and others feel marginalized or minimized when we start talking about diversity. This part of the module is offered to help you better understand and explain to others why diversity is important for everyone, not just for those who are considered different than the dominant norm.

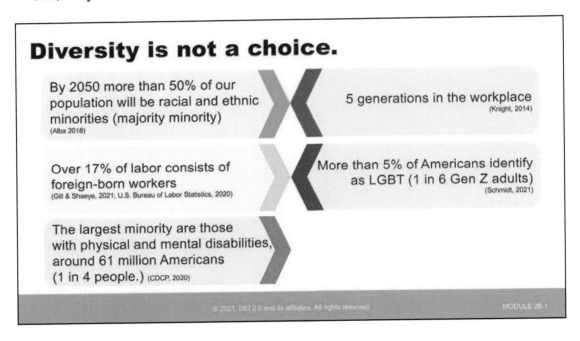

Diversity Is Not a Choice

My first answer to the question of why you should care about diversity is that diversity is not a choice. The United States is and has always been the most diverse nation in the world—and that trend is increasing. In fact, census projections claim that by 2050, there will no longer be one racial majority but, rather, the majority of Americans will be of various racial and ethnic groups of people (Alba, 2018).

In terms of our labor force, foreign born workers make up more than 17% of our labor force (Gill & Shaeye, 2021; U.S. Bureau of Labor Statistics, 2020).

Here's an interesting statistic: the largest minority in the United States are those with physical and mental disabilities—that's around 1 in 4 people (Center for Disease Control, 2020).

Although accurate LGBTQ+ statistics are hard to find, a recent Gallop poll found that more than 5% of Americans identify as LGBTQ+. And about 1 out of every 6 Gen Z adults identity as something other than heterosexual (Jones, 2021; Schmidt, 2021) . In fact, I'd venture a bet that everyone in this course is in some way connected to this identity group, either through your own sexual orientation or that of a friend, family member, or colleague.

And, finally, for the first time in America's history, we have five generations in the workforce (Knight, 2014). Perhaps you've already encountered some differences related to work styles, priorities, and communication preferences among colleagues from different generations.

My point with all these statistics is this: diversity is not a choice, it is the reality we live in. If individuals and organizations are going to be successful, they are going to have to be able to communicate, collaborate, and build relationships with people from backgrounds different from their own. When we understand and embrace our differences, there are wide-ranging benefits for all, as we will now discuss.

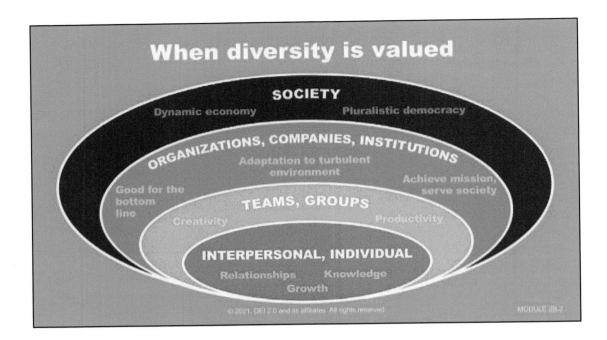

When Diversity Is Valued

To understand the value of diversity, we need to understand how a culture that is welcoming and inclusive of individual and group differences can impact our lives at various levels. Starting at the core, the individual and interpersonal level, when individuals feel valued for what they bring to the table, we can all learn and grow as individuals and enhance our relationships with those around us. Research shows that the more contact we have with diverse ideas, information, and people, the better we can think and learn (Astin, 1993; Gurin et al., 2002; Milem, 2003). We each have so much to gain, so much to offer, and so much to learn from each other.

Now think about these individuals who value diversity working in teams or groups. There is a ton of research that shows that diverse teams can be more productive, more creative, and better at problem-solving than homogenous teams (Freeman & Huang, 2015; Tadmor et al., 2012). Why do you think this is? Because the more varied the insights and perspectives we have at the table, the more possibilities that open up.

And think about what this means for organizations. A culture that is welcoming and inclusive of diversity is good for business, makes organizations more adaptive to turbulent environments, and supports the mission to add value to society (Soares et al., 2011.; Henderson & Herring, 2013; Hunt et al., 2015).

And finally, valuing diversity is the heart of a democratic, pluralistic society (Milem, 2003). We can only thrive by understanding how our individual and group differences makes us stronger as a society.

My point in showing this model is to illustrate that the benefits of diversity start with our individual relationships but extend far beyond to our shared society. In this light, no one can really say that diversity doesn't impact their lives. We all stand to gain by working toward a culture that is diverse, welcoming, and inclusive. Unfortunately, there is a lot of stuff that gets in the way.

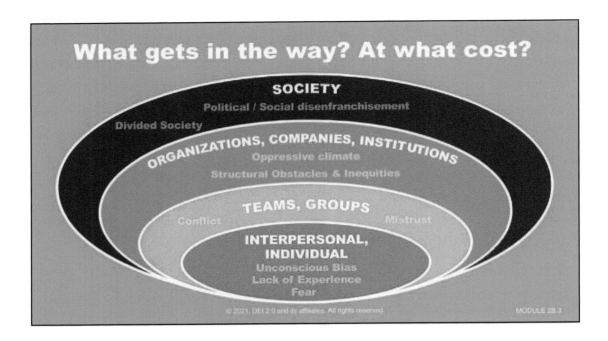

What Gets in the Way? At What Cost?

At the individual and interpersonal level, we may have fear, a lack of experience, and bias that inhibit personal growth and create barriers to relationships. This can create conflict and mistrust in groups and teams and can inhibit group function and job satisfaction. At the organizational level, we have structural obstacles and climate issues that impede our ability to benefit from diversity. And if these hindrances continue outward, we create a divided society marked by political and social alienation.

This is where our work lies, because you can see a lot of this happening on our campus, in our community, and in our society at large. Okay, that's a lot of gloom and doom, but I think it's important to understand what's at stake.

So now the question is: how do make sure that we are headed in the right direction? The good news is that it starts with each of us! And the fact that you are here, participating in this course with a cohort of other people, means that we are already on the right path. Throughout this course, I will encourage you to think about how these different levels are all interconnected. In the next video, we'll start at the core: diversity at the individual and interpersonal level.

In the following excerpts, participants grapple with the complexity of the multiple meanings of diversity and how it impacts individuals, teams, and organizations. This thread provides a great example of how much the online discussion contributes to their learning as they respond to their peers' posts with additional insights, questions, and feedback.

Discussion Prompt

What are your thoughts, questions, or reactions to the module videos?

Examples of Participant Discussion Forum Posts

[Amelia, 32 years old, White, Jewish, female faculty member] It's interesting because, while I agree entirely that diversity is important at all the levels discussed in the two videos, in my day-to-day life, I think about it less at the organizational level. If I were going to define diversity, that might be an arena I would forget about, even though I'm currently doing this course for our company/organization, and it's clearly a focus when discussing hiring faculty members or picking graduate students for our department. So that may not make sense. But I still think about caring about diversity for either individual or team/group purposes (I associate team=department) more than doing them for the good of the organization. For example, I'm not doing this course because I think it's good for the university to have people doing the training, even though it clearly is.

On the other hand, "diversity" the word also feels a bit like a catchphrase at higher levels to indicate something broad (so more the organizational and societal levels), and I think in my own personal life (individual and interpersonal level), I often try to be more specific as to what I'm discussing (i.e., race, ethnicity, culture, gender, gender orientation, sexual orientation, disability, SES, religion, etc.), and I think I've been trying only to use the word diversity when I truly mean it in the broadest sense.

I realize that those two thoughts might be at odds with one another, and I'm trying to understand that a bit more in my head. I look forward to hearing what other people have to say!

[Marie, 40 years old, White, French, faculty] Emily, I had similar thought(s) as you, when I was watching the 2nd video ("why should I care about diversity"): my first motivation in taking this course is more for understanding, self-improvement, and the improvement of how I engage with my students, and I do not/did not typically pay attention to the "business case" aspect of it for the university—but now I feel like I understand a bit more (and have some references to support!) the idea that diversity (and inclusion) is "good for business." I feel a bit uncomfortable with the argument (although of course I don't disagree with the claim itself) that diversity is good for business/the bottom line (and for our enrollment numbers)—but at the same time, it is a reality, and it is a good argument to get people on board with more diverse/inclusive hiring or recruiting practices who may otherwise not be! Thanks for sharing your thoughts!

[Carrie, 48 years old, White, female staff] Amelia and Marie, I was also struck by the "Good for Business" argument. I find myself thinking that it doesn't have to be good for business because embracing diversity (whichever form that might be) is just the right thing to do. However, I do realize I am a bit narrow-minded in that. Having never worked in a for-profit business setting, I see the drive for profits through a distorted nonprofit or academic rose-colored classes. Given the pandemic and the devastation it has caused many, I have started seeing that good for business often means good for employee pay, job opportunities, allowing people to feed house and care for their families. So yes, the good for business argument is definitely true and definitely has value and could move some in the correct direction. The problem then becomes now that businesses are benefiting from diversity how do we make sure that those benefits are being inclusively distributed. That is a rabbit hole I will avoid for now.

[Marie] I appreciated getting a brief history of the term *diversity* because it is such a "catchall" term. I agree that diversity means a lot to different people, and I've often been struck about how "diverse" (as an adjective) is sometimes used by individuals to define themselves (as individuals) or others; which is interesting, considering how the defining trait of diversity is that it involves multiple different characteristics, typically multiple individuals from different backgrounds. We all "contain multitudes" for sure—but I think "diversity" or "diverse" in this sense is often used to mean not white or not belonging to dominant groups (diverse then meaning "minority" or from a mixed ethnic background). I don't mean to erase/deny the reality of those power dynamics/structure reflected in that use of "diverse" because they do impact people's lives—but, as the video says, I think it is helpful to think of diversity as something that everyone can contribute to, because we all have somewhat complex identities and experiences that can help us think outside of the box and bring something to the table (as long as it doesn't silence what others bring to the table, too). Thanks for reading, and looking forward to reading your insights!

Elisa [30 years old, White, female faculty] Marie, thank you for your thoughtful response. I agree the term "diverse" is used often to describe "minority" amongst whiteness. Moving beyond racial diversity is important. I like how you state "diversity as something that everyone can contribute to, because we all have somewhat complex identities and experiences." We may appear similar on the outside but be more diverse than is on the surface.

[Sheila, 58 years old, African American, female faculty] Thinking about diversity from a variety of lenses helps to provide variety in the discussion but also makes the lens blurry to the reader. We don't think or talk about diversity at the different levels. When I think about diversity, I always think about it at the individual or group level. Thinking about diversity at an even broader level was impactful. The "identity" regarding "diversity" is very important and causes individuals/families/communities to treat those organizations according to their reputation of what is perceived versus what is real.

There are many that are comfortable talking about diversity as long as it does not require that they change their behaviors or their biases. I believe that everyone should care about diversity, but I often get frustrated that those who are in "majority" culture get to "choose" when they want to participate when others must think about diversity all of the time.

I had the opportunity to talk to a small group about diversity and topics that they would like to discuss in the future related to diversity. The insights from the group were great in that they brought up examples such as diversity in religion/churches, neighborhoods/communities, health professions, veterans, sports, etc. Bringing up this variety of groups forces you to think about diversity in a way that is more focused on the culture someone was brought up in or chose to join. The group brought up these differences because it makes it very difficult to mix groups from different denominations or faith traditions or health professions. Discussing these differences in how this makes conversations richer as well as outcomes greater when we move outside of homogenous groups was really reinforced with the group and the video.

[Amelia] I really like the points you made, Sheila! I also really appreciate the thoughts from the group when you asked about diversity. I agree that it's really important to think about diversity within different communities (religious, occupation, neighborhood) rather than just thinking about it in a broad, overarching, societal framework, or just within an individual examining their own identity/biases/behavior. I agree that some of the most difficult conversations I've had about diversity are from within smaller groups who all have a common focus in some way (same religion, same profession, are all parents of kids with X characteristic).

[Stephen, 37 years old, White, male faculty] Shelia, I appreciate your thoughtful post, and one thing really stood out to me: "There are many that are comfortable talking about diversity as long as it does not require that they change their behaviors or their biases. I believe that everyone should care about diversity, but I often get frustrated that those who are in "majority" culture get to "choose" when they want to participate when others must think about diversity all of the time."

100% agree and hopefully I/we can help make a difference by showing our care and passion for diversity. The diversity/inclusion example of a dinner table at the end of video 1 really made me think about what I need to do in order to be better at making sure everyone is given equal opportunities to participate and equal access, even in groups that appears diverse.

[Trevor, 42 years old, White, male faculty] "What is diversity"—I certainly learned that there are multiple ways that people use the word. Often seems used without context and that creates confusion. I'm not sure, but I think I tend to use it with more context. When talking about workplace, I may speak about specific areas—such as racial or gender diversity. And I actually use the word regularly in teaching—because many levels of diversity are taught in biology (organismal, habitat, genetic, species, etc.). I think many of the lessons there actually are relevant and helpful when thinking about societal diversity issues.

I don't need to be convinced why I should care about diversity—but I would be interested to show the second video to some individuals who are not already clearly interested in diversity and see what their response is to try to learn more about how to affect people. For me, that's certainly part of why doing this is important to me.

[Kelly, 27 years old, White, nonbinary, staff] That's so interesting, Trevor. I had the same thoughts regarding the similarities in biological diversity as well (I studied biology/ecology in college, so maybe it is ingrained in me to view most things through that lens). I think it most closely compares to the "Business Case" aspect the video talked about—just like in biology, we all benefit from working and interacting with diverse people.

[Amy] It was encouraging to learn that our definition of diversity is expanding along with our increasing awareness of equity and inclusion. Whereas at one time it may have been more limited to racial and gender differences, today it is much broader in scope. It is important to learn about diversity because it affects us in our interpersonal relationships, our workforce, our society, our national and global economies. I think it is important to create safe and healthy communities in which we value each other for what we each have to offer, bringing forth our individual value, to add to the greater whole of society. Thus creating, as it was mentioned in the video, a stronger, and more productive society, as well as a more inclusive culture.

I asked three people of different generations, and these were their definitions: An 83-year-old said that diversity is about trying to understand the people of different cultures and getting along with others. A 55-year-old said that diversity is about inclusion, different opinions, different lifestyles, cultures and subcultures. A 30-year-said that diversity is leading with empathy as we explore the unique backgrounds of others and look to find common grounds despite the differences that make us uniquely human.

What I learned is that people from different generations have different views about what diversity is according to their own perceptions and life experiences. The older person in the group did not think diversity was a positive thing--they associated it more with racial differences and biases—and the younger person has a more expansive perception of diversity. This supports the video's premise that diversity has changed and become more expansive over time.

[Stephen] It was interesting to think about diversity from the business standpoint and how being diverse actually is a very good thing for a business, especially, as video 1 states, "in terms of the bottom line." It makes sense when you think about all the different ideas and viewpoints people can bring based on their various backgrounds and experiences.

Another part of the video I found interesting was the section about workplace diversity and how in the 80s companies needed to learn how to manage culture differences in order to survive. I feel we are in a very similar situation now as companies must find a way to not only manage culture differences but also create environments where both employees and customers from diverse backgrounds feel welcomed and understood.

Most people I asked to define diversity had somewhat similar answers, likely because they were all from a similar demographic. The common definition I heard was: a group comprised of people from various genders, races, ethnicities, religions and sexual orientations. Also common was the thinking that no single group should dictate the group's actions or thoughts.

I feel most people have similar basic definitions of diversity, but once you get beyond the basic "dictionary" definition, that is likely where the variations occur. One area I found interesting was asking about inclusion for everyone (from end of video 1). That is one area I feel gets overlooked or misunderstood. Hopefully this is an area we will discuss more later on. I struggle with how to make sure everyone is given a chance to participate and has equal access without limiting another group or oppressing someone else's views/thoughts.

[Kelly] The videos were very interesting! It is helpful to break down and learn the different perspectives that the word "diversity" can hold. I appreciated the history section, as I hadn't ever considered before how the word has become such a catchall and buzzword for us to use these days. I thought it was interesting how the "Business Case" perspective seemed to arise in the 90s, when the internet came into use more, and thus people could start more easily interacting on a global scale; it makes me think about how this is even more the case today, with so many social media platforms and even more people having access to the internet than ever before. Perhaps it influenced the progression toward the inclusion perspective that is common now—more accessibility to hear others' voices and perspectives may not only encourage people to recognize the "business" benefits but also humanize everyone and help us recognize that we should all have a seat at the table and equal access to the food/conversation.

As discussed in the section about online facilitation, you should consistently read all the discussion posts but refrain from responding to individual posts in order to encourage a peer-centered conversation. Your role in contributing to the group conversation is to highlight some of the themes discussed among the participants, as well as to share your own insights and, hopefully, push all involved to take their thinking a bit further.

For efficiency, we recommend that you save one version of your group feedback post and adjust it as needed for upcoming groups according to the particular conversation of that group. Below, we provide the written text from one version of a response to the Module 2 discussion.

Facilitator Note: Our group feedback tends to be very long, so it is helpful to use headings to identify the main topic of each section. You might also consider doing a video recording response in addition to or rather than a written text. Regardless of which approach you take, be sure to demonstrate enthusiasm, encourage ongoing participation, and include reminders for upcoming tasks.

Discussion Forum Feedback: Sample Text

Thank you for a thoughtful and generous discussion! As I've said before, your participation in the discussions makes or breaks the value/effectiveness of this course, so I am excited and heartened that you have already been so willing to share your stories and learn from each other. We are off to such a good start!

Over the next few days, for the sake of inclusion and learning in our community, please make sure that every person has at least two replies—including the folks who have not yet had a chance to post.

It is hard for me to hold back from responding to all the interesting things you share, but I try to take up as little space as possible in the ongoing discussion because, as you can already see, you all have so much to learn from each other. This feedback is the space I carve out for myself to comment on your discussion, to try to push your thinking a bit further, and perhaps provoke more discussion. I welcome responses to my post, but none are required. I thank you in advance for taking the extra time to read my lengthy thoughts.

What Is Diversity?

I appreciate your comments about the content in the video, about the various meanings of the word *diversity*. It has been really interesting reading through your responses to the *What is diversity?* activity! It sounds like you had some interesting conversations by simply asking the question. It seems like everyone has an idea about what diversity is and perhaps thinks that we are all on the same page about it, but your conversations reveal that this is not the case. I hope this encourages you to continue asking this question and having these discussions because the way we talk about diversity has powerful implications for our workplace policies and practices, as well as for the way that individuals are labeled and treated.

Clarity is important.

When it serves as a stand-in for almost anything, diversity ceases to carry real meaning and can obscure the underlying issues. So, for example, when people say, "we need to hire more diverse employees," they are likely talking about the need for more women and minorities because the fact is that White men are overrepresented in many industries and in many of the upper levels of the organizational chart.

This is not to say that White men are not capable or deserving of their positions. But I am saying that if we consider the fact that women and minorities are EQUALLY capable and deserving—yet underrepresented numerically—then it becomes clear that there are structural and cultural issues that we need to address. Quite frankly, simply hiring more women and minorities in these positions will not necessarily change these issues, but it would be a good start.

In any case, hiding behind the ambiguous word *diversity* allows us to avoid thinking and talking about the root causes of underrepresentation of women and minorities (and most notably women minorities) in various areas. We need to be clear about naming the problems of unconscious bias, racism, and sexism in order to do the necessary work of addressing the disparities that they cause.

And when we are talking about "integrating diversity" into our curriculum, we are probably talking about the inclusion of diverse viewpoints and perspectives from a multitude of standpoints for the purposes of enhancing learning and knowledge. This is very different from racial/gender diversity in faculty hiring.

And when we say, "diversity is important" (i.e., in the classroom or workplace), we are probably talking about "inclusion" or how people with all different kinds of identities and backgrounds are treated, as well as how our policies and practices support and/or create obstacles for full engagement in organizational life.

And when we are talking about "harnessing diversity" (the business case) it means that we are intentionally and strategically trying to integrate a variety of perspectives, experiences, talents, and skills in context-specific ways for goal-oriented purposes.

My hope is that if we are more precise and more nuanced in how we talk about "diversity" issues, we can have more effective conversations that lead to more effective actions.

But in all honesty, I, too, am guilty of shorthanding to the word *diversity*. Sometimes it's just easier to say "diversity" because it is a term that people recognize and that, frankly, has some legitimacy in our institutionalized practices. But I do think that questioning our usage of the word will lead to some of those deeper conversations that we need to have.

Meet people where they are.

One of the most important lessons I have learned in doing DEI work is that of meeting people where they are. This module was developed to help you do just that. First, you had the opportunity to start conversations about diversity with people you may not normally discuss this type of issue with. This is a key step—opening up the conversation. In these discussions, you learned that people define diversity differently depending on their own experiences, beliefs, identities, and values. The first step towards meeting them where they are is to find out where they are!

Why should I care about diversity?

The video "Why should I care about diversity?" was meant to broaden your toolbox of reasons and rationales for explaining the importance of DEI to different people. In my experience, people are motivated by self-interest, whatever that may be; it could be in their own learning, it could be morality, it could be relationships, it could be the bottom line, etc. Having this framework of understanding the multiple layers that can be impacted when diversity and inclusion are valued should help you meet people where they are and gain their buy-in or maybe just help them better articulate what they already believe.

By the end of Module 2, participants have begun the process of transformative learning by challenging some of the ways that they think about diversity. Importantly, they begin to understand and are better able to articulate the relevance of diversity in their own lives. In the next module, they delve deeper into the concept of diversity at the organizational level, in this case, on campus.

Module 2 Conclusion: Sample Text

This module focused on enhancing your capacity to be specific about the meaning of diversity when you or others use the word, as well as being able to articulate the importance of diversity and inclusion in various contexts. Here are some ideas for putting these concepts into action:

Write a diversity statement for your syllabus. If you teach classes, try writing a diversity statement for your syllabus to help students understand the value of diversity and inclusion in the classroom and in relation to your subject matter.

Write a diversity statement for your department/office. Try writing or rewriting one for your office/department/work unit. Be sure to clearly articulate what diversity means and how it impacts the work that you do.

Module 2 References

Alba, R. (2018). What majority-minority society? A critical analysis of the census bureau's projections of America's demographic future. *Socius: Sociological Research for a Dynamic World, 4,* 1–10.

Astin, A. W. (1993). Diversity and multiculturalism on the campus: How are students affected? *Change: The Magazine of Higher Learning, 25*(2), 44–49.

Centers for Disease Control and Prevention. (2020). *Disability impacts all of us.* National Center on Birth Defects and Developmental Disabilities. https://www.cdc.gov/ncbddd/disabilityandhealth/infographic-disability-impacts-all.html

Freeman, R. B., & Huang, W. (2015). Collaborating with people like me: Ethnic coauthorship within the United States. *Journal of Labor Economics, 33*(1), 289–318.

Gill, F., & Shaeye, A. (2021). Relative wages of immigrant men and the Great Recession. *Journal of Economics, Race, and Policy, 5*(1), 1–12.

Gurin, P., Dey, E. L., Hurtado, S., & Gurin, G. (2002). Diversity and higher education: Theory and impact on educational outcomes. *Harvard Educational Review, 72*(3), 330–367.

Henderson, L., & Herring, C. (2013). Does critical diversity pay in higher education? Race, gender, and departmental rankings in research universities. *Politics, Groups, and Identities, 1*(3), 299–310.

Hunt, V., Layton, D., & Prince, S. (2015, January 1). Why diversity matters. *McKinsey & Company.*

Jones, J. (2021, February 24). LGBT Identification Rises to 5.6% in Latest U.S. Estimate. *Gallup.* https://news.gallup.com/poll/329708/lgbt-identification-rises-latest-est imate.aspx

Knight, R. (2014). Managing people from 5 generations. *Harvard Business Review, 25*(9), 1–7.

Litvin, D. R. (1997). The discourse of diversity: From biology to management. *Organization, 4*(2), 187.

Milem, J. F. (2003). The educational benefits of diversity: Evidence from multiple sectors. In M. J. Chang, D. Witt, J. Jones, & K. Hakuta (Eds.), *Compelling Interest: Examining the Evidence on Racial Dynamics in Colleges and Universities* (pp. 126–169). Stanford Education.

Prasad, A. (2001). Understanding workplace empowerment as inclusion: A historical investigation of the discourse of difference in the United States. *The Journal of Applied Behavioral Science, 37*(1), 51–69.

Schmidt, S. (2021, February 24). 1 in 6 Gen Z adults are LGBT. And this number could continue to grow. *Washington Post,* 1–5.

Soares, R., Cobb, B., Lebow, E., Regis, A., & Wojnas, V. (2011, December 13). *2011 Catalyst Census: Fortune 500 women board directors (report).* Catalyst. Retrieved October 17, 2021, https://www.catalyst.org/research/2011-catalyst -census-fortune-500-women-board-directors/

Tadmor, C. T., Satterstrom, P., Jang, S., & Polzer, J. T. (2012). Beyond individual creativity: The superadditive benefits of multicultural experience for collective creativity in culturally diverse teams. *Journal of Cross-Cultural Psychology, 43*(3), 384–392.

U.S. Bureau of Labor Statistics. (2020, May 29). *TED: The Economics Daily.* Retrieved October 7, 2021, https://www.bls.gov/opub/ted/2020/foreign-born -workers-made-up-17-point-4-percent-of-labor-force-in-2019.htm

Module 3

DIVERSITY AT THE INTERPERSONAL LEVEL

Strength lies in differences, not in similarities.
—Stephen Covey

Many people come to a course about diversity with expectations to learn about *diverse others*. This module's content is intended to destabilize this preconception by focusing on self-awareness rather than on learning about other identity groups. This challenge to participants' preconceived ideas provides a catalyst for transformative learning. At the same time, the activity and discussions are designed to promote self-awareness and self-disclosure to help develop a sense of trust among participants, a critical component of a learning community.

The module builds self-awareness, complicates the notion of diversity and identity, and starts the conversation about the way we approach people who are different from ourselves. This video includes an identity mapping activity designed to increase participants' level of awareness of themselves and others, a critical starting point for any conversation on diversity or cross-cultural competence. In completing this activity, participants explore their own multilayered, complex identity and how these identities may play out in the different settings they inhabit, such as their workplace, the classroom, and the broader community.

Facilitator Note: In the sample script in this chapter, the first author shares her identity map as an example. Facilitators should create their own map to share with their participants. An editable slide with the identity map template is provided in the accompanying slide deck.

Module 3 Overview: Sample Text

Diversity and Identities

The module builds self-awareness, complicates the notion of diversity and identity, and starts the conversation about the way we approach people who are different from ourselves. The module video includes an identity mapping activity designed to increase your level of self-awareness and awareness of others, a critical starting point for any conversation on diversity or cross-cultural competence.

Essential Questions

- What is identity?
- Why do our identities matter in the workplace?
- How do other people's ideas about our identities impact the way we see ourselves and lead our lives?
- How can our lack of knowledge about other people impact the way we perceive their identities?
- How can we try to see someone as they see themselves?

Activities

While watching the module video, you will be walked through an identity mapping activity. In completing this activity, you will explore multilayered, complex identities and how these identities may play out in the different settings such as the workplace, the classroom, and the broader community. Please print the worksheet posted in the module or refer to your participant workbook and have it available while you watch the video.

Videos

The module video, "Diversity and Identity," focuses on the innermost level, the interpersonal level, of the Value of Diversity model we explored in the previous module.

Discussions

Please post your initial responses to the discussion prompts by _____ .
A synchronous dialogue will take place on _____ .

Additional Resources

If you are ready to delve deeper, you can explore the collection of multimedia resources about identity and intersectionality.

Facilitator Note: This mini-lecture has an engagement activity embedded in the video.

Diversity and Identity

When we encounter someone new, there's almost an automatic process that we go through of sizing up the other person. Are you like me or not like me? Friend or foe? We size people up in different ways depending on who we are, who they are, and the context in which we meet. But I think the essence of it is that we are asking ourselves: are we going to understand each other? Are we going to be able to get along? In other words, when we encounter someone who is different from ourselves in ways that are immediately apparent, we tend to have uncertainty about what to expect.

For some of us, this can create anxiety because we might be afraid of doing or saying the wrong thing; or we think the other person might do or say something in contradiction to our own beliefs or values. Or we just feel unsure that we'll be able to relate to each other. Ironically, even though these uncertainties and anxieties are a result of "not knowing," our natural tendency is to pull back rather than to move forward and seek more information that might reduce that uncertainty. But I'm going to let you in on a little secret: the key to understanding others is to better understand yourself.

I do not mean to suggest that you don't know yourself. In fact, quite the opposite. You probably know yourself so well that you have not stopped to really think, "Who am I?" If you haven't, I'm going to give you that chance right now.

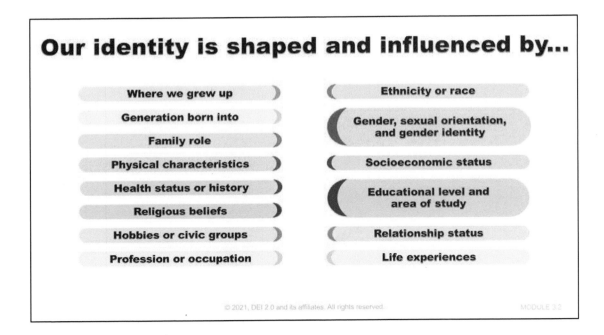

Our Identity is Shaped and Influenced by . . .

When we are talking about the question "Who am I?" we are talking about our identity. Our identity, the fabric of who we are, is an intricate weave of various experiences, values, and beliefs that shape how we see the world and how the world sees us (Ashforth & Mael, 1989; Eisenberg, 2001; Tajfel, 1978).

Our identity is influenced by so many things, including when we were born, where we grew up, the body we were born into, and that which we choose to do in life. If you think about it, each of these aspects of our identities contributes in some way to our values, the way we communicate and act towards others, and the way we conduct ourselves in the world (Allen, 2011). In order to bring this into clearer focus, we're going to do an identity mapping activity.

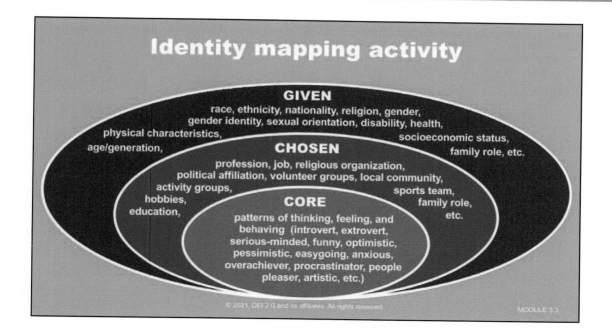

Identity Mapping Activity

To do this activity, you'll need a piece of paper and something to write with or you can print out the Identity Map handout provided in this module.

Identity can be thought of like an onion with three main layers. I'll explain this model, use myself as an example, and then ask you to create an identity map of yourself. The outer layer is our given identities, many of which are visible to the world. These are the cards we are dealt at birth—we do not choose our race, gender, or sexual orientation. We have no say in our mental or physical physiology, nor the generation into which we were born. And, of course, we don't choose our birth family.

And yet, all of these given identities can have a strong impact on how we experience the world and how the world sees us. So, in my case, I would describe some of my given identities as White, American, East Coaster, cisgender woman, middle class, Gen X, sister, daughter, able-bodied, healthy, and average size.

The next layer consists of our chosen identities. These are the activities, life choices, and affiliations that we choose. Some of these social identities are more important to us than others, but they all can say something about who we are because we have chosen them. Some of my chosen identities are PhD, diversity trainer, world traveler, bilingual, married, city dweller, and child-free.

And finally, at the core is the essence of our personality, our emotional traits, the ways in which we learn, and our deep personal values. Here, I might include introvert, critical thinker, compassionate, and socially conscious. My husband would probably add a few things to this core list such as impatient, stubborn, and control freak . . . and he would be right. But this is my map, so I'm going to keep it nice. Still, there's a good point here: there are parts of ourselves that we prefer not to see but nonetheless are still parts of who we are.

Okay, now it's your turn. Pause the video now and fill your map in with as many aspects of your identity as you can think of. You can use the examples I provided, but feel free to add others. When you are done, start the video back up for the next part of the activity.

Now, take a look at your identity map. What a multifaceted individual you are! Each of these aspects is a part of you, but some aspects of your identity are probably more meaningful to you than others.

My identity map

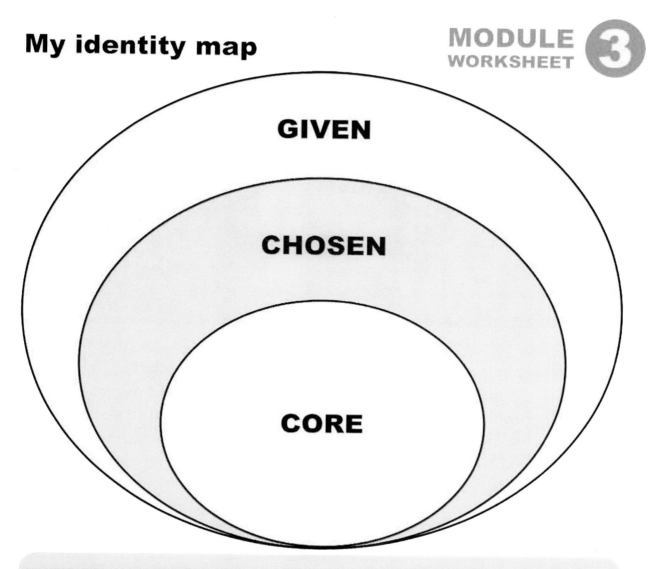

When we talk about our identities we're really answering the question "Who am I?" This is a complex question that deserves a complex answer. Our identities are made up of core, chosen and given aspects about ourselves. Core aspects are specific traits and characteristics that describe our unique selves. There are also chosen aspects of our identities such as groups and activities that we've chosen to be a part of. Given identities are the groups or characteristics that we are born into. Here are some examples to help you map your multiple levels of identities.

CORE: Personality traits (introvert/extrovert, spontaneous, organized), learning style, values, etc.

CHOSEN: profession, job, religious organization, political affiliation, volunteer groups, local community, activity groups, sports team, hobbies, family role (i.e., choosing to have children or to get married), education, etc.

GIVEN: race, ethnicity, nationality, religion, gender, gender identity, sexual orientation, disability, health, age/generation, physical characteristics (tall, short, thin, hefty), family role (i.e., your role as youngest, middle, oldest, or only child), socio-economic status, etc.

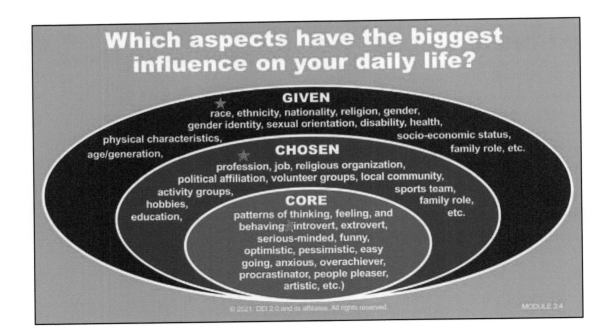

Which Aspects Have the Biggest Influence on Your Daily Life?

For the next part of the activity, I'd like you to contemplate which parts of your identity are the most salient or important in how you see yourself. I'd like for you to pause the video for a minute and draw a little star by the 4 or 5 aspects of your identity that have the biggest impact on how you view the world and what you think is important. When you are done, start the video again, as there is one final part to this activity.

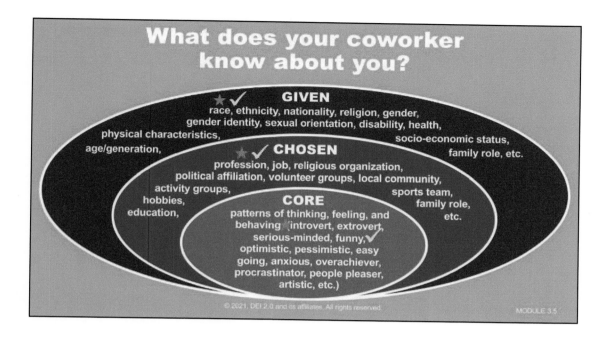

What Does Your Coworker Know about You?

Okay, now this is the final part of the exercise. I'd like for you to think of someone you work with or have worked with in the past who you would say does not know you very well. This might be someone you've worked with for a long time or someone new to the workplace. Or maybe you are the new person. Now, obviously this person must know some things about you. Pause the video and put a check mark by the aspects of your identity that you think this person does know about you, based on what you have told them or what they can observe. When you are done, start the video again for the final slide.

Looking at your map, how many of the aspects of your identity that you just checked are the same as the ones with a little star--the most important parts of who you are? How many of those aspects are part of your given identities? How much or how little does this person know about you?

Now flip this thought experiment for a minute and imagine what the other person's identity map might look like. How much could you fill in about that person's core or chosen identities?

Now, consider the implication of our identities in the workplace for a minute. All the core, chosen, and given aspects of our identity blend together to make us who we are, how we see the world, how we work, and how we communicate. What happens when we work with people who only know limited aspects of who we are and we know just as little about them?

How Well Do We Know Each Other?

Here's my point. When we talk about diversity at the individual/interpersonal level, we can readily see a good number of differences, but there is so much more to us than meets the eye. As I mentioned earlier, when we encounter someone who seems different from us, we don't tend to dig deeper to those other levels. Consciously or unconsciously, we make quick judgments about people based on what we can observe.

But think about how much we don't know about each other: these are likely the aspects of our identity that are the most important to us.

As we move forward, I encourage you to contemplate your identity map and how this influences the way you view other people, but also think about the people around you and how you might go about learning more about the various aspects of their identities beyond the ones that you can see. This might take a little courage, but I assure you that it's worth it!

In the following excerpts, participants share insights from their experiences doing the identity mapping activity. Peer learners respond to each other with additional insights, questions, and feedback. Transformative learning comes through these quotes, as participants reflect on their identities in new ways and gain a heightened sense of awareness about how their identities impact workplace relationships.

Discussion Prompts

1. How was the Identity Mapping Activity for you? Did you gain any insights that you can share with the group? Did you struggle with it?
2. How do you think your identities might play out in your work relationships (with supervisors, students, colleagues, clients, patients, etc.)? Can you give some examples?

Examples of Participant Discussion Forum Posts

[Megan, 58 years old, White, Jewish, female faculty] I enjoyed the activity—it made me think about how few people really "know" me. My husband, kids, brother, and very close friends. Perhaps we should all make an effort to expose the parts of our identity that are most important to us—and find ways to help others feel comfortable doing the same.

I think that I deliberately keep my core identity and most of the things that are most important to me to myself with some coworkers. Primarily the ones who I know don't agree with my politics, religion (or lack thereof), and my thoughts about other divisive topics. I guess I am trying to avoid conflict and confrontation. But this is a direct contradiction to the statement I made about exposing our most important parts of our identity! I'm looking forward to seeing what others have to say about this.

[Dara, 36 years old, Asian American, female faculty] I love what you say here, Megan, about "exposing the parts of our identity that are most important to us—and finding ways to help others feel comfortable doing the same." I think when we do that, that is where we are able to gain understanding and have valuable discussions with each other.

[Julian, 44 years old, African American, male staff] It was a thought-provoking exercise that made me think about who I am and how I am perceived in the world. It was easier for me to quickly identify the chosen and given aspects of myself. Even at 44, I am still learning my core. I think it has become clearer as I've gotten older, but there are conflicting aspects of myself. On the one hand, I can be very sensitive to other's feelings but there are times when I am very selfish with my time and energy. I am an outgoing introvert, meaning that my job and family require that I engage in extroverted ways, but I need time to recharge and if I don't get that time, I can be pretty irritable.

When I thought about what people know about me, I realized that I am probably not revealing as much of myself as I should be. The exercise is prompting me to think about how to create opportunities for self-disclosure.

Our identities are very important in the workplace. I currently work in an environment where I feel there is space for me to be me, but there is also accountability. I have worked in places where I felt I was not seen. Those experiences were unfulfilling and frustrating. And I felt as if, even if I tried, people were not interested in seeing me. So I value my current workplace and work harder because I feel valued and respected

[Renee, 55 years old, White, female faculty] Hi Julian! Your reflection prompted me to think of something. I'm pretty introverted, and I tend to NOT ask questions of people—but I wonder if there are opportunities I'm missing because of that.

When you wondered how to create opportunities for self-disclosure, what kinds of things would you want to expose to your workmates? And when you say you felt you were not seen in your previous workplaces, what kinds of interaction might have changed that?

[Andrea, 36 years old, White, female staff] I thought that the activity was very eye-opening, but I also felt like it put me into a box in my current state. I felt that my core and my given will remain constant, but my chosen will change as I move throughout life and make choices or evaluate my current chosen state. I also think that I have developed my identity. This mapping would have been completely different for me if I were to have taken it 5–10 years ago. I feel that my identity is evolving. I find it useful because it gave me an opportunity to sit and think about who I am. It was really hard to think of words that describe me because in my mind "I am just me," but I feel that if I am able to thoroughly think about who I am in this context, I can have a deeper understanding of who I am. I think that this can impact workplace relationships and practice because I can articulate who I am to others and express my needs and be accepted by others because they have a better understanding of where I am coming from. I also think that the given is what everyone always sees and [uses to judge and compare themselves to others] as the online presentation stated. I think that by having a deeper understanding of yourself, you can create better relationships to communicate who you are and also use your own understanding of this mapping to ask questions to learn about others. It's a two-way street!

[Judith, 51 years old, White, female staff] I believe the given and core areas in this exercise can also evolve as we progress through life. For example, my core values now as a middle-aged, middleclass, nonreligious, mildly healthy parent with two kids, are very different from the values of a physically healthy welfare child in an extremely religious family. The aging process alone, as part of our given, evolves daily—if I am alive in another 40 years, my given physical abilities will be very different from what they are today. Regardless, this mapping identity exercise certainly is a great tool for self-reflection and improved personal communication skills!

Discussion Forum Feedback: Sample Text

First of all, thank you for your thoughtful engagement in the small group discussions. I saw a lot of honesty, vulnerability, and some aha moments. There is still a lot of juice in those discussions, including maybe some folks who have not had the benefit of being replied to. So, perhaps over the weekend and next week, you can take a minute to revisit those discussions.

Now, I will provide some additional thoughts to deepen your thinking and perhaps provoke more questions!

Individuals and Systems

This week's focus on identities, how we see ourselves and how others see us (and vice versa), is located at the center of the multilayered model that we explored in the last module. As we move forward, keep in mind how this level impacts and is impacted by the outer layers (group, organizational, social). The purpose of this approach is to try to keep our attention on and draw connections between personal experiences and systemic experiences. This can be very challenging because we are socialized to see ourselves as independent individuals making our own way in the world, succeeding or failing based on our hard work, tenacity, and talent. We are not socialized to understand how we (as individuals) are shaped by institutions, systems, history, broad social values, and stereotypes.

For example, many people do not realize that "race" is not a biological construct but rather the result of a series of laws from the early twentieth century that determined who could be categorized as White and therefore receive particular rights and privileges. Racial labels were created to identify everyone else who was not considered White, and these labels have continually changed and shifted over time, illustrating the fluid, contextual, historical nature of race as a category of difference and as a tool for discrimination. In other words, identities such as race and gender only mean what society has decided they mean. In this light, we are all products of history, systems, the institutions that reproduce dominant ideas about who we are.

At the same time, race, gender, and other aspects of our identity may also be important to our sense of self and may have meanings for us that are different than what society tells us. This is why there is often a tension between how we see ourselves and how others see us, and vice versa. We should always strive to liberate people from the boxes, stereotypes, and assumptions put upon them and learn to see people as they see themselves. But that's not always easy because identities are complex.

Identities Are Complex

As you may have noticed, the identity map model does not allow for easy placement of all aspects of our identity, as one aspect of identity might overlap several layers. For example, one's religion might be given (by family), as well as chosen (or rejected) later in life, and may develop into a core aspect of one's identity. Also, many aspects of our identities change over time. For example, you may have a "given" identity as lower socioeconomic status and at the same time a "chosen" middle-class identity that you worked to achieve.

One doesn't erase the other: the way we grew up will always be a part of who we are. As we grow, age, and change, some aspects of our identity simply "layer over" other ones. And, as some of you mentioned, some change over time.

Seeing Ourselves, Seeing Each Other

As we discussed, differences may exist between how we see ourselves and how others see us. This becomes particularly complex when we add the concept of "identity salience," which refers to the degree to which an aspect of our identity is important to us in a particular context. For example, my last name, "Goldstein," is a Jewish name. Without knowing me, one might make certain assumptions about my religious beliefs and practices that are not necessarily true. In fact, most of the time, being Jewish is an identity that I would not "star" or consider very important to who I am.

However, the salience or importance of that "given" identity for me changes in two contexts: 1) when there is anti-Semitic activity and 2) when I am around other Jewish people. When my "group" is threatened, I feel threatened. And when I am with people who share this group identity, I feel a certain connection that is different than what I may feel with people who do not share that identity/culture/experience (even though Jewish people's connection to and experiences of being Jewish differ!). So sometimes being Jewish is a very important part of my identity, even though on a day-to-day basis it usually is not. Yet, someone who doesn't know me might make assumptions about me based on the identity marker of my name. In fact, I once got a call from a well-meaning colleague who was trying to find out what the local "Jewish community" is like. I had to tell her that I literally have no idea.

The point I'm trying to make is that we cannot assume what people's chosen or given identities mean to them. And we cannot assume that, if we share or disclose aspects of our identities to someone else, others will see us as we see ourselves. And when we reduce someone to one or two aspects of their identity or we try to put someone in a box, we minimize their humanity.

The Complexity of Learning about Other People

Sometimes our well-intended curiosity about "others" can have the opposite effect, as our assumptions of "otherness" (which can mean other than ourselves or "other" than the dominant norm) can actually serve to diminish a person by making them feel unreasonably questioned or put-upon. For example, when those of us who are fascinated by foreign cultures meet someone who has an accent, we may want to ask, "Where are you from?" Now, stop and think for a minute. Many people who come to the United States as teenagers or young adults never lose their accent. I know many people who have lived in this country for 30–40 years and still speak with an accent. Now, imagine how tiresome it must be to constantly get asked over the course of decades—Where are you from? Maybe they thought it was nice at first, but, come on, it must get old. Although you might be curious, as well as have good intentions, it may not be very interesting for them to have to answer that question over and over. And so if your purpose is to connect with them, this might not be the most effective way to do so. Also, it is important to remember that many people who moved here from other countries did so because they had no choice—they may be survivors of trauma, such as refugees who had to leave everything dear to them behind—so, in these situations, your asking someone about where they are from because you discerned an accent people might trigger unwanted or even painful feelings.

That noted, the lesson here is not to stop being curious about others and refrain from expressing interest in learning more about them; it's simply to be more mindful, to think beyond your own curiosity and try to see the whole person, not just to delight in the novelty of cultural difference.

What is the curious person supposed to do? How can we hope to learn about those who are "different" from ourselves without offending?

There are no easy answers to this question, given everything we've discussed. But as a starting point, I think referring back to the identity map idea is helpful. How might you find out about someone's "starred" identities, those most important to them? Questions to get under the layers (even simple ones such as "What do you enjoying doing in the town/state where you live?") can open up all sorts of possibilities for connection.

As we discussed, sharing parts of ourselves (and learning things about others) may not always have the desired effect. For example, if I am a staunch antigun person and I ask someone whom I have just met what they enjoy doing in their free time, and they reply that they enjoy going to the firing range to practice their accuracy with a high-powered handgun, my effort to get acquainted might inadvertently have created more of a barrier than a bridge.

The reality is that in the course of our lives we will encounter some people with whom we fundamentally disagree at the core level. The core level of identity is enmeshed in deep-seated values. So, when we encounter someone whose core (value-laden) identity conflicts with our own, it can raise our guard—to say the least. Again, I'm not talking just about people who are "different" but those whose values "conflict" with our own. This, for me, is really challenging. However, I learned a powerful lesson recently.

Creating Connections and Maintaining Differences

I have a friend who is very different from me on the surface (different age, race, religion), but we have found a lot of common ground in terms of our (core) values around social justice issues, and we have similar senses of humor, so we really enjoy each other's company. Therefore, I was completely taken off guard when we were talking one day and she mentioned her position on a "hot button" issue that is the opposite of mine.

More precisely, this issue is a "trigger" for me, as in I tend to get very upset when people express the opposite view. I know, I know, not very tolerant of me, but this is a value so deeply held that I tend to dismiss people who hold the opposing one. However, because I honestly already liked this woman and already knew we share some other core values, I found a way to "let it go." For the sake of our friendship, we agreed that I would not try to change her mind and she would not try to change mine. My esteem for her allowed me to not judge her. We simply acknowledged that, okay, we feel differently about this, but now, let's move on.

The point I'm trying to make is that we are not always going to want to embrace or celebrate some of our differences, but sharing and knowing more about each other's multiple levels of identity can open up points of connection that can be useful for working, learning, and living together in community. And, of course, at the foundation of this must lie trust and respect.

Perhaps an open acknowledgement of fundamental differences and disagreements, if respected by both sides, is okay. There is no reason that we can't try to individualize, humanize, and connect with people with whom we may disagree. And, since we are thinking about engaging authentically with others who are different from ourselves, I'd like to share one of my favorite passages from an article listed in the "additional resources" for this module:

Our greatest weakness is the tendency to take constructions of self, other, and the world too seriously and to allow our attachment to a chosen world view to irreparably divide us from diverse others . . . but bridging these gaps is not easy because . . . authentic dialogue is always chancy, because identity, not just meaning, is always at stake. (Eisenberg, 2001, p. 101)

In other words, sometimes to truly engage with someone who is very different from ourselves, we might need to become softer, more flexible, in order that we might bump up against those with different opinions and values without damaging each other.

I hope that my post is not too frustrating for you. I do believe that it is important to make these matters of identity as complex as possible in order to avoid the boxes into which we typically put ourselves and others. I also believe that questions are more valuable than answers, so, on that note, I hope this discussion has raised a few questions for you!

By the end of Module 3, participants have a more nuanced understanding of diversity, inclusion, and identity and why these matter in the workplace and in classrooms. It is important to note that the content in the first three modules is intentionally non-controversial and nonconfrontational. Participants have had time to engage with each other about topics that are thought-provoking but not emotionally laden. This lays the foundation for the more challenging topics that lie ahead.

Module 3 Conclusion: Sample Text

Congratulations on finishing Module 3! Now that you've gained a deeper understanding of the multifaceted nature of our identities and considered the impact of our identities in our work, it's time to put these ideas into action by getting to know people beyond their visible identities and by learning more about what aspects of their identity are important to them. You may also think about ways to bring your *whole self* to work. When you take the brave steps to fully be who you are, you help create an environment where others can do so as well.

To put the knowledge you gained in this module into practice, try writing a diversity statement. A diversity statement is a personal essay that is a depiction of your past experiences and explains how these experiences have contributed to your personal and professional growth. It is often asked for on job or educational program applications. See the additional resources section for some guidance. Before you move on to the next module, please make sure you have replied to at least two of your colleagues' posts in the discussion board and read/replied to people who have posted to yours.

Module 3 References

Allen, B. J. (2011). *Difference matters: Communicating social identity.* Waveland Press.

Ashforth, B. E., & Mael, F. (1989). Social identity theory and the organization. *Academy of Management Review, 14*(1), 20–39.

Eisenberg, E. M. (2001). Building a mystery: Toward a new theory of communication and identity. *Journal of Communication, 51*(3), 534–552.

Tajfel, H. (1978). Social categorization, social identity and social comparison. In H. Tajfel (Ed.), *Differentiation between social groups: Studies in the social psychology of intergroup relations* (pp. 61–76). Academic Press.

Module 4

INTRODUCTION TO UNCONSCIOUS BIAS

All of us have implicit biases to some degree. This does not necessarily mean we will act in an inappropriate or discriminatory manner, only that our first "blink" sends us certain information.

Acknowledging and understanding this implicit response and its value and role is critical to informed decision-making and is particularly critical to those whose decisions must embody fairness and justice.

—Malcolm Gladwell, *Blink*

The content in this module facilitates transformative learning by helping participants start to think about their thinking in new ways. This meta-cognitive approach helps mitigate some of the defensiveness that people may feel when they hear the term *unconscious bias*, which is sometimes misunderstood and misused. The content is informed by social science research into the effects of unconscious biases to help participants understand the systemic impact of individual instances of unconscious bias.

Who Does What? Matching Game

Unlike other modules, this module starts with an engagement activity. The "Who Does What?" activity is an easy way to highlight some of the mental shortcuts (cognitive biases) that people use every day. Participants are asked to match pictures of people with a variety of jobs (e.g., white collar, blue collar, service industry, and academic) based solely on what they can see in the pictures.

When we debrief this activity, we tell people that there are no right answers. Any of the pictured people could do any of the listed jobs. And yet, those who do this activity tend to associate certain people with certain jobs and not for others. Although this is frustrating to realize, it makes a point.

Facilitators should be prepared for the mixed reactions this activity provokes. Some participants react very strongly and negatively against being asked to pigeonhole people into certain jobs. They feel it is wrong and unfair to do this, so they express some anger or frustration about the activity. Other participants get a little "aha" moment when they realize that their conscious feelings (that it is wrong to stereotype people in terms of jobs) may conflict with some of their unconscious biases (that were revealed in the selections that they made). Below are the debrief questions and example responses from previous participants.

Module 4 Overview: Sample Text

An Introduction to Unconscious Bias

Unconscious (or implicit) bias is a hot topic in diversity, equity, and inclusion education, as well as a thriving area of research in such fields as healthcare, education, media representation, employment, and law enforcement. The concept of unconscious bias really began to enter the public discourse in the wake of a consistent stream of police shootings of African American boys and men. The concept of unconscious bias has been used to explain why White police officers could so frequently make fatal errors when assessing the threat in encounters with Black people. Unfortunately, in some of these discussions, the concept of *unconscious bias* was used as if it were synonymous with *racism*. For example, after one of the 2016 presidential debates in which Hillary Clinton stated that "I think implicit bias is a problem for everyone, not just police," a *Washington Times* headline trumpeted, "Hillary Clinton Calls the Entire Nation Racist" (Riddell, 2016). This headline represents a common and unfortunate misperception about what unconscious bias is and what it means.

To counter the idea that unconscious bias is an insult or character flaw, this module draws upon neuroscience research to explain that unconscious bias is a product of our natural brain functioning. The video is largely based on the book *Thinking, Fast and Slow* by Daniel Kahneman, a Nobel Prize-winning behavioral economist. The content is also informed by social science research into the effects of unconscious biases to help us understand the systemic impact of individual instances of unconscious bias.

Essential Questions

- What is unconscious bias, and why does it matter?
- How do unconscious biases (positive or negative) play out in your daily life?
- How does unconscious bias affect you, others, and society as a whole?
- What can we do about unconscious biases?

Activities

To begin the module, you are asked to do a matching activity called "Who Does What?" It will only take a few minutes to do the activity, but then you should take a few minutes to reflect on the experience. We'll talk about it in our group discussions!

Videos

The module video, "Fast and Slow Thinking," explains what unconscious bias is, how it functions, and steps we can take to help ensure that we don't make faulty decisions based on unconscious biases.

Discussions

Please post your initial responses to the discussion prompts by _____ . A synchronous dialogue will take place on _____ .

Additional Resources

There is a rich set of additional resources (videos, articles, books, online tools) provided to help you explore this topic further.

Module 4 Activity: Who Does What?

Activity Instructions: Sample Text

For this activity, your task is to associate each one of the people pictured with one of the jobs on the worksheet. There are an equal number of people and jobs, so it's a one-to-one match-up. You don't have much to go on, so you'll have to rely on ideas, images, experiences, and even stereotypes stored in your brain. Please don't overthink it; just go with your gut impulse. When you are done, please reflect on the discussion questions, then post to the discussion forum.

Who Does What? Reflection Questions

Please reflect on these questions and post your reaction to the activity to the discussion forum.

- What information did you use to match people to certain jobs?
- Who was it easy for you to match with a particular job? Why?
- Who was it harder for you to match to a job? Why?
- Who did you put into the "professional" class jobs?
- Who did you put in the lower-wage jobs?
- What cognitive shortcuts did this reveal?

Who does what?

Associate each person with one of the jobs listed.

Marta

Bob

Amara

Kelly

Jennifer

Amber

Larry

Dan

Damion

Sasha

Steve

David

Who looks like the
chemist?

Who looks like the
web designer?

Who looks like the
flight attendant?

Who looks like the
CEO?

Who looks like the
soldier?

Who looks like the
stockbrocker?

Who looks like the
community activist?

Who looks like the
hair stylist?

Who looks like the
math teacher?

Who looks like the
doctor?

Who looks like the
minister?

Who looks like the
hotel desk clerk?

Examples of Participant Discussion Forum Posts

[Tanya, 42 years old, African American, female faculty] I automatically thought about gender first, choosing fields with high percentages of women or men and assigning the pictures. Secondly, I looked at clothing. The clothing in the pictures gave me ideas as to what I picture certain professions wearing. After doing this exercise I somewhat feel guilty. Guilty that I did pick a male CEO and a woman hairstylist. I would hope someone would look at picture of me and think I could be a CEO. In split-second decisions, this is what I went with.

[Maria, 59 years old, Latina, female faculty] My reaction to the "Who does what" activity was that I found it fun and eye-opening. It gave me the opportunity for a hands-on experience activity. I always had thought of myself free of biases mainly because of my background. However, I realized that I also stereotype people while matching the professions with the people I was influenced by. What they were wearing as well as given characteristics as a decision factor influenced me.

[Danny, 43 years old, White, male staff] Regarding my thoughts on the game . . . I, like many others have stated, found myself feeling uncomfortable at having to make assumptions based on looks. However, it did force me to think critically about where my own internal biases lie. Maybe I don't mean "biases" necessarily but rather unfairly (sometimes) categorizing people due to my own past personal experiences.

[Elsa, 30 years old, White, female faculty] This exercise was very hard! It forced me to face my "hidden biases." As I was matching people with their career choices, I came to realize how our beliefs and assumptions play a huge part in the way we make decisions. The phrase "we don't believe the world we see; we see the world we believe" came to mind. It's human to hear what we want to hear and see what we want to see. For many of us, we may view the world through our biases and fail to recognize how automatic our responses are as a result.

[Matt, 52 years old, White, male faculty] My reaction to the "Who does what?" activity is that it leaves the door open for a large amount of assumptions. Perhaps this was the idea when the activity was created, which on its face does what you want it to do because people are left with deciding who does what based on the physical appearance of the people in the pictures. This I think is what we do as a society more often than we would care to admit. We fit people into what we would think of as stereotypes based on some attribute of their being.

Mini-Lecture Slides & Scripts: Fast and Slow Thinking

Let's talk about your unconscious biases!

- Define unconscious bias

- Types of unconscious bias

- Impact of unconscious bias in our daily lives

MODULE 4.1

Let's Talk about Your Unconscious Biases!

When the topic of unconscious bias is raised, the reaction often is "What? Who, me? How dare you!" I think this defensive reaction stems from the fact that unconscious bias is not well understood and is often misused. In this module, we learn what unconscious bias actually is, discuss some typical types of biases and when they may come into play, and explore why it is important to think about biases in our daily lives.

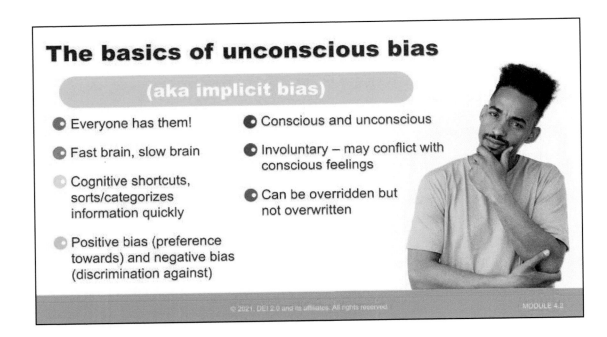

The Basics of Unconscious Bias

Let's start with the basics. First, you may also have heard the term *implicit bias*. *Unconscious bias* and *implicit bias* are synonymous. From what I have seen in the literature, there is no distinction between the two. I just happen to prefer *unconscious bias* for now.

Okay, so first thing to know . . . everyone has biases. It doesn't mean you are a bad person . . . just that you have a brain.

In fact, it's almost as if you have two brains or at least two types of brain functioning. For the sake of simplicity, I'll refer to these two types of functioning as fast brain and slow brain (Kahneman, 2011).

Biases are cognitive shortcuts that our fast brain uses to sort and make sense of a lot of information very quickly (Gowin, 2012). As we'll discuss later, we rely on these shortcuts routinely in order to go about our day.

All of us harbor both positive biases and negative biases. We are fully aware of some of our biases or preferences, a case in point being my bias for any dessert containing chocolate. But what concerns us here are our unconscious biases, for they can operate outside of our conscious awareness.

And this is the worst part: our unconscious biases are involuntary and can in fact conflict with our conscious feelings (Banaji & Greenwald, 2016). I think this is why unconscious bias is almost a taboo topic, because admitting our biases, even to ourselves, can provoke feelings of guilt or shame—things that all of us would prefer to avoid.

The good news/bad news scenario is that our biases can be overridden but not overwritten. In other words, our biases are deeply engrained neuropathways that cannot be erased. However, through ongoing mindful effort, we can learn to override our biases by perceiving them but choosing not to act upon them, and, eventually, through intentional efforts, they can get weaker, even if they do not vanish completely (Rudman et al., 2001). So, that's the big overview. Now, let's delve in a little deeper.

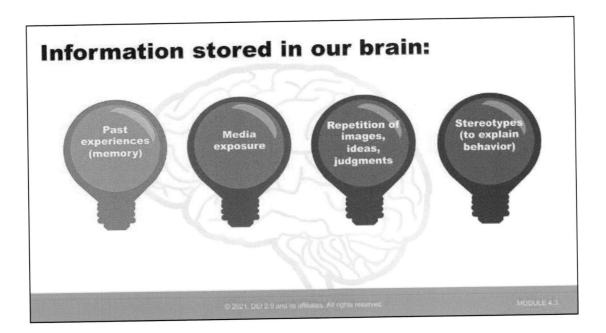

Information Stored in Our Brain

Our brains store a lot of information. When we encounter something or someone, especially something or someone with whom we are not already familiar, our fast brain processing is kicked into gear to assess information very quickly. Our fast brain does this kind of immediate assessment in a nanosecond by finding any bits of information already stored in the brain to associate with the type of person or situation at hand so that you can make some quick judgements and decisions about how to act or react in the given situation.

Among those bits of information are our past experiences in the form of memories, which are often distorted (Kahneman, 2011). For example, we might have several pleasant encounters with people from a particular culture, but if there is one negative encounter, that might be the bit of information our fast thinking finds. In other words, memory is skewed toward the negative as a protective mechanism to help us avoid similar negative people or situations (Banaji & Greenwald, 2016), even if our own experience tells us that positive experiences are more common with people in that culture.

We also retain a barrage of images, ideas, and judgments that are constantly reinforced through media exposure. And, again, it's important to remember that even if we may not consciously agree with some of these ideas and judgments, they still can make their way into our unconscious minds and cause us to say or do things that may be inconsistent with how we feel consciously.

Our fast brain also relies on stored information in the form of stereotypes it uses to form quick explanations (Kahneman, 2011). For example, if we see what we assume is a homeless person asking for money on the street, our fast brain might immediately associate that person with drug addiction or mental illness—and, out of concern for our personal safety, we may avoid the person rather than help them. However, we also know very well that there are myriad reasons that someone can end up homeless, from domestic abuse to home foreclosure to a chronic illness not covered by health insurance. But, typically, our fast brain does not search for disconfirming or additional information after it has reached the most readily available and seemingly appropriate conclusion.

Now let's take a look at some of the ways that these bits of information come out in the form of biases.

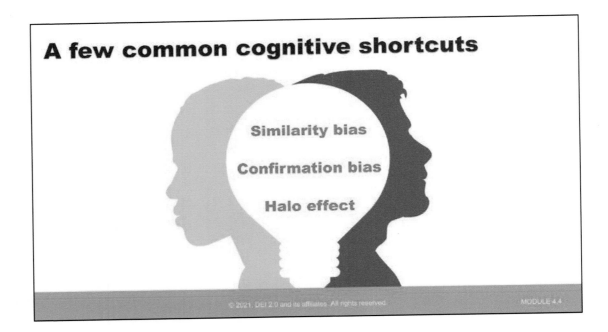

A Few Common Cognitive Shortcuts

What do we do when are pressed for time? We take shortcuts. That's what our fast brains do as well. Similarity bias, confirmation bias, and halo effect are three common shortcuts that end up affecting our decision making, whether we know it or not.

Similarity Bias

Similarity bias refers to our unconscious preference for those whom we perceive to be similar to us in some way. And that's not just because we think we are awesome and others like us surely are as well. It's because, when we perceive similarity, a whole lot less cognitive work needs doing to figure things out. When someone seems similar to us in terms of some aspect(s) of our identities, we quickly feel more at ease, as we perceive a sense of shared understanding (Moreland & Zajonc, 1982). Similarity bias is often apparent in the processes of hiring and promotion, when people who are making the decisions feel drawn to those whom they perceive as similar to themselves in one or more ways.

MODULE 4.6

Confirmation Bias

Confirmation bias is the effect of immediately focusing on that which confirms an already held idea or opinion about what someone or something is like and, by extension, filtering out information that contradicts the previously stored information that our brains have readily at hand. If we have a similarity bias towards someone who appears to look or behave like us, chances are that we will pick up on things that confirm that bias and might miss other important pieces of information that contradict our assumptions or judgments. And the same can apply when we harbor negative biases towards groups of people: we pick up information that confirms that negative bias and miss or dismiss information that contradicts that negative bias. Confirmation biases often come into play when we are evaluating another person's behaviors or their work. We tend to pick up on things that confirm what we already believe about them and miss other things that may be important.

Halo Effect

The last type of common bias we'll discuss is the halo effect, which is closely related to the previous ones. The halo effect occurs when we perceive one characteristic that we like about someone, such as their appearance, their pedigree education, or some commonality we share with them such as where we grew up or went to school (Nisbett & Wilson, 1977). Our fast brain clings to this positive association in such a way that we are predisposed to interpret the rest of the available information that we might gather through the golden light of this halo. When we are reviewing someone's résumé, for example, and we see that they grew up in the same place that we did, we may unconsciously be predisposed to be highly impressed by the rest of their résumé rather than assess each piece of information from an objective perspective.

Overriding Unconscious Bias

As I mentioned at the beginning of the video, unconscious biases are created from bits of information stored in our brain. Unfortunately, we cannot overwrite these bits of information—the neuropathways are permanent—but we can actively override them so that we might minimize their capacity to affect our decision-making and behavior (Rudman et al., 2001). There are three steps that are useful for overriding biases. Let's break them down one at a time.

Recognize conditions ripe for unconscious bias errors

STEP 1

- Shortage of time; quick action/decisions needed
- Personal and environmental stress
- Multitasking
- Routines

MODULE 4.9

Step 1: Recognize Conditions Ripe for Unconscious Bias Errors

First, it is important to recognize those work conditions that are ripe for the rise of unconscious biases. Errors related to unconscious biases tend to come into play in situations in which you are pressed for time and need to complete a task quickly (Kahneman, 2011). Sound familiar? We are also at risk under other stress-inducing conditions, such as conflict at work, issues at home, or environmental stress such as loud or otherwise annoying noises, other people's unbridled emotions, or a series of other distractions, big or small. Multitasking poses another risk factor. When we do several things at a time, we throw our automated processes into overdrive and then are highly prone to unconscious bias (Kahneman, 2011). Even going about our standard daily routines might invite unconscious bias because routines are by nature automated processes: we don't ordinarily have to put much thought into them, we seemingly do them on autopilot (Kahneman, 2011). This, then, is clearly a time during which our fast brain takes over and our slow brain goes elsewhere.

Since these are work conditions that most of us find ourselves in at some point or another, if not most of the time, I'd like for you to pause the video and take a moment to take inventory of some of your work-related or daily-life tasks that involve big or small decisions or judgment calls. Think about the work conditions when you are doing those tasks or making those decisions. Which of those might be prone to similarity bias, confirmation bias, or the halo effect?

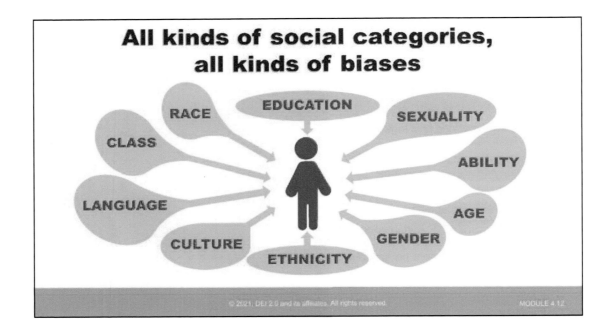

All Kinds of Social Categories, All Kinds of Biases

As you will see in the additional resources section, most of the research on unconscious biases focuses on gender and race. However, it is important to note that we have positive and negative biases about all kinds of identities and appearances.

And here's a really important point to remember: regardless of one's race, gender, social class, age, etc., we are all socialized in the same society. While our individual experiences differ, we are still raised in a society that tells us that pink is for girls and blue is for boys, that the typical firefighter is male and that women are the best primary caretakers of children.

We are told that if you work hard enough you can succeed. We are told that Black men are dangerous. We are told that a man, a woman, and children constitute a family. We are told that obese people are lazy and lack self-control.

Whether we believe these things in our conscious minds is another matter, but these ideas, images, and assumptions are unconsciously embedded in our minds whether we like it or not. So, yes, women can have unconscious bias against women, African Americans can have unconscious bias against African Americans, and so on. The fact that we unconsciously harbor ideas and assumptions that work against our beliefs, values, and self-interest is a hard thing to grapple with. But can we only resist it if we face it.

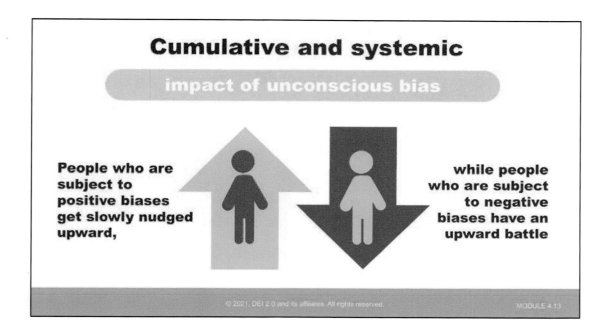

The Impact of Unconscious Bias Is Cumulative and Systemic

It is critically important that we learn to resist or override our biases because their impact is cumulative and systemic. Negative and positive biases reoccur over the lifetime of a person in a wide variety of contexts. People who are subject to positive biases get slowly nudged upward, while people who are subject to negative biases have an upward battle. And when people in a particular identity group are widely and consistently subject to biases, it creates systemic disparities in many areas of society such as education, employment, healthcare, and housing (Staats, 2013).

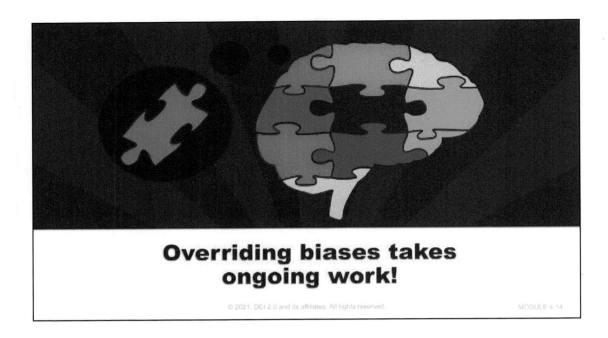

Overriding biases takes ongoing work!

MODULE 4.14

Overriding Biases Takes Ongoing Work

Overriding biases is ongoing work. The good news is that by taking this course, you are already on the right path. The bad news is that this is not enough. Getting better at overriding biases takes ongoing effort. It means being mindful as often as you can. It means grappling with feelings of discomfort. It means intentionally exposing yourself to people and ideas that are different from those with which you are already comfortable. I promise you, however, that the work and effort are worth it. Not only will your own life be enriched, but you may well improve the lives of others and make a valuable contribution to our institution and society overall!

Module 4 Discussion Forum

Discussion Prompts

1. Which of your work-related tasks involve making (small or large) decisions or judgment calls?
2. Which of these tasks might be prone to errors based on unconscious bias?
3. What questions and/or processes might help to identify and override biases?
4. How can mindfulness help us mitigate the influence of unconscious bias in our actions?

Below is an exchange between two participants that provides an example of how they engaged with content from previous topics covered in the course, as well as with their individual experience and knowledge base.

Examples of Participant Discussion Forum Posts

[Janet, 37 years old, Asian American, female faculty] I appreciated the explanation in the unconscious bias video about how our brains work in terms of categorizing things; there is nothing wrong with this, as our brains need to do it, but examining the judgments we make as a result is really important.

I'd say the most common decisions/judgment calls I make happen when I meet with students. It could be things like which courses to recommend to them, or how heavy of an academic load to recommend, or how to approach a difficult conversation (for example, a student isn't graduating when they intended, or they aren't competitive for the program they are applying for).

When I am meeting with students and am trying to figure out which courses to recommend, or how heavy of a load to recommend, I take into account their past performance in courses but also ask questions about their interests and strengths, how their past performance happened—Did something click for them to do well in certain classes? Did something happen in a given semester to make them struggle?—as well as their outside obligations. These are the types of questions that I ask each of the students I meet with because you have to know these things to be able to give the best information.

I do try to remind myself often that while the information that I use to best assist a student (like grades and test scores) tells part of the story, and that is helpful, it doesn't tell all of the story. I also think that talking through situations with colleagues can be helpful when someone else can lend fresh ears to a situation, they can help introduce a new perspective.

I think that mindfulness relates very strongly to the topics covered in this course because, for example, the more that we can be aware of ourselves in a moment, the more in touch we are with our own identity, which includes some privilege. The more mindful we are, the more empathy we can have, I believe, because our minds aren't moving forward to the next thing we can be in the moment with others. We can make conscious decisions to override unconscious bias if we notice it, and we can advocate for and include others if we are cognizant of what all is happening in a given scenario.

[Matthew, 28 years old, White, male staff] Hi Janet. You wrote in your post: "We can make conscious decisions to override unconscious bias if we notice it . . ." . . . which is a cool observation and keen analysis. This course has taught us to be more aware and (for me to) explore resources, such as the Harvard Implicit Association Tests.

In your post, you also wrote about identity. I have thought more about identity throughout this course and have wondered if the general population recognizes or espouses one identity vs. multiple identities. Moving forward, I prefer to think in terms of multiple identities but realize that some folks have a viewpoint or inclination to strongly identify with one prominent identity. I wonder why? Anyway, I enjoyed your post.

[Janet replying to Matthew] I am not the most articulate person, but I think you were understanding the point I was trying to get across with the comment about being conscious of unconscious bias—that sometimes, if we take a step back and analyze a situation, we may become more aware of various things at play than meet the eye.

Regarding identity, I, too, prefer to think in terms of multiple identities, but I think there are certain situations or settings in which we may strongly identify with one prominent identity, even if we don't in other situations. I feel like mother is always a significant part of my identity, though typically I would consider it to be one part of many.

The facilitator kind of touched upon that earlier in one of her discussion follow-ups about how in certain instances, some parts of our identities can become more prominent, and I think that concept can apply to people identifying strongly with one part of their identity vs. multiple parts. I would guess that in times of great pride for a group we identify with, and in times of great fear, we might be more prone to identifying more with just one part. It may also be different for different groups. I don't always immediately consider being white to be part of my identity, even though it is because that is part of my privilege. But someone who is commonly racially profiled, for example, may have a harder time pushing that identity to the side in various circumstances. I'm not really sure; that's just a thought. Again, I am probably not explaining myself all that well, but hopefully that makes some sense. Thanks for your reply!

Discussion Forum Feedback: Sample Text

Thank you for taking the time to work through this challenging module. I'd like to share some additional thoughts that may push your thinking a bit further as you continue processing.

You may remember this old riddle:

A father and his son are in a car accident. The father dies at the scene, and the son is rushed to the hospital. At the hospital, the surgeon looks at the boy and says, "I can't operate on this boy; he is my son." How can this be?

Back in the 70s and 80s, this riddle was a real head-scratcher. Female surgeons were such a rarity that it was beyond the imagination of many Americans that the surgeon in this scenario could have been the boy's mother.

Luckily, times have changed, so I was certain that when I presented this same riddle to a group of millennials, the question would seem ridiculous. Indeed, they very quickly came up with the answer "The boy has two dads," but it was only after some prodding that they landed on the "surgeon is the mother" response.

One takeaway from this story is that even though we may be exposed to new ideas and images of people, some long-standing, broadly held stereotypes, images, and ideas are still deeply ingrained and can prevail over new ideas.

Although many people feel uncomfortable doing the "Who Does What?" activity, it can help reveal stereotypes and archetypes that our brains have stored and can implicitly impact our evaluations of people and who belongs where. Increasing awareness of our biases is critical for being able to mitigate their impact on our decisions and actions. You will find a few resources in the module closing to help you start that process.

By the end of this module, participants typically are starting to get more comfortable with being uncomfortable. Understanding that unconscious bias is something that everyone has to grapple with helps destigmatize the concept so that people can move from denial that they have them toward active steps to mitigate unconscious bias. This module closing should encourage them to keep learning about their biases and prepare them for the next module, which is closely related.

Module 4 Conclusion: Sample Text

Thank you for your thoughtful and honest engagement with the activity and discussion in this module. I know that this topic can provoke feelings of discomfort for many people. Fortunately, this discomfort is a good sign! It means you are coming up to a learning edge. Managing your discomfort and remaining open to learn from that discomfort presents an opportunity for real personal growth.

The next couple of modules will provide you with more opportunities for discomfort and growth. I encourage you to recall our community norms and guidelines and be patient with yourself and each other.

In the meantime, here are some practices that you can implement to mitigate, override, and/or weaken implicit bias.

Learn more about your biases. Take a few of the Harvard Implicit Association Tests to discover implicit biases that may be impacting your decisions and actions. https://implicit.harvard.edu/implicit/takeatest.html.

Do a bias self-audit. Look through your social media contacts and connections. Who are the people you know, follow, read about? If most of the people are similar to you, try expanding your circles!

Please reply to at least two of your colleagues in this module's discussion before moving on to the next module.

Module 4 References

Argyris, C. (1992). Overcoming organizational defenses. *The Journal for Quality and Participation, 15*(2), 26.

Banaji, M. R., & Greenwald, A. G. (2016). *Blindspot: Hidden biases of good people.* Bantam.

Blair, I. V., Ma, J. E., & Lenton, A. P. (2001). Imagining stereotypes away: The moderation of implicit stereotypes through mental imagery. *Journal of Personality and Social Psychology, 81*(5), 828–841.

Gowin, J. (2012). The neuroscience of racial bias. *Psychology Today.* https://www.psychologytoday.com/blog/you-illuminated/201208/the-neuroscience-racial-bias

Kahneman, D. (2011). *Thinking, fast and slow.* Farrar, Straus, and Giroux.

Moreland, R. L., & Zajonc, R. B. (1982). Exposure effects in person perception: Familiarity, similarity, and attraction. *Journal of Experimental Social Psychology, 18*(5), 395–415.

Nickerson, R. S. (1998). Confirmation bias: A ubiquitous phenomenon in many guises. *Review of General Psychology, 2*(2), 175–220.

Nisbett, R. E., & Wilson, T. D. (1977). The halo effect: Evidence for unconscious alteration of judgments. *Journal of Personality and Social Psychology, 35*(4), 250.

Oyler, D. L., Price-Blackshear, M. A., Pratscher, S. D., & Bettencourt, B. A. (2021). Mindfulness and intergroup bias: A systematic review. *Group Processes & Intergroup Relations,* 1368430220978694. https://doi.org/10.1177/1368430220978694

Riddell, K. (2016, September 26). Hillary Clinton calls U.S. racist in debate. *Washington Times.* https://www.washingtontimes.com/news/2016/sep/26/hillary-clinton-calls-us-racist-debate/

Rudman, L. A., Ashmore, R. D., & Gary, M. L. (2001). "Unlearning" automatic biases: The malleability of implicit prejudice and stereotypes. *Journal of Personality and Social Psychology, 81*(5), 856.

Staats, C. (2013). State of the science implicit bias review (p. 104). *The Kirwan Institute for the Study of Race and Ethnicity.* http://kirwaninstitute.osu.edu/?my-product=state-of-the-science-implicit-bias-review

Module (5)

INTRODUCTION TO MICROAGGRESSIONS

> More insidious than those moments of outright hostility, though, and maybe more powerful, are the constant, low-level reminders that you're different. Many of us feel different in some way, but it's really jarring when one of your differences is obvious at a glance—other people can tell you're different simply by looking at you . . . Even when you feel like you belong, other people's reactions—even stares and offhand remarks—can make you feel that you don't, startlingly often.
>
> —Celeste Ng, *Everything I Never Told You*

Microaggressions are a hot, and sometimes contested, topic, particularly in higher education contexts. Microaggressions are defined as "brief and commonplace daily verbal, behavioral or environmental indignities, whether intentional or unintentional, which communicate hostile, derogatory, or negative slights, invalidations, and insults to an individual or group because of their marginalized status in society" (Sue, 2010). The term came into popular usage in the past decade or so when students across the country took to social media to give voice to their ongoing experiences of microaggressions on college campuses. The intention was to draw attention to the offhand and demeaning comments and behaviors that they experience.

This uprising of student voices sparked a backlash in the media by voices purporting the dangers of the politically correct (PC) culture taking hold on college campuses (Chait, 2015). It is argued that the increasing rhetoric of microaggressions, safe spaces, and trigger warnings are antithetical to free speech and academic freedom, and that student demands for these protections will leave them unprepared and unable to cope in the real world (Lukianoff & Haidt, 2015). In the mix of this debate are also stories of college professors, such as a film professor at Northwestern whose provocative comments sparked student demands for her official censure (Goldberg, 2015).

Outside of this controversy over microaggressions playing out in the media, there is a significant body of research that illustrates the harmful psychological and physiological effects that microaggressions can have on individuals from marginalized identity groups (Jay, 2009; Sue et al., 2008; Sue, 2010; Yosso et al., 2009). Therefore, it is an important topic to address in a course about diversity, equity, and inclusion.

The video addresses some of the common points of pushback against the concept of microaggressions. First, the video discusses how microaggressions, like unconscious biases, can create an obstacle to inclusion and therefore it should be everyone's concern. Second, the video explains that we should not point fingers because all of us have likely perpetrated microaggressions, even those of us who may be the targets. And, finally, we explore why microaggressions are a bigger deal than they may seem.

Module 5 Overview: Sample Text

On campuses and in workplaces, there are several types of communication and behavior that are damaging to individuals and organizations. In this module, we're going to explore the concept of microaggressions. Microaggressions come in the form of things like subtle slights, backhanded compliments, well-intentioned comments, and unintentional insults that are actually based on harmful stereotypes and unconscious biases related to race, sex, gender, sexual orientation, age, nationality, weight, disabilities, and so on. Microaggressions are harmful to individuals and organizations. Therefore, this module will raise your awareness about microaggressions and provide you with some strategies for addressing them.

Essential Questions
- What are microaggressions, and why do they matter?
- Do intentions matter?
- Why are microaggressions an obstacle to inclusion?
- What can we do about microaggressions?

Activities
The Do-Over activity in which you are asked to practice responding effectively to a microaggression that you have experienced or witnessed in the past.

Videos
The module video, "The Little Things We Say," provides a conceptual framework for understanding what microaggressions are, why they can have such a damaging impact, and what we can do about them.

Discussions
Please post your initial responses to the discussion prompts by _____ .
A synchronous dialogue will take place on _____ .

Additional Resources

There is a rich set of additional resources (videos, blogs, articles, and books) provided to help you explore this topic further.

To help illustrate microaggressions in action, we use video clips found on YouTube. To find video clips to illustrate microaggressions, simply use the search term "microaggressions," and you will find many to choose from. You will also find a curated list of them on the resource website for this book (www.dei360consulting.com).

Destructive Workplace Communication & Behavior

In the workplace, there are several types of communication and behavior that are damaging to individuals and organizations. In this module, we're going to explore the concept of microaggressions.

© 2021. DEI 2.0 and its affiliates. All rights reserved.   MODULE 5.2

Examples of Microaggressions

Microaggressions come in the form of things like subtle slights, backhanded compliments, well-intentioned comments, and unintentional insults that are actually based on harmful stereotypes and unconscious biases related race, sex, gender, sexual orientation, age, nationality, weight, disabilities, and so on.

Think about Your Thinking before You Start Speaking

One of the first steps to stopping yourself from saying a microaggression is to recognize how they start with our thoughts. This is really a key point if you think back to the module on unconscious bias when we discussed how our fast brains often make these automated connections between the person we are talking to and some bit of stored information in the brain, such as stereotypes. Whether we consciously believe these stereotypes or not, our fast brains might use them to make associations and assumptions about people. And you might also recall that one of the steps to take to override unconscious bias in our decision making, for example, is to think about our thinking. In terms of microaggressions, perhaps we can't stop the thought from popping into our heads . . . but we can take an extra step to think a little more carefully about that thought before we let it come out of our mouths and do some damage.

It's also important to remember that no one is immune from making microaggressions. I can almost guarantee that every person in the course, myself included, has committed a microaggression at one point or another . . . even those of us who may just as often be targets of microaggressions. So we have to be careful about pointing the finger at other people and start with examining our own thought processes and behaviors.

Intent vs. impact

MODULE 5.4

Intent vs. Impact

One aspect of microaggressions that is really challenging for folks is that our intention, or lack of intention, does not change the fact that the microaggression caused some pain. It's like, if I accidently step on your foot, I did not intend to hurt you, but that doesn't change the fact that you now have a throbbing toe.

Microaggressions can be made with positive intent, such as curiosity, a compliment, or an attempt to connect with someone. They are also often made thoughtlessly without any intent at all.

So you may wonder why such small or unintentional comments can have such a negative impact. That is due to what can be referred to as "the bucket effect."

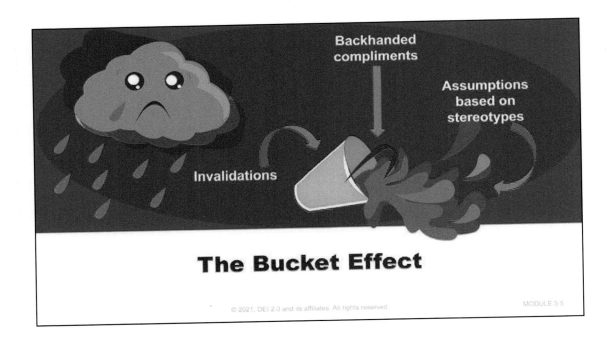

The Bucket Effect

MODULE 5.5

The Bucket Effect

People who complain about microaggressions are often told to "Shrug it off," "Don't worry about it," "You shouldn't let it bother you." That may seem like reasonable advice, but the problem is that microaggressions are like little drops of water in a bucket: they add up over time, and the bucket becomes a very heavy burden that people have to carry around.

Eventually the bucket will overflow and spill out in ways that may seem like overreaction when, in fact, the reaction is not to a single comment but a bucket full of them.

One more thing about the bucket effect: notice the little sad cloud graphic. That is meant to represent the overall cultural and political climate that consistently sends negative messages about people in marginalized groups, whether it be through political debate, print or broadcast entertainment, advertising, media image, or policy discussions.

In other words, the microaggressions committed by individuals are simply adding to buckets already being filled by the climate in our workplaces, in society, and in the world at large.

Microaggressions Can Lead to Macro-Effects

There is a growing body of research that focuses on the damaging impact of microaggressions. The ongoing experiences of microaggressions increase individuals' stress levels, and ongoing stress is directly linked to both physical and mental health issues (Clark et al., 1999; Sue et al., 2008).

Team effectiveness can be impacted as well. Microaggressions can take up a lot of a person's cognitive energy as they try to process what happened, to manage emotions, and to negotiate ongoing relationships with the microaggressors. This depletion of cognitive energy has an impact on both productivity and problem-solving, so you can imagine how that plays out in teams and groups (Dovidio, 2001; Salvatore & Shelton, 2007).

And when microaggressions are commonplace, yet go unrecognized and unaddressed, it creates a hostile and invalidating climate, which then produces direct and indirect inequities for those targeted by microaggressions and has a damaging impact on our organizations and society overall (Purdie-Vaughns et al., 2008).

Identity dominance

✓ Race/Ethnicity
✓ Nationality
✓ Gender, Gender Identity, Sexual Orientation
✓ Religion
✓ Socioeconomic status
✓ Physical appearance
✓ Physical ability
✓ Education

POWER
Social/Cultural
Political
Economic

Mainstream Norm

Marginalized "other"

© 2021. DEI 2.0 and its affiliates. All rights reserved.

MODULE 5.7

Identity Dominance

The final thing to know about microaggressions is that even when the intent is positive, there is a power dynamic at play, which often goes unrecognized by the person who makes the microaggressions but is definitely felt by those on the receiving end.

In our society, each of our social identity groups is structured by two binary poles. And the poles do not occupy an equal position in our society. One side of the scale is mainstream or "the norm," and it is closer to the center of social, cultural, political, and economic power. On the other side of that power scale, the other group is on the margins of power. What does all this have to do with microaggressions? Microaggressions reinforce this dynamic of the mainstream "norm" and marginalization of the "other."

While microaggressions such as "I can't tell Asians apart," "You're English is so good," or "You don't sound Black" minimize or invalidate the people at whom they are directed, they also serve to normalize the ways that the dominant group looks and sounds.

To visualize this dynamic, think about kids roughhousing in the swimming pool. When they push someone under, they simultaneously are pushing themselves up—closer to the air and sunshine. Now, the kids may not intentionally be pushing themselves upward, but that in fact is the dynamic that occurs when we push someone down, even verbally.

While we all need to do our best at avoiding making microaggressions—and being accountable for them when we do say them—we also need to find the courage to speak up when we are targeted by or witness to microaggressions because microaggressions prevent people from feeling that they belong and can thrive in our organizations. Now, we'll discuss how to navigate through the challenges of addressing microaggressions.

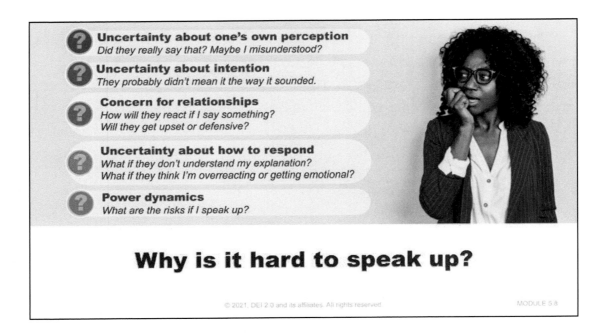

? **Uncertainty about one's own perception**
Did they really say that? Maybe I misunderstood?

? **Uncertainty about intention**
They probably didn't mean it the way it sounded.

? **Concern for relationships**
How will they react if I say something?
Will they get upset or defensive?

? **Uncertainty about how to respond**
What if they don't understand my explanation?
What if they think I'm overreacting or getting emotional?

? **Power dynamics**
What are the risks if I speak up?

Why is it hard to speak up?

MODULE 5.8

Why Is It Hard to Speak Up?

Microaggressions create obstacles to inclusion, which means that, when left un-addressed, they can create an environment that prevents colleagues from feeling like they belong and can bring their best. The negative impact is felt by individuals and can be seen in overall organizational performance. From this perspective, it is everyone's responsibility to address microaggressions. But sometimes that's easier said than done.

There are a lot of reasons that it can be hard to speak up. We may be uncertain about what we heard or the intentions behind it. We may have concerns about making the relationship uncomfortable or about not being able to explain what the problem is. And finally, there may be power dynamics at play, which can be risky for those in positions of less power.

Addressing microaggressions

(• Intentional or not, words hurt.

(• Silence perpetuates the problem.

(• Rights and responsibilities.

MODULE 5.9

Addressing Microaggressions

Although there may be risks, we have to do something to address microaggression. Why? Because intentional or not, words hurt. They can make people feel isolated, excluded, and minimized. None of these feelings help people thrive in our organizations. Moreover, silence perpetuates the problem. Letting things go normalizes and reproduces destructive communication practices that create a toxic environment. And finally, we all have a right to work in a place where we feel safe, valued, and included. We also have a responsibility to create that environment for ourselves and others.

Be ready with quick one liners.

Repeat back
"So you're saying that..."

Separate intent from impact
"I'm sure you did not mean to be offensive,
but when you said..."

Play dumb
"I'm sorry, I don't quite understand what you mean.
Can you explain?"

**Show support directly
to the person harmed.**

**Ask for third party
assistance or report it.**

**People with privilege and
power should be particularly
vigilant, responsible, and
accountable for speaking up.**

Strategies to address microaggressions

Strategies to Address Microaggressions

In order to address microaggressions, it is helpful to have a set of strategies for different situations.

In some situations, such as when a colleague makes an off-the-cuff remark or joke that is based on harmful stereotypes, a quick one-liner in the moment may gently let them know that what they said was not okay. For example, you can ask them to explain or clarify what they said, which may help them realize the inappropriateness or offensiveness of the comment. If it was a joke, you can play dumb and say you don't understand.

In other situations, such as when the person really was not aware that their comment was offensive or they meant to give a compliment, you might ask them to meet for coffee and explain the impact of their words, even if their intention was positive. Approaching them with genuine regard and an intention to educate may help diffuse the defensiveness they are likely to feel.

If it is not safe for you to address the perpetrator directly, you can still speak up by showing support directly to the person harmed, asking for third-party assistance, or reporting it.

It is especially important that people with privilege and power are particularly vigilant, responsible, and accountable for speaking up when they hear a microaggression . . . even if the people being targeted are not in the room.

And finally, just a reminder that all of us have perpetrated a microaggression, whether intentional or not. The more you learn about microaggressions, the better chance you have of noticing. If you catch yourself, hit the pause button and apologize. Just a simple "Ouch, I'm sorry. That wasn't right. What I meant was . . ."

If someone cares enough and is brave enough to let you know that you said something hurtful or offensive, manage your feelings of defensiveness and take it as a gift rather than a criticism. Don't try to prove your perspective, just listen intently, learn something, and take responsibility.

I hope these strategies provide you with ideas and encouragement for addressing microaggressions so that they do not continue to do damage to your colleagues and your workplace environment.

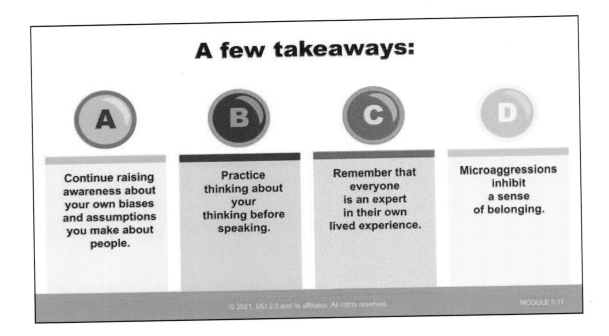

A few takeaways:

A — Continue raising awareness about your own biases and assumptions you make about people.

B — Practice thinking about your thinking before speaking.

C — Remember that everyone is an expert in their own lived experience.

D — Microaggressions inhibit a sense of belonging.

MODULE 5.11

A Few Takeaways

This brings us to the end of this short overview of microaggressions. I'll just leave you with a few thoughts to take with you. Since each of us occupies some mainstream and some marginalized identities, we are all potential perpetrators of microaggressions. To avoid making unintentional microaggressions, we need to continually work on recognizing our own biases and assumptions about people who are different from us, because that's the stuff that our fast brain picks up on before we've had a chance to think. If we practice thinking about our thinking before we speak, we will get better at catching ourselves before saying something that might hurt, minimize, or invalidate someone unintentionally.

Module 5 Discussion Forum

Facilitator Note: We have found that by the time we reach this module, participants usually have enough trust in one another and feel safe enough to open up and share their experiences of microaggressions with their learning communities. These discussions tend to include microaggressions that participants themselves have experienced, witnessed, and/or perpetrated. By providing a space for participants to recall and reflect on these experiences, we provide learners with the opportunity to learn more about others' experiences as well as explore ways to approach these situations more effectively. Below we share some examples of stories from faculty, staff, and students about being on the receiving end of microaggressions, as well as stories that participants shared about past experiences that they now realize were microaggressions that they either witnessed or unintentionally committed.

Discussion Instructions: Sample Text

To contribute to this dialogue, please start by responding to one or more of the discussion prompts below and/or anything else related to the module. Then, read and reply to at least two of your colleagues. Be sure to read replies that people write in response to your post and reply if needed.

Please ensure that all of your colleagues receive at least two replies. And, as always, keep the Community Norms and Guidelines in mind when participating in the discussion.

I invite you to contribute to our learning community by sharing any/all of the following:

1. Share your story. If you feel comfortable, share an experience when you were on the receiving end of a microaggression.
2. Share your do-over story. Now that you've had a chance to think about microaggressions you've experienced or seen others do, take a minute to think about things you've said. Describe a microaggression you may have committed and take a shot at writing up an apology to that person that illustrates that you truly understand why what you said may have been hurtful, despite your intention.

Examples of Participant Discussion Forum Posts

[Juan, 20 years old, Latino, male student] Microaggression: "So you are from Mexico? Are you even here legally?"

How I would respond: "Well, I got a green card when I was 16 and then moved to the US soon after, so I would say, 'yes!' I am. Thank you for your concern."

[Jeffrey, 26 years old, African American, male student] I remember one microaggression that sticks with me to this day and bothers me. This incident happened at one of my jobs. I just started a job at a hotel called Wingate Inn. My position was front desk clerk. It was my first day on the job. I was getting my work uniform and going over the schedule and the work handbook. The manager of the hotel had the nerve to tell me, "You want to know the reason why I hired you?" I asked her why and her response was "Because you articulate very well. Most people of your kind don't articulate well. Usually, you people have your pants sagging and speak some slang I don't understand. You don't present yourself as a slob."

[Latrice, 31 years old, African American, female staff] One comment that really gets under my skin is when people would always say, "You look like the other black girl that works here" or "I thought you were. . . . " This makes me so angry! We literally look nothing alike, face, body shape, size, etc. So when I hear this comment, I just say, "Oh, I don't see it" or "You think so?" They would always answer back, "Yeah, you guys wear your hair the same." I would leave the conversation alone because it's ridiculous that hair makes you look the same.

[Thomas, 29 years old, African American, male student] I'm in the Army National Guard, and one day I was at drill when I found myself in a situation to where my peers were discussing black people. They told me that I wasn't like other black people because I go to college, I don't act "hood," and that I don't get into any illegal trouble. At the time, I didn't say anything because I was the only African American guy in our unit and I didn't want to cause a scene or bring unwanted attention to myself. I knew that they meant no harm by what they were saying, but it made me feel terrible, because outside of myself, they automatically assumed the worst about my race. I thought, "Why can't we be thought of as being educated, upstanding citizens?"

[Sabastian, 49 years old, Latino, male faculty] My main takeaway from the content of microaggressions is that everyone, including me as a member of a "marginalized" group, is guilty of committing microaggressions to family, friends, and some other people in general. I am wondering if microaggressions will end once we start treating everyone with respect and part of the same community.

Background information: I moved to a college town after being born and raised in small towns without knowledge of what diversity meant. My college had a great international diverse population and I was so fascinated to learned about everyone that sometimes I would ask too many questions. So, this is a real situation in my life when I met an African friend who came from the Republic of Congo, and I said . . .

"So, how do you like living in a city like this instead of living in the jungle?" To which my friend replied: "Oh, come on, not all people in my country live as you see it in TV. I actually come from a bigger metropolitan city, so I am getting used to living in this small college town."

This is what I should had asked instead: "So how do you like living in this college town compared to your hometown?"

My friend and I had a long conversation about our backgrounds after this naïve question. I still feel so embarrassed when talking about it, but we continue to be friends and sometimes talk about that funny dumb question I asked a long time ago.

[Kaitlyn, 19 years old, White, female student] Every year during Thanksgiving break my summer camp friends and I celebrate together at my house in Chicago. It also happens to be the time of year where my family puts up our Christmas tree, so my friends and I help haul the boxes of ornaments up and set up the tree with my family. We had just finished setting up the tree and were about to start putting on ornaments when my brother told my friend Jack, who happens to be gay, "Make the tree fabulous!" Everyone giggled, myself included, but I saw Jack's face tighten up a bit. I didn't say anything back because I didn't want to get into a fight with my brother while trying to decorate the Christmas tree.

[Scott, 32 years old, White, male faculty] One time I witnessed a microaggression was when I was at a bar and my friends and I were all sitting around a table. My roommate's girlfriend was talking about one of her good friends and said: "Yeah, [NAME] is Black, but she doesn't act Black at all." She was saying this to our other friend who is African American. Neither of us responded to her comment but we just looked at each other and smirked, and both of us knew that what she had said was offensive, but she still had no idea. I regret not saying anything or sticking up for my friend in the moment, but at the same time I knew that he and I were on the same page.

Discussion Forum Feedback: Sample Text

Thank you for a robust and honest discussion about responding to micro-aggressions. As many of you acknowledged, speaking up is a hard to do for a variety of reasons: uncertainty about what to say or simply being too shocked to say anything; power dynamics; and not wanting to start an argument or embarrass someone further. Speaking up can be difficult, even frightening, for the fear of not doing so well. It is challenging to find the right balance between not coming off as a "holier-than-thou-know-it-all" or making too much light of the situation in order to avoid discomfort.

I think it helps to analyze the situation as best as we can in the moment. If you think the person committing the microaggression really does not know better, then a more empathetic/educational approach might be appropriate. If you think the person probably does know better but was either being thoughtless or was assuming that it would be all right to make the comment in your presence, then perhaps a little humor or a simple "Really? Did you just say that?" will suffice and let the person know that it is not OK. However, the reality is that no matter what action we take, there may be a price to pay.

If we say SOMETHING: No matter how effectively we respond to the micro-aggression that we've witnessed or experienced, it is very unlikely that the person will say, "Awesome, thanks so much for letting me know what a jerk I am!" and go merrily on their way. It is more likely that the person will feel embarrassed or ashamed and will feel "some kind of way" about you, at least for a while. They may even get defensive and lash out at you. Ideally, they will ponder your comment, be self-reflective, and learn/grow from it, and in time be grateful for it. But there is always a risk that it will cause a (hopefully) temporary rift between you.

If we say NOTHING: Your relationship with that person may remain "comfortable," but your feelings toward that person may begin to change and even grow negative as the offensive behavior becomes normalized, which is damaging not only to your relationship but to the overall environment/climate.

I think the lowest risk move, but perhaps one of the most challenging, is when we recognize and take responsibility for the microaggressions that we do. I really appreciated that some of you took the opportunity to apply what was learned about microaggressions to reflect on your own past comments/behavior.

When we own up to the microaggressions we make, not only do we model the kind of behavior that the world needs more of, but we also empower the person (who we just disempowered through our microaggression) by making ourselves vulnerable to them, by showing remorse and owning our mistake. And truth be told, sometimes it is hard to catch ourselves in the moment; it is only later that we realize that we said or did something regrettable. But like any apology, it still can go a long way to follow up with that person even after the fact.

And if you have been lucky enough to have been told by someone that you said a microaggression, then you are a few steps ahead of the game. I say "lucky enough" because speaking up to tell someone that they have said or done something offensive, especially someone you like enough to have a relationship with, is really a hard thing to do. So, if this person took the initiative to say something to you, it means they care enough about you to have bothered.

Speaking of whether to bother or not, a few of you shared examples of microaggressions you experienced or witnessed by strangers. My personal advice is to pick your battles. If you have an opportunity to be an ally and stand up for someone else, then you probably should try to rally. If someone says something to you, you have to consider whether it will cost you more cognitive energy to carry it around without saying something or to address it in some way. My personal advice would be that if you say something, don't bother with too much of an educational approach, just a simple one-liner (such as from the list) to let them know and so you don't have to carry as much around.

And, finally, I want to provide you with a little fodder to push back on people who say things like "What about freedom of speech?" or "I'm tired of all this PC oversensitive BS." I would say this:

The things we say have the power to build bridges or walls; it's as simple as that. If your goal is to connect with people through inclusive, compassionate, and effective communication, then you should try to minimize or at least be more aware of microaggressions. If you prefer to only consider your own perspective and feelings, then you are within your right to do that.

A little snarky perhaps, but I just get a little tired of people refusing to see beyond their own perspective/experience.

At this point, participants may already be struggling with guilt or feeling resistant to the content. It is important to acknowledge their challenge, communicate gratitude, and keep them motivated to tackle another challenging topic.

Module 5 Conclusion: Sample Text

Whew! You've made it through another very challenging module. Hopefully, you gained some important insights into how our thoughts and behaviors can negatively impact others in ways that we did not realize and did not intend. This is a hard thing for many of us well-meaning folks to grapple with. However, this heightened sense of awareness will help you avoid making microaggressions and also notice (and hopefully speak up) when they occur around you. In this next module, we'll tackle one more challenging topic that will raise your awareness even more and give you some important tools for inclusion.

In the meantime, here are some ideas for putting your learning into practice:

- **Prepare to respond to microaggressions**. Although it can be challenging to speak up effectively in the moment, it will be easier if you actually do your homework ahead of time by familiarizing yourself with common microaggressions and thinking about strategies for speaking up that might work for you. Check out the additional resources for this module for examples and strategies to consider.
- **Start implementing the power of micro-affirmations**. Accentuating the positive is one strategy for counterbalancing microaggressions. Learn more about this evidence-based practice for counteracting the cumulative negative impact of microaggressions in the additional resources section.

Before you move on to the next module, please make sure you have replied to at least two of your colleagues' posts in the discussion board and have read/replied to people who have posted to yours.

Module 5 References

Chait, J. (2015, January 27). Not a very P.C. thing to say: How the language police are perverting liberalism. *New York Magazine*. http://nymag.com/daily/intelligencer/2015/01/not-a-very-pc-thing-to-say.html

Clark, R., Anderson, N. B., Clark, V. R., & Williams, D. R. (1999). Racism as a stressor for African Americans: A biopsychosocial model. *American Psychologist, 54*(10), 805.

Dovidio, J. F. (2001). On the nature of contemporary prejudice: The third wave. *Journal of Social Issues, 57*(4), 829–849.

Goldberg, M. (2015, March 16). The Laura Kipnis melodrama. *The Nation.* https://www.thenation.com/article/laura-kipnis-melodrama/

Jay, M. (2009). Race-ing through the school day: African American educators' experiences with race and racism in schools. *International Journal of Qualitative Studies in Education, 22*(6), 671–685.

Lukianoff, G., & Haidt, J. (2015, September). The coddling of the American mind. *The Atlantic.* https://www.theatlantic.com/magazine/archive/2015/09/the-coddling-of-the-american-mind/399356/

Purdie-Vaughns, V., Steele, C. M., Davies, P. G., Ditlmann, R., & Crosby, J. R. (2008). Social identity contingencies: How diversity cues signal threat or safety for African Americans in mainstream institutions. *Journal of Personality and Social Psychology, 94*(4), 615.

Salvatore, J., & Shelton, J. N. (2007). Cognitive costs of exposure to racial prejudice. *Psychological Science, 18*(9), 810–815.

Solórzano, D., Ceja, M., & Yosso, T. (2000). Critical race theory, racial microaggressions, and campus racial climate: The experiences of African American college students. *The Journal of Negro Education, 69*(1/2), 60–73.

Sue, D. W. (2010). *Microaggressions and marginality: Manifestation, dynamics, and impact.* Wiley.

Sue, D. W., Capodilupo, C. M., & Holder, A. (2008). Racial microaggressions in the life experience of Black Americans. *Professional Psychology: Research and Practice, 39*(3), 329.

Yosso, T., Smith, W., Ceja, M., & Solórzano, D. (2009). Critical race theory, racial microaggressions, and campus racial climate for Latina/o undergraduates. *Harvard Educational Review, 79*(4), 659–691.

Module (6)

INTRODUCTION TO PRIVILEGE

To be white, or straight, or male, or middle class is to be simultaneously ubiquitous and invisible. You're everywhere you look, you're the standard against which everyone else is measured. You're like water, like air. People will tell you they went to see a "woman doctor" or they will say they went to see "the doctor." People will tell you they have a "gay colleague" or they'll tell you about a colleague. A white person will be happy to tell you about a "Black friend," but when that same person simply mentions a "friend," everyone will assume the person is white. Any college course that doesn't have the word "woman" or "gay" or "minority" in its title is a course about men, heterosexuals, and white people. But we call those courses "literature," "history" or "political science." This invisibility is political.
—Michael S. Kimmel, *Privilege: A Reader*

Learning and engaging in discussions about privilege can be a pivotal moment in the transformative learning process, but it can also provoke strong resistance from participants in both dominant (i.e., those who identify as White) and marginalized (i.e., those who identify as persons of color) identity groups in the United States. For example, White participants may experience cognitive dissonance, or inconsistent thoughts and attitudes, between the concept of privilege and their belief in meritocracy and a sense of personal hardship (Case & Wise, 2013). Individuals from nondominant groups may also react negatively to the topic of privilege because they may perceive it as making them appear or be thought of as disadvantaged or oppressed, minimizing their own sense of agency (Case & Cole, 2013).

Importantly, many people have never been asked to reflect on their own privileged identities, so, when asked to do so, it might invoke feelings of discomfort. To help mitigate resistance and defensiveness, we take a very broad approach to the concept of privilege so that all participants are able to identify aspects of their identity that afford or deny them privilege in particular contexts. This process is very enlightening for many people because it is often easy for them to recognize the areas in which they *do not* have privilege but much more difficult for them to see the areas in which they *do*. For example, participants who may not have privilege based on race may discover that they have privilege based on socioeconomic status, education, able-bodied status, religion, gender identity, or sexual orientation. This process also helps mitigate White participants' defensiveness

153

against the idea that they have privilege because of their race, as they can see the other areas in which they, too, may have experienced a lack of privilege related to gender, age, sexual orientation, socioeconomic status, body type, and health status.

Ultimately, this module helps participants understand privilege as a set of unearned, and often invisible or unrecognized, social advantages related to different aspects of one's identity. After participants have gone through the process of identifying their own areas of privilege, this module provides them with some guidance for what they can do about it so that these new insights do not mire them in guilt or despair. When participants engage in the module with a sincere intention to learn, it can empower them to transform the ways that they understand their own experiences as well as those of people different from themselves.

Module 6 Overview: Sample Text

Introduction to Privilege

In this module, you are asked to critically examine aspects of your daily lives that you may consider to be normal or natural yet in fact are aspects of *unearned privilege*. Unearned privilege refers to the advantages that an individual receives by identifying with or being born into a specific group. This type of privilege is different from the advantages or privileges that you earn as a result of your own hard work (McIntosh, 1989).

After you learn more about privilege and do an activity to help you identify your areas of privilege, we'll discuss what you can do about it.

Please note as we go through this module that it is normal and appropriate if the content makes you feel a bit uncomfortable. As we grow in our self-awareness, we learn to see things in new ways—and we may not always like what we see. The good news is that by becoming more aware of ourselves and others, we are taking the first important step toward being more inclusive!

Essential Questions

- What is privilege, and why does it matter?
- Why is it so hard for some people to talk about privilege?
- How does privilege play out in our daily lives?
- What is the effect of privilege on individuals and society as a whole?
- How does privilege create obstacles to inclusion?
- What can we do about privilege, our own and other people's?

Activities

- Privilege Self-Audit: The activity will help you identify areas of privilege that you may not be aware of and in the process gain insights into the experiences of people who do not have those same privileges.
- Managing Privilege: This is guidance to review after your audit. People tend to feel guilty or angry after the audit. This guidance will help you channel those feelings into something more productive.

Videos

This module's video, "Margins and Mainstreams," explores the concept of privilege and clarifies some misconceptions that people may have.

Discussions

Please post your initial responses to the discussion prompts by _____ .

Readings, Handouts, and Additional Resources

There is a rich set of additional resources provided to help you explore privilege and allyship.

Mini-Lecture Slides & Scripts: Margins and Mainstreams

Margins and Mainstreams

People tend to get upset when the word "privilege" is used to describe their experiences. This is understandable because most of us have worked hard to be where we are and might not feel that we have had any special advantages. But privilege doesn't mean being born with a silver spoon in your mouth. Privilege means being born into a group that holds more economic, social, and political power in a given society. This dominant group comes to define mainstream or "the norm," while groups on the margins are "different" or "other" than the norm. And this is what creates privilege for dominant groups. Let me put this another way . . .

Privilege is like being right-handed

Allen, B. J. (2010). *Difference matters: Communicating social identity.* Waveland Press.

MODULE 6.2

Privilege Is Like Being Right-Handed

To understand how privilege functions, think about the experiences of right-handed vs. left-handed people. Think about the ways that most tools, utensils, and desks favor the dominant majority of right-handed people. Right-handed people don't ever have to think about the issues of handedness. Left-handed people, on the other hand (no pun intended), face challenges throughout their lives. In school, teachers might try to force them to use their right hand to write, which can be uncomfortable. Later in life, left-handers have to adjust to handshakes, maybe driving a car with a stick shift (on the right, of course), or how to not bump people with their elbows at dinner parties. Right-handed people are often unaware of their privilege because, well, it just seems natural. In other words, privilege is the stuff you don't have to think about because it doesn't really affect you, even though it benefits you in ways in which you may not be aware.

MODULE 6 3'

Privilege Means . . .

Privilege means that you don't have to consider the way in which your life differs from others because your day-to-day activities are not hindered or questioned. Privilege does not mean that you don't have to work for what you have. It does not mean that you don't suffer or have hard times. Privilege means never having to be aware of your skin color when you go to a store, drive a car, walk through campus. It means being able to hold hands with your romantic partner as you walk down the street without people staring. It means not having to worry about whether you will physically be able to get into or out of a particular building or room. It means knowing that your name won't raise an eyebrow when an employer sees it on your résumé. It means being free of derogatory names that people might call you or assumptions that people might make about you based on your given identities. You get the gist. But let's be clear here, privilege is contextual: most of us have privilege in some contexts and not in others. All of us at the university have some degree of privilege in the broader social context by the very fact that we draw a regular paycheck. And individuals taking this course have more privilege than others by the very nature of having computer literacy and access to this course. But the point for our current discussion is that privilege often functions below our level of awareness. As stated earlier, it seems natural, it's the way things are, the norm. By not recognizing how privilege functions, we may overlook the fact that our organization is a right-handed world where not everyone can function naturally or comfortably.

And while left-handed people can be just as successful as right-handers, it is also true that they face struggles and indignities that right-handed people may never notice. So let's take a minute to identify your areas of privilege.

Mapping privilege

Given
Chosen
Core

Put a "+" by aspects of your identity that:

+ have little impact on daily life; you don't have to think about

+ do not cause obstacles or challenges

+ you have in common with the majority of people you work with

+ you have in common with people in the upper levels of your organization chart

© 2021. DEI 2.0 and its affiliates. All rights reserved.

GIVEN IDENTITIES

- Country of citizenship
- Age/generation
- Ethnicity or race
- Physical characteristics/stature
- Physical abilities/disabilities
- Religious or spiritual affiliation
- Gender/sex
- Gender identity
- Sexual orientation
- Socioeconomic status/social class

MODULE 6.4

Mapping Privilege

Pause the video for a minute and jot down each of the aspects of your given identity: your nationality or country of citizenship; your age or the generation you were born into; your ethnicity or race; your physical characteristics such as body size and other normative standards of appearance; your physical ability status; your religious affiliation; your socioeconomic status; your sexual orientation, gender, and gender identity. If you are unsure about gender identity, you'll learn more about that in the next activity in the module.

This is not an exhaustive list, so feel free to write down any other aspects of your given identities that you can think of. When you are done, come back to the video for the next part of the activity.

Look at your list of given identities, the cards you were dealt at birth, and mark a "plus" by any of those given identities that you feel have very little impact on your daily life, that do not cause obstacles or challenges in your work life or in society, and that you have in common with most people you work with and with most people in positions of power at the university such as deans, division heads, and administrators.

The categories that you marked with a plus are those identities that afford you privilege as defined in this video. Again, please understand that these aspects of your identity are not something to be ashamed of, whether they are privileged or not. Rather they highlight some areas that you may want to increase your awareness about in the next part of this module.

Concepts for moving forward

- Everyone has some forms of privilege; some have more than others.
- It's easy to see the privileges we do **NOT** have—but very hard to see the ones we do.
- No blame, no shame: It's no one's fault. We were born into a system based on privilege that we did not create.
- Guilt is not productive. Taking action is!
- Privilege is **NOT** a zero-sum game. We can spread it around without losing anything.
- Conversations about privilege are hard—but necessary.

MODULE 6.5

Concepts for Moving Forward

I want to close with a few reminders for you to take with you to help you engage in conversations about privilege with the people in your life. First, everyone has some forms of privilege, whether they know it or not. In the previous activity, you may have discovered forms of privilege that may never have even crossed your mind because, as was mentioned previously, privilege is like right-handedness; it just seems normal. That's why it's very easy to see the privilege that we don't have and much harder to see the ones that we do. The third point is really important. When some people first learn about privilege, they can become defensive because they feel as if they are being blamed for something that they didn't do. I urge you to remember the "no blame, no shame" mantra. We were all born into a system that we did not create. Therefore, guilt about privilege is not only unnecessary, it's also not productive. But taking action is productive, as we will discuss at the end of this module. And the truth is that we have nothing to lose by trying to ensure that everyone is afforded the privilege of belonging and feeling safe. In fact, if we actively make sure that everyone feels safe, welcome, and accepted, we all win! That said, conversations about privilege can be hard and uncomfortable. But I promise, it's worth it. We have so much to gain by increasing our awareness of privilege because it enhances our capacity for empathy and our ability to improve our campus and our community. So let's get started!

Module 6 Activity: Privilege Checklists

This activity does not involve a video. The following instructions should appear in the course site as written text. The privilege checklists are provided in the online DEI tool-kit as well as in the Participant Workbook.

Activity Instructions: Sample Text

In the previous activity, you identified aspects of your given identities that are associated with privilege both in our organizational context and society at large. Now we're going to take a deeper dive into how privilege plays out in our daily lives in order to increase your awareness, understanding, and empathy for people who do not share your areas of privilege. Read through the Privilege Checklists that align with your identified areas of privilege from the previous activity. As you read through the checklists, you might find yourself thinking things like "Oh, that's ridiculous" or "That's not how it is for me" or "What's the big deal?" You are encouraged instead to think about what it might feel like if those things that seem natural, normal, or insignificant were not your reality. In other words, try to use the lists to build your capacity to imagine what walking in someone else's shoes might be like.

Now that participants have identified their areas of privilege and learned more about what it means to benefit and not benefit from those areas of privilege, they may be feeling a bit overwhelmed with guilt, shame, and/or uncertainty about what to do with this information. These challenging emotions and insights can serve to break down previously held beliefs and perceptions, so it's natural that they may cause a sense of emotional and cognitive disequilibrium, which is a critical part of transformative learning processes. However, this experience can also be counterproductive or detrimental if learners do not move past these potentially upsetting, even immobilizing, feelings. Providing participants with concrete guidance about how to manage privilege—and the awareness thereof—can also help them manage this accompanying discomfort of these feelings.

Post-Activity Discussion: Sample Text

Managing Privilege

Many people struggle with feelings of guilt when reading the privilege checklists. None of us chose the areas of privilege into which we were born, so there's no need to feel guilty about that. However, the fact that we did not choose it does not mean that it is not so or that we do not hold any measure of responsibility for what we do with it. Rather than own up to this responsibility, some folks end up struggling with feelings of guilt about their privilege. This is really not a productive response to privilege. Rather than feel guilty, here are some guiding principles that can help you be responsible with your privilege:

Manage your talk time. Recognize that people in privileged identity groups have historically been the ones to dominate discussions and dictate norms and expectations of organizational life. If you are in a group with people from nondominant identity groups, be mindful of your participation in the conversation. Share the floor, open the space, and don't make the conversation about you.

Listen through discomfort. It can sometimes be uncomfortable to really listen to the experiences of people in nondominant identity groups, especially if you or people in your group are being criticized. Privilege means that you have the choice to ignore it. Being responsible with your privilege means that you do not ignore or dismiss what you are being told.

Educate yourself. Seek out resources (books, blogs, movies, articles, events, conferences) to educate yourself about the experiences and issues faced by people in various nondominant identity groups. Do not ask people from those groups to educate you, and do not expect them to pat you on the back for educating yourself.

Speak up. When you hear disparaging, degrading, or dehumanizing comments, such as slurs, jokes, and stereotypes based on an identity group, speak up against it, whether there are people from that identity group present or not. This can be uncomfortable, but if you say nothing, you are in fact condoning and perpetuating that behavior. Finding ways to effectively call attention to this inappropriate behavior in your peer or work group is an important aspect of taking responsibility for your privilege.

Cultivate critical self-awareness. Our areas of privilege have been taught to us and reinforced throughout our lives. All of us have internalized ideas, thoughts, and behaviors that reinforce our privilege at the cost of someone else's oppression.

This means that even though we have very good intentions, we may sometimes get it wrong—especially in the quickness of the moment (when our fast brain is in control). If you think you may have unintentionally hurt someone or simply reinforced a power dynamic, take the time to rethink and question yourself. If possible, backtrack to the people involved and check in about it. These are important learning and trust-building situations. Don't miss the opportunity!

Module 6 Discussion Forum

In the section below, we share the discussion prompts provided to participants, along with several excerpts. The excerpts below do not reflect a particular thread in one discussion forum but rather they were selected as prime examples of the transformative learning that often occurs in the online discussions following this module.

Discussion Prompts

1. In what ways, if any, did your understanding of privilege as a concept change or evolve as a result of what you learned in this module?
2. Describe any areas of privilege discussed in this module that you had not previously thought about.
3. What are some things that you might do as a result of gaining new insights about privilege?

Examples of Participant Discussion Forum Posts

[Sabastian, 49 years old, Latino, male faculty] Wow . . . that was an eye-opening exercise. I didn't realize how many privileges I have, and [it] also tells me that what I have thought of as normal could be a disadvantage for others. That gives me a different perspective of my daily life.

For me the only two privileges I felt that were granted to me over my lifetime were being a citizen of the US and all of the privileges that entailed and being a good athlete, which seemed to allow a lot of privilege.

The privilege categories and checklists were eye-opening. I realized that I was in several privilege groups; however, on the 100-point assessment, I scored only 60. I thought it would be higher, but childhood poverty and life circumstances I had not considered as impacting privilege impacted my score. I am very aware of some impacts of disability, and we have far to go to make accessible housing and communities a given, not something you have to search for.

[Nina, 32 years old, White, female staff] The info on privilege increased awareness that everyone has some amount of privilege [and] some have many more than others. I liked the example of right-handedness. I did find myself feeling guilty after taking the quiz, which indicated I have been "quite privileged." As a Catholic, I often find myself feeling guilty for one thing or another. I appreciated the video recognizing guilt as unnecessary and not productive. I do think the exercise helped to increase empathy—I honestly haven't considered myself "quite privileged." But writing down the answers and considering what it would be like to be in a category where I would be exposed to more ridicule or be concerned about being myself in public increased my awareness.

Watching the privilege video was uncomfortable. I realized that I do take offense when someone says that I'm privileged in a certain area [when] they don't even know me or my background. This is something I need to work on.

[Danielle, 38 years old, White, female faculty] I often didn't know how to respond beyond explaining how I am privileged (I am upper middle class, highly educated with highly educated parents who could support my college education, I am White, I am able-bodied and fit, I am CIS and married to a White man, and we have two able-bodied children). Everything about me exudes privilege and certainly helped pave my way, even though I certainly worked hard, too. I recognize that I did it with help and without discrimination or societally imposed obstacles along the way.

[Irene, 61 years old, White, female faculty] This was definitely a loaded module! I really benefited from the privilege videos, charts, etc. . . . I have always felt a sense of guilt for "white privilege," so I liked how the videos taught me to switch my focus away from my guilt, to greater awareness, and, importantly, using this as privilege as a way to help or be an ally to others with less privilege, depending on the context. What I also learned is that privilege is so contextual . . . where one might be privileged in one situation could be very different in another situation and that we need to bring greater awareness to how our privilege changes depending on the situation/context.

Physically listing out my identities and then reviewing the checklists really made me realize how much privilege I actually have. I really enjoyed the graphic that showed that you can be privileged in some aspects and not as much in others.

I also thought it was interesting to have Christian privilege and other subsections spelled out. I had never really thought about those other categories. In the news you usually hear the term "white privilege," and other types are not mentioned.

[Harry, 39 years old, White, male staff] Boy oh boy! This module made me do a lot thinking and rethinking and overthinking. I never viewed myself as "privileged," but then I started putting everything on the list, and my mind started up. On my list, I am the following: American-born, white, Christian, male, and middle class. [Despite] all of those things, I never considered myself privileged. My mind is going 100 miles a minute, and I hope that I can say what I am wanting to say and not be confusing. All the things listed, I never considered as privileged, I just thought that it is who I was born to be. I always look at some people and think, "Man, I wished that I had what they have," such as wealth, not realizing that there are people thinking the same about what I have. Is it jealousy, or is it just a dream? That is what I struggle with. My parents worked very hard and sacrificed a lot to get where we are today. I also believe the way that my parents raised us was never to take for granted what we have. This is such a learning experience for me, and I am determined to be more aware and to help more.

[Gerald, 26 years old, African American, male staff] I found this module really important, and I learned a great deal about myself and how to better listen (really listen) to others. I had to stop and think a few times over the past few days as I have gone through it. I think my learning grew the most when considering and understanding what is meant by privilege. I used the checklist to consider what it means [when] we talk about privilege, and even though I grew up poor (waiting in line to get expired free food kind of poor) and worked hard through college and grad school, I can now see my own privilege.

[Alice, 31 years old, White, female staff] After this module, I am much more aware of what "privilege" means and realize that, knowingly or unknowingly/intentional or unintentional, microaggressions exist and occur regularly. I definitely think I have more empathy for others after reading all of the checklists and taking the

Privilege Test. I have taken for granted many of the privileges I have, such as being able-bodied, but I will be much more aware of them and how I can stand up for others and help others just like the lady did at the grocery store when her sister was being unfairly discriminated against for the color of her skin.

[Becky, 40 years old, White/Jewish, female faculty] I challenged myself after the election to speak up more. I'm not a confrontational person and would rarely speak up when I heard someone say something inappropriate, believing it wouldn't make a difference, so why make myself uncomfortable. Having a choice to speak up or not is privileged in and of itself. I try to think of it as emotional credit in a bank account. In areas where I am privileged, I have more credit to spend, so the effects of spending are less on me.

[Gena, 55 years old, White, female staff] I get so embarrassed about inequality and bigotry, I think I sometimes try to sweep it all away, pretend it doesn't exist, at least not in the moment. I suppose that's another indicator of privilege.

[Jeffrey, 56 years old, African American, male staff] The privilege exercise was great. It made me look at myself in a different light. Though the activity said I was not privileged, and I knew that going into it, I was surprised by some of the questions asked. I have thought about how me being able-bodied or not being crucified because of my religion or being heterosexual is a privilege for me, I do not take it for granted and would stand up or with those who may be judged because of it.

Discussion Forum Feedback: Sample Text

Thank you for your honest and generous discussion about privilege. It sounds like most of you discovered some areas of privilege that you might not have been aware of. This new or heightened awareness is a critical part of your learning because this awareness and new knowledge can then be harnessed to lead to behavioral changes, such as those mentioned in the managing privilege section of the module.

Now that you have a greater understanding and awareness, here are some additional thoughts to deepen your thinking further:

Privilege Is Not an All-or-Nothing Game

As some of you mentioned, we all have and don't have some forms of privilege, so it's not as if one is either privileged or not.

For example, I have privilege based on my (perceived) race, socioeconomic status, family background, education, marital status, physical ability, gender identity, and body size. At the same time, my gender and ethnicity (Jewish) are not privileged identities in broader society.

Does this mean that my gender and ethnicity always were and always will be an obstacle for me? No, of course not. But sometimes these identities are targets of discrimination and violence, even though not directed at me personally (thus far). The point is that race, class, sexual orientation, gender, and physical and mental ability all work together in a system that sometimes works for us and sometimes against us.

Individual Experience vs. Systemic Evidence

Most of the time, I feel that being a woman is great, no problems. To my knowledge, I have never been excluded or discriminated against for being a woman. That said, I also know that in society overall, women are paid less than men, are harnessed with more housework and childcare, make up the majority of people who are targets of domestic violence and sexual assault, and are missing from many of the top ranks in business, education, and government. This tells me that no matter what my personal experience is as a woman, the evidence shows that, overall, women have less social, economic, and political power than men.

The same thing goes for race. There are many individual African Americans who have better jobs, make more money, and have more social, political, and economic power than do many individual White people. However, that does not undo the reality that, at the societal level, African Americans face a high degree of discrimination, exclusion, bias, racism, and state-sanctioned violence as evidenced in a myriad of statistics that could fill several pages.

The fact that some women, people of color, and other marginalized identity groups have achieved great things is proof of their resilience within a system that is not stacked in their favor, but it is not evidence that the system is fair and equitable for all people.

The Privilege of Not Having to Think About It.

Having privilege not only means that you do not face violence or discrimination based on a particular aspect of your identity, it also means that you have the choice to ignore injustices, indignities, and other unpleasant realities that other people have to endure. Men can choose to be concerned about sexual violence or not; White people can choose to be concerned about racial inequality or not; middle-class people can choose to be concerned about issues related to poverty or not. The privilege to "not think about things" frees up a lot of cognitive energy to pursue other things. Just think about our privilege lists and imagine all of the things that you don't have to be concerned about on a daily basis! I don't say this to make you feel guilty but rather to open your mind to the truth that we all have a choice either to do nothing or to be concerned, to learn, and to take action. But speaking of feeling guilty . . .

Guilt Can Be Productive or Unproductive.

As some of you may have experienced, learning about privileges you were unaware of can provoke feelings of guilt. Guilt can be a mixed bag. On one hand, guilt can be an effective motivator to action. Trust me on that—I probably would not be where I am today were it not for my mother constantly having laid guilt trips on me as a teenager. It was the only way to get me to do the things I needed to do. My self-imposed guilt in adulthood still serves as a motivator to do good things.

That said, guilt has also been known to be a hindrance to action. First, guilt can all but immobilize some people, who instead of taking action to alleviate it (by doing something about it), hang on to the feelings of guilt and let it stop them in their tracks. Second, guilt is an external motivator, meaning that we decide what we should or shouldn't do based on external opinions and judgments. Research has shown that external motivations to do (or not do) promote action to some degree, but this type of motivation tends to break down or weaken under duress (stress, limited time, cognitive overload).

In other words, guilt as a primary motivator to action will only get you so far. Therefore, we need more intrinsic motivation. Which brings me to my next point.

The Liabilities of White Privilege

While the idea of White privilege still rankles some folks who grew up White and poor, once they delve in and see that White privilege does not mean that you have not suffered or had to overcome hardships, it becomes a bit easier to digest. In doing this work, I tend to spend a lot of time focusing on how privilege means we "enjoy" unseen (by us) advantages. But there is another side to this.

A few years ago, at The White Privilege conference, I attended a session that really resonated with me because I realized that I was missing an important piece to my educational endeavors about privilege. Although the session focused on White privilege, I think the lesson is broadly applicable.

The session was called "Completely Unpacking the Invisible Knapsack: How White Privilege Hurts White People." The presenter described "unearned liabilities" as "The societal and cultural disadvantages that put white people in a state of blurred reality, separateness, and internal damage, which in turn affects all the rest of humanity."

I was intrigued by this description because, as I said, I spend a lot of time talking about and thinking about the unearned advantages. This approach to White privilege is like a mirror to someplace much deeper. Here are a few of the liabilities that stood out to me: you can see the full list here (https://myhumanity.live/2016/01/02/liabilities-of-white-privilege-how-white-privilege-hurts-white-people/).

- White privilege tells us we are entitled and deserving.
- White privilege allows us to deny peoples' lived reality.
- White privilege tricks us into thinking the playing field is level.
- White privilege restricts our ability to see and be comfortable with all of humanity.
- White privilege limits our ability to understand parts of our own identity.
- White privilege limits our awareness of how people really feel or what they think.
- White privilege deceives us into seeing beauty only in some places.
- White privilege limits our ability to have a true connection to many people of color.

Wow, right? Sit with this for a few minutes.

I think this is important because resistance to acknowledging privilege is rooted in fear of losing something, so people become invested in protecting themselves when, in fact, we (individually and collectively) have so much to gain by dismantling our own privilege.

Become a Privilege Awareness Advocate!

I think one of the best ways that we can use our privilege is to get better at talking to people who share similar privileges as you do (e.g., White privilege, Christian privilege, middle-class privilege, cisgender privilege, male privilege, etc.) about privilege. Here are a few strategies to add to your toolbox:

1. Your personal understanding is a great starting point. ("I've started learning about something that has a real impact on how I see things . . .")
2. Be able to articulate a clear definition and framework for explaining the very complex nature of privilege.
3. Metaphors are also useful. (Privilege is like being right-handed in a right-handed world; privilege is like air: you don't think about how much of it you have at your disposal until it's gone.)

Consider your spheres of influence (family, friends, students, coworkers) and how you might use these and other strategies to help increase privilege awareness and deflect privilege resistance.

By the end of this module, participants may be feeling a little tired and overwhelmed with the content and the emotions it may have raised, so it's important to acknowledge and validate their feelings, as well as remind them that this is the type of learning that needs to happen for both personal and organizational change and growth. It also important to encourage them to keep learning about this broad and critically important topic. In the module closing, be sure to let them know that the next module is all about things they can do to harness this newfound awareness and knowledge into action.

Module 6 Conclusion: Sample Text

Congratulations! You've made it to the end of this challenging set of modules. The things we say, the ways that we think, and the ways that we go about in the world can unintentionally create obstacles to inclusion. In the past three modules, you did the challenging work of recognizing how these obstacles to inclusion play out in your own communication, thoughts, and behaviors. We are all good people trying to do our best, so it can be painful to recognize that we may say and do things that run contrary to what we want to put out in the world.

While we may engage in these obstacles to inclusion (bias, microaggressions, and privilege) unintentionally, by raising our awareness and understanding, we can choose to intentionally avoid doing them or mitigate their impact. The good news is that there also are things that we can intentionally say, think, and do to promote inclusion. The next module introduces a framework for *inclusive excellence* to help you identify areas where you can put inclusion into action.

In the meantime, start exploring the additional resources provided in this module. Obviously, there is a lot to learn, and it can be overwhelming. My recommendation is to choose two articles or videos to chew on this week, then come back in a couple of weeks and choose two more. It can be helpful to choose one article that helps you understand a particular aspect of privilege or oppression, then choose another article that provides ideas or action steps that you can take.

Remember, our new knowledge and awareness are only beneficial to creating a more inclusive campus if we actually put them into action!

Module 6 References

Case, K. A., & Cole, E. (2013). Deconstructing privilege when students resist: The journey back into the community of engaged learners. In K. Case (Ed.), *Deconstructing privilege: Teaching and learning as allies in the classroom* (pp. 34–48). Rutledge.

Case, K. A., & Wise, T. (2013). Pedagogy for the privileged: Addressing inequality without shame or blame. In K. Case (Ed.), *Deconstructing privilege: Teaching and learning as allies in the classroom* (pp. 17–33). Rutledge.

McIntosh, P. (1989). *"White privilege: Unpacking the invisible knapsack"* and *"Some notes for facilitators."* National SEED Project. https://nationalseedproject.org/Key-SEED-Texts/white-privilege-unpacking-the-invisible-knapsack

Module 7

INCLUSIVE EXCELLENCE

A school that prepares students for academic and life success has a democratic, inclusive spirit. The spirit, or climate, of a school is greater than the sum of its parts.
—Maurice Elias, Psychology Professor

The previous modules focused on diversity at the interpersonal and individual levels. This module expands the focus out from the individual level to the organizational level. In higher education, this means the campus as a whole; in other contexts, the organizational level might refer to the entire company or agency. This module introduces an Inclusive Excellence Framework (Smith, 2020), which is being implemented on many campuses to guide institutional efforts at integrating diversity and inclusion into all aspects of operations and functioning.

In developing this Inclusive Excellence framework, Daryl Smith used a transdisciplinary approach to the topic of diversity, drawing on research and resources from a wealth of literatures and fields. She argues that to become more relevant to society, the nation, and the world while remaining true to their core mission, higher education institutions must begin to see diversity as central to teaching and research. Her research-based framework offers an innovative approach to developing and instituting effective and sustainable diversity strategies.

In order for such a framework to be implemented, organizational members must understand what it is and why it is important. To that end, the purpose of this module is to introduce the framework and have participants start exploring how it relates to their daily lives on campus. Having participants focus on their specific campus and department environments makes the topic come alive and feel relevant to their work, a key principle of adult learning (Knowles et al., 2015). In this chapter, we will provide one example of how we approached this topic in our campus context. This module is very campus specific, so unlike the content provided in the other modules of this book, you will need to develop your own materials and script. That said, the activity provided in this module is applicable to any campus context. The activity in this module is called a *Diversity Audit.* It provides an opportunity for participants to learn more about diversity and inclusion efforts on their respective campuses and asks them to take a closer look at their department or work unit through the lens of inclusion.

The script below offers one example of how to contextualize the importance of diversity and inclusion to higher education in general and on a specific campus. In your module lecture, providing information about your campus's climate survey if they have done one or other institutional research data or surveys about student success helps paint a picture of diversity on campus. Your module lecture should also include your university's diversity statement, as well as its mission and values statements.

Module 7 Overview: Sample Text

This module introduces an Inclusive Excellence framework (Smith, 2020), which is being implemented on many campuses to guide institutional efforts at integrating diversity and inclusion into all aspects of operations and functioning. In order for such a framework to be implemented, it is important that organizational members understand what it is and why it is important. To that end, the purpose of this module is to introduce the framework and allow you to explore how it relates to daily life on campus.

Essential Questions
- What does a diverse and inclusive campus environment have to do with institutional excellence?
- How does the work you do relate to inclusive excellence?
- What do diversity and inclusion currently look like on your campus and in your department?

Videos
"Diversity on Campus"

Tasks and Assignments
Diversity Audit Activity (3 parts)

Post and reply to Module 7 discussion by ——————— .

Diversity and Inclusion on Campus

As previously discussed, diversity is only half the equation; the other half is inclusion. How might we discern if our campus is inclusive or not? One can gauge the level of inclusion in terms of who has access to different institutional spaces or resources, who feels like they truly belong here, who thrives here, what kinds of knowledge are created here, and whether our campus is headed in the right direction to achieve its mission in a diverse society and globalized world. Only when a wealth of diverse people, experiences, knowledge, and perspectives are integrated into everything that we do can we truly serve society and achieve our institutional mission. As you can probably tell, there are a lot of pieces to this puzzle. Luckily, we have a framework for guiding our learning journey.

Inclusive Excellence

Education & scholarship

Access & success

Institutional Mission

Climate & intergroup relations

Institutional infrastructure

© 2021, DEI 2.0 and its affiliates. All rights reserved.

MODULE 7.1

Inclusive Excellence Framework

This nationally recognized Inclusive Excellence framework (Smith, 2020) illustrates the four key areas that work together to guide our university toward creating an institution of inclusive excellence. And as you can see, the heart of this model is our institutional mission, which can only be achieved if diversity and inclusion is embedded throughout the different aspects of our institutional functioning. Let's break these down one at a time. As we go through each one, I'll describe some associated activities and goals. Keep in mind which aspects of your work touch upon each of these areas.

Access & success

Inclusive excellence goal:

Achieve a more diverse & inclusive undergraduate, graduate, faculty, and staff

• Valuable networks
• Enriched decision-making
• Role models & Leadership

MODULE 7.2

© 2021, DEI 2.0 and its affiliates. All rights reserved.

Access and Success

One area of inclusive excellence has to do with making sure that people from different racial, ethnic, economic, and other backgrounds have access to the wonderful educational resources that our campus offers. "Access and Success" means looking at enrollment, academic performance, recruitment and retention, and hiring practices to make sure that there are no barriers to access for certain groups of people. We also have to make sure that our culture, policies, and practices facilitate the success of all members of our campus community. This means taking a hard look at the way we do things, the things we take for granted, and even some cherished traditions, some of which may create unintentional obstacles or barriers to people's ability to thrive on our campus.

But let me be clear here: this is not about doing people favors; this is not about giving special advantages to different groups; and it's not even entirely about doing the right thing. I'll list just a few of the ways that access and success of diverse faculty, staff, and students is directly tied to institutional excellence.

First of all, people from different backgrounds bring networks, connections, and associations with different communities. These networks are a valuable resource for advancement, recruiting, and our reputation in various communities.

Second, our decision-making processes are enriched and improved with the inclusion of people from diverse backgrounds who bring important insights and perspectives. When there are more voices and perspectives in any given decision-making process, not only is the process better informed, it also increases people's trust in that process and in the institution itself.

Third, when institutions foster the leadership of women and minorities, not only do others in those groups benefit from seeing someone who "looks like them" in important positions, it also benefits constituents from dominant groups.

We live in a society that implicitly and explicitly sends a constant stream of positive images of White people, particularly men, and an equally persistent stream of negative ideas, images, and messages about women and people of color. These positive and negative images create and reinforce particular ideas in our conscious and unconscious minds. Therefore, exposure to and relationships with people from diverse backgrounds in teaching and leadership positions helps all of us develop healthier and better-informed images of people who are different from ourselves.

Education and Scholarship

Beyond the few important contributions that I just mentioned, it is important to remember that diversity in faculty, staff, and students is integral to the main purpose of higher education: the discovery and dissemination of knowledge and scholarship. Diversity in terms of education, research, and scholarship needs to be understood in a few different interrelated ways.

Cultural competence refers to the ability to learn from, communicate with, serve, and collaborate with people with a great many different backgrounds. Cultural competence is indispensable to being effective as leaders and professionals in today's diverse workplace. Faculty and staff need to have cultural competence skills in order to help students develop those same skills themselves. And all of us can only develop these skills if we are living, learning, and working in community with people from different backgrounds.

Integrating various domestic and global perspectives and forms of knowledge into our curricular activities not only enhances our knowledge about the subject area under study but also expands our understanding of the world and ourselves.

And, finally, when people from diverse backgrounds are enabled to thrive alongside one another in higher education, it drives research and innovation. In this light, our survival and vitality as an institution of higher education depends on the integration of diverse ideas, perspectives, talents, and life experiences to help us create knowledge, develop innovations, and serve our society. In other words, the access and success of diverse faculty and staff is directly tied to our excellence in education and scholarship.

It's important to remember that every single one of us plays an important role in creating an environment in which faculty, staff, and students from all backgrounds feel that they belong, which brings me to the next area of inclusive excellence.

Campus climate & intergroup relations

Inclusive excellence goal:

Create and sustain an organizational environment that acknowledges and celebrates diversity and employs inclusive practices through its daily operations.

MODULE 7.4

Campus Climate and Intergroup Relations

One of the biggest factors in people's ability to succeed in any given working or learning environment is a sense of trust, safety, and belonging. If, so far in the presentation, you have not been able to identify where your work fits into the inclusive excellence framework, here it is: every single one of us contributes to our campus and departmental cultures and environments; all of us have relationships with people on campus; and all of us have the ability to help make people feel like they belong here.

The most talented person will be set up to fail in a place where they do not feel valued and respected. And, actually, they probably won't stick around long enough to fail. Smart people who do not feel valued simply take their talent elsewhere. We cannot afford to bleed diverse talent by tolerating working and learning environments is which faculty, staff, and students feel that they are not enabled to be their best. Therefore, it is contingent upon every person who draws a paycheck from the University to do their part to make sure that we create and foster learning and working environments where people want to be. By participating in this course, you are enhancing your capacity to do just that! So thank you! Okay, one final piece to this inclusive excellence framework.

Institutional Infrastructure

Our institutional infrastructure is what facilitates all of the other aspects of inclusive excellence. Having an institutional infrastructure that creates and sustains diversity and inclusion means that we have the structures, policies, and resources to ensure that we are continually evaluating, learning, and improving our strategic initiatives so that they might lead to meaningful change. This entails engaging multiple stakeholders in decision-making, advancement, and outreach efforts. It also means institutionalizing processes for reporting, analyzing disaggregated data, and ensuring accountability for continuous improvement.

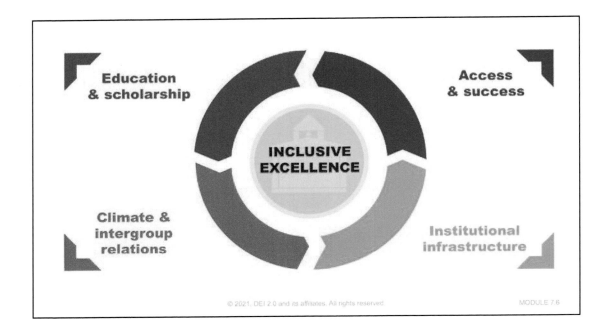

MODULE 7.6

Inclusive Excellence

No matter where your work lies in this Inclusive Excellence framework, your efforts touch upon all four of these interrelated areas. The next part of this module will help you develop a better sense of diversity and inclusion in your own department and campus so that we can start doing the work of moving toward inclusive excellence.

Module 7 Activity: Diversity Audit

The Diversity Audit activity is designed to help participants start noticing how diversity and inclusion is or is not reflected in their campus's physical and virtual environment (its webpage). Not all parts of this diversity audit activity may be appropriate for your institutional context. For example, if the presence of your institution is primarily online, then the questions focusing on the physical department space might not be applicable.

Activity Instructions: Sample Text

Diversity Audit

This part of the activity involves taking a close look at where you work on campus through the lens of diversity and inclusion. To do this, you are asked to look at the same people, places, building, and walls that you see every day with a new set of eyes and with some new questions on your mind.

For this activity, we are using a very broad sense of the word *diversity*. Think about the privilege mapping activity and all the areas of privilege that are denied to people from various identity groups.

This may be a difficult activity for many of you—and please don't let that worry you; it's okay. The point here is to sharpen your skills at noticing, wherever you find yourself, who is there, who is not there, and what your physical and/or virtual environment communicates to our various constituents and stakeholders who identify in many different ways.

Please reflect on the following questions. You will not be asked to share your responses, but you will be asked to share what you learned by exploring these questions. You should take notes as you do this three-part activity so that you can share some your findings with the rest of the group. These notes will also come in handy at the very end of this course when you do your action planning.

Diversity Audit Activity Part 1: Department/Unit Questions

1. As far as you know, what types of diversity do and don't exist among the people in your office, department, lab, or work unit?
2. In what ways does or doesn't the physical environment reflect inclusion? Who would likely feel most comfortable and welcome there? Who might feel less comfortable and welcome there?
3. Who is pictured, or most often pictured, in promotional or educational materials (electronic or paper)?

4. Are entrances, exits, water fountains, vending machines, classrooms, and bathrooms accessible for people with physical disabilities?

5. Do transgender people have access to bathrooms they can use without any concerns over harassment or safety?

6. Is there a designated place where babies can be nursed?

7. Does your department celebrate holidays? If so, which ones and how are they celebrated?

8. Are any non-Christian holidays celebrated or acknowledged? If so, how?

9. How often do you and your colleagues have discussions that center on diversity and inclusion (either formally or informally)?

10. How often do you hear comments or jokes that are potentially offensive to others, even if they were not intended to be?

11. How comfortable do you and your peers/colleagues feel voicing a different opinion or perspective than that of the majority in a meeting or class?

Diversity Audit Activity Part 2: Campus Website

For this part of the audit, you are asked to find resources on your campus's website that relate to the different areas of the Inclusive Excellence Framework. For example, for the first area, "Access and Success," you might try the keywords "access AND underrepresented" or "programs for minority students" or "student success."

For "Education and Scholarship," you might do some keyword searches (diversity, multicultural, cultural, social justice) in your campus course catalog, research areas of faculty, and/or professional programs for faculty, staff, and students.

For "Campus Climate and Intergroup Relations," you might try keyword searches related to specific identity groups (i.e., LGBTQ, international students, African American students) or programming designed to increase knowledge and awareness.

For "Institutional Infrastructure," you might search for "diversity AND policy" or "diversity AND scholarship" or "diversity AND funding" or instead of "diversity," use specific identity groups.

The purpose of this little sleuthing activity is twofold. First, it will give you a chance to discover some things on your campus of which you might not have been aware. And, second, it will help familiarize you with the Inclusive Excellence framework so that you'll be better able to think about your own work and goals in terms of how they influence the different areas.

Chances are that your search results will pull up things that can fit in more than one category. Again, you will not be asked to share your responses, but you will be asked to discuss what you learned in the discussion forum at the end of this three-part activity.

Diversity Audit Activity Part 3: Institutional Mission Statement

For the final part of this activity, you are asked to read your institution's mission statement. Often such statements include vision and values statements as well. As you read these guiding principles, think about how diversity and inclusion are integral to meeting your institution's mission, vision, and goals. You might also look at the strategic goals of your department. Write down keywords or phrases from the mission statement (as well as vision, values, and goals statements, if available) related to diversity and inclusion in general and the areas of inclusive excellence.

Module 7 Discussion Forum

A few examples of participants' responses are provided here. Responses to these prompts will vary widely from institution to institution, so these examples provide just one glimpse from a specific institutional context and may not be relevant to your particular context. Be sure to revise the activity and the discussion prompts to reflect your campus's culture and context.

Discussion Prompts

1. What did you learn from doing this audit activity?
2. Did anything surprise you? If so, what?
3. Did any ideas for areas of improvement occur to you?

Examples of Participant Discussion Forum Posts

[Lisa, 46 years old, White, female faculty member] I learned that there were so many different aspects to diversity and inclusion. It was interesting to see what appeared on the campus website when I typed the word *diversity*. Besides the Office of Diversity and Inclusion, I saw there were other departments/units on campus that focused on cultural diversity, leadership diversity, diversity links, cultural diversity course requirements, and human origin/cultural diversity. The questionnaire on diversity and inclusion department/unit audit showed that the campus should always be reviewing the diversity in physical accessibility, public restroom accommodations, cultural/religious holidays, and reflection of inclusion on campus, and true diversity/inclusion in promotional or educational materials.

[Tiffany, 26 years old, Biracial, female staff member] I think about inclusion, but the Inclusive Excellence Framework was a learning experience in seeing how it can be broken down further into different categories. Also, when working on the audit, I can see how things may be easier as an employee (e.g., the majority of employees in my unit have private offices, so having privacy as a nursing mother is fairly simple; a student may struggle to find privacy outside of a restroom (personal note: gross!) with the exception of a few designated nursing spaces on campus). The audit was hard. It is tough to imagine anyone feeling uncomfortable as they work here. But digging deeper into thoughts of transgender restroom use, holiday celebrations, and the limited time spent on discussing diversity and inclusion helps me to realize how much work we still need to do to ensure this is an inclusive environment.

Discussion Forum Feedback: Sample Text

There were several objectives to this module, the first of which was to provide some fuel for a new conversation about diversity on our campuses. As we discussed in Module 1, the word *diversity* carries a lot of different meanings. Sometimes these various meanings can bog us down when it comes to moving forward with diversity efforts.

While compliance efforts (Title IX, affirmative action, reporting, etc.) are important parts of the institutional infrastructure, they are not enough to create healthy and vibrant organizations in which everyone can thrive.

The Inclusive Excellence framework is not only a tool for how we must think about our work, it is also a way to change the conversation so that we can move forward. Not everyone will take this course, so it is incumbent upon you to bring this conversation to your colleagues as you work together to define your goals, create your processes, and define what excellence looks like in your particular areas.

The first part of the audit activity provided some thought-provoking questions for developing an inclusive lens. Inclusion, like so many worthy pursuits, starts with questions and then moves to actions. In this part of the audit, you focused on your immediate area of influence.

The second part of the audit was meant to be an opportunity to learn more about diversity and inclusion efforts outside of your immediate area. Some folks have jobs that naturally lead them to find out what is happening on different parts of campus, but there are also a lot of people who function in organizational silos—departments or offices with relatively little interdepartmental communication and cooperation. This so-called silo effect is counterproductive to organizational goals because it is only through collective and collaborative action across all areas of organizational functioning that we can achieve inclusive excellence.

And, finally, the last part of the audit asked you to think about how diversity and inclusion are implicitly or explicitly tied to the overall mission, vision, and values of our campus. In this light, inclusion is not an add-on but an integral part of our organizational goals.

It was fantastic to hear that some of you gleaned some additional insights into ways to look at inclusivity more broadly in your local context. And some of you shared some of your current practices that provided some additional food for thought to your peer learners. This was a great opportunity to learn from each other. Thank you!

The inclusive excellence framework and the diversity audit tend to motivate participants to take action. It is helpful to collect a list of campus and community resources to encourage them to take action steps.

Module 7 Conclusion: Sample Text

After completing this module, you have gained a deeper understanding about why diversity and inclusion are integral to the mission and values of the university. Using the Inclusive Excellence framework, you have done a deep dive into what diversity and inclusion currently look like on campus and in your department. As a next step, consider engaging in one or more of the following practices to apply your learning from this module:

Start filling in the knowledge gaps. It is likely that during the diversity audit activities you encountered a topic or two about which you were not very knowledgeable. Choose one and start learning more about it!

Familiarize yourself with campus resources. Take the time to visit your campus's website to get information about student resources on campus. The more familiar you are with these resources and services, the more you can help others access them.

Before you move on to the next, please make sure that you have replied to at least two of your colleagues' posts in the discussion board and read/replied to people who have posted to yours.

Module 7 References

Knowles, M. S., Holton, E., & Swanson, R. A. (2015). *The adult learner: The definitive classic in adult education and human resource development.* Butterworth-Heinemann.

Smith, D. G. (2020). *Diversity's promise for higher education: Making it work.* JHU Press.

Module 8

INCLUSION IN ACTION

As a whole, this course is intended to increase participants' sense of self-efficacy in terms of diversity and inclusion, because people are more likely to take action or change behaviors when they feel confident in their ability and are motivated to do so (Bandura, 1994; Combs & Luthans, 2007). The content in this module provides a framework and resources for building a culture of inclusion: *inclusive attitudes*, *inclusive practices*, and *inclusive language*. The culmination of this module and the course is a personal action plan for inclusion. Action plans are an important part of professional development programs intended to promote transformative learning and organizational change (Cranton & King, 2003), because the course is only beneficial to the campus or workplace if people apply what they learned.

Module 8 Overview: Sample Text

In previous modules, we learned about how unconscious bias, microaggressions, and privilege create obstacles to inclusion in our organizations. We gained an awareness of things we need to avoid doing and some strategies for mitigating those obstacles. In this module, we'll explore concepts for intentionally and actively building a culture of inclusion. We'll explore three concepts for building a culture of inclusion: inclusive attitudes, inclusive practices, and inclusive language. And then you will be asked to create a personal action plan for inclusion, because this course is only beneficial if you apply what you've learned!

Essential Questions

- What kinds of attitudes are conducive to being more inclusive?
- How can we be more inclusive in our everyday actions at work, at home, and in our community?
- Why is language so important to an inclusive campus?

Activities

The activity in this module involves creating your 90-day action plan. You are provided with several ideas and asked to choose at least three that you can realistically commit to and accomplish within the next 90 days.

Videos

The video in this module, "Building a Culture of Inclusion," explains the concept of inclusion and how to put it into action in our daily lives.

Discussions

Please post your initial responses to the discussion prompts by _____ .
A synchronous dialogue will take place on _____ .

Readings, Handouts, and Additional Resources

There are several handouts for the action planning activity.

Inclusion means that ALL members of the university community can say:

I feel valued and respected by my peers and superiors. Standards, norms, policies, and practices allow for my full engagement in working and/or learning activities and do not create obstacles to my ability to learn, do my job, or advance in the organization.

DIVERSITY → ← INCLUSION

MODULE 8.1

Inclusion Means . . .

An inclusive organization is one in which all members feel valued and respected. Inclusive organizations ensure that structures such as standards, policies, processes, and practices allow for full participation and do not create obstacles to any organizational member's ability to do their job or advance in the organization.

Inclusion Involves Both Structures & Culture

Inclusion also entails intentionally fostering a culture of belonging through daily practices, norms, expectations, and values. In other words, inclusion involves both a culture and the supporting structures to create an environment in which everyone feels like they belong and everyone can thrive.

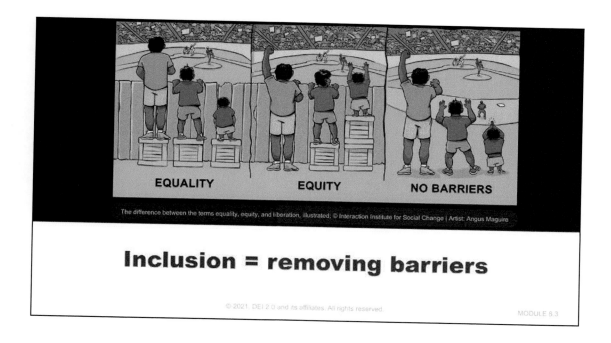

EQUALITY   EQUITY   NO BARRIERS

The difference between the terms equality, equity, and liberation, illustrated: © Interaction Institute for Social Change | Artist: Angus Maguire

Inclusion = removing barriers

© 2021, DEI 2.0 and its affiliates. All rights reserved.

MODULE 8.3

Inclusion Goes Beyond Equality and Equity

Here's another way to think about inclusion. Equality is about treating everyone the same way. Unfortunately, equal treatment doesn't always lead to equal outcomes. Equity takes into account that people are not the same and individuals may need differing levels of support to be successful in the existing structures.

Inclusion entails removing the barriers and obstacles to full participation, so everybody gets what they need, and everybody can succeed.

In this video, we'll discuss three building blocks for inclusion that all organizational members can practice every day to help foster a culture of inclusion.

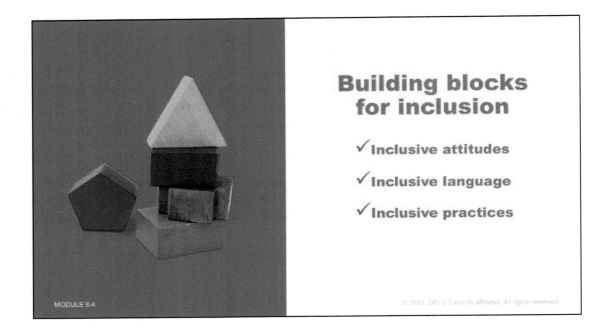

Building Blocks for Inclusion

Building a culture of inclusion involves our attitudes, our daily practices, and our language. As we go through this presentation, think about particular things that you might do to grow in each area. In the additional resources section, you are provided with some ideas and resources that will help you develop an action plan for putting these ideas to work.

Inclusive Attitudes

An openness to learning is critical for any organization's mission and success. Openness to learning means not just learning about the area in which you work and the tasks needed for your job but also learning about the people around you.

Diversity is all around us: in the people we work with, provide services to, and share a community with. There are all those differences and aspects of identity that we can readily see, plus all the ones we can't see.

The only way we can make sure that everyone feels valued and respected is if we are open and curious enough to learn about people, the ways that they identify, and the issues and concerns that they have.

An openness to learning also requires a sense of humility and an understanding that everyone is an expert in their own lives, so we all have something to learn from each other. This means seeing beyond organizational role and rank and seeing each other as full humans with unique and equally valid experiences, perspectives, and dreams. And in this way can we open ourselves up to the richness of the human condition of those with whom we share a community.

Attitudes That Do Not Promote Inclusion

To put a finer point on the importance of inclusive attitudes, it's helpful to think about the opposite. Attitudes such as defensiveness, self-righteousness, judgment, fear, and indifference toward people who are different from ourselves creates barriers to learning, to building relationships, and to our ability to thrive as individuals and organizations.

We all experience these attitudes occasionally, so it is important that we recognize when they show up and actively choose another approach to a person or a situation.

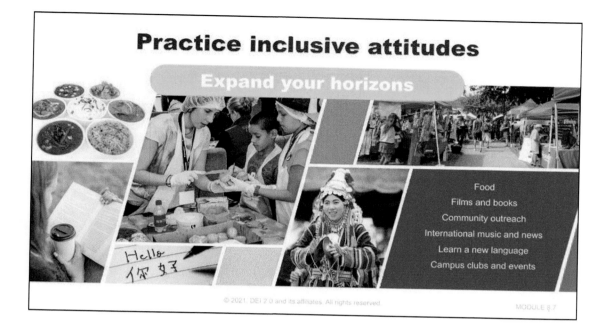

Practice Inclusive Attitudes

Putting inclusive attitudes into action means making a consistent and intentional effort to expose yourself to new people and cultures. Yes, it does take effort to deviate from our normal habits, but this really *is* the fun stuff. Learning about people through films and books is both entertaining and informative. So maybe you can't travel to Afghanistan, but you can gain a deeper understanding of the culture and politics of the people of a nation whose lives are truly intertwined with our own.

And what about all the cultural diversity in your own town? There are markets, neighborhoods, restaurants, and community groups ready for exploration. Are you a religious person? Try going to services at another religious institution, and learn how your practices and beliefs are similar and different.

Food is another great way to expand your horizons. Try a new ethnic restaurant with your friends or family. Whether you like the new tastes or not, it's a fun cultural excursion.

Learning a new language, even a few words or phrases, provides amazing insights into another culture and helps create bridges across difference when you meet someone who speaks that language.

These are just some of the fun things that you can do to build your knowledge and put inclusive attitudes into practice in your daily life. The more you integrate inclusive attitudes into your life, the more fun you have, the more informed you become, and the more you have to contribute to a culture of inclusion.

Inclusion Takes Work

Building a culture of inclusion takes work. It means rethinking and reevaluating the way we do things in all of our common practices to make sure that everything works for everyone. It means considering perspectives and ideas that have previously been invisible or excluded. It means creating spaces for and encouraging respectful disagreement.

Inclusive practices start with questions

✓ Whose voices are not being heard, whose perspectives not being considered?

✓ How might this policy/standard/norm have a negative impact on some groups of people?

✓ What accommodations have we not considered?

✓ What can I learn about my colleagues, students, or clients to ensure they feel included/valued/respected?

✓ What things do I take for granted that may not be so easy for other people I work with or care for?

© 2021, DEI 2.0 and its affiliates. All rights reserved.

MODULE 8.9

Inclusive Practices Start with Questions

Inclusive practices start with asking tough questions. Given our limited resources and time, it often feels necessary to plunge forward. But think about what you might be missing. The next time you are in a meeting, take a look around the table and take notice of who is there and who is not.

Think about how the missing perspectives might add to the discussion.

Or the next time you are planning an event or a meeting, take an extra step to make sure it doesn't fall on any important religious holidays and that the room is accessible to people who use a wheelchair.

Or maybe gather some colleagues, along with some people outside your department, and take an inventory of some of your norms and informal policies. Think about what you learned through the Diversity Audit activity. What ways can you make your department or office look and feel more inclusive? Challenge yourself to learn and ask questions so that you can identify things that might differentially impact individuals from nondominant groups.

Looking through a lens of inclusion

MODULE 8.10

Looking Through a Lens of Inclusion

Another way to think about inclusive practices is like a lens that you use to see things in a new way, to try to catch things that you may have been missing, and to create a fuller picture in your work area. In the resources section, you are provided with a tip sheet of a few small steps for inclusion that can go a long way. Please consider adding a few to your action plan! But first, let's talk about one more building block for inclusion.

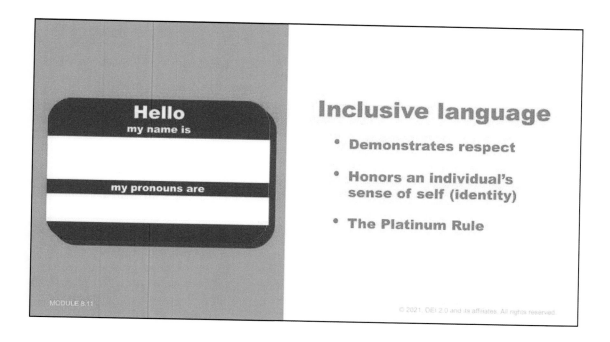

Inclusive Language

Words have the power to hurt us as well as to make us feel empowered and give us a sense of belonging. Since we strive for a culture of inclusion, it is important that we are conscious of the language that we use in talking about or describing people in terms of their race, ethnicity, socioeconomic status, gender, gender identity, sexual orientation, disability, and so on.

Simply put, inclusive language means using terminology that is preferred by the people about whom you are talking. As straightforward as that sounds, I have found that this topic can provoke some negative reactions.

Some people get very nervous because they are afraid of saying the wrong thing and feel frustrated that they have good intentions but might not know all the preferred words.

Some folks just get mad because words and phrases that they grew up saying to refer to other groups of people are no longer acceptable, and they think this is just about being politically correct.

While I can certainly understand these negative reactions, I think that those who experience them might be missing the point.

Inclusive language isn't about being politically correct, it is simply a good way to demonstrate respect to other human beings. It shows that their identity and experience is valued. Another way to think about this is in terms of the Platinum Rule. You probably know the Golden Rule, that we should treat others as WE would like to be treated.

The Platinum Rule takes it up a notch by contending that we should treat others how THEY would like to be treated, such as using language and labels that they prefer. If we want to show others respect, make them feel valued, and uphold their dignity, we will want to use inclusive language.

Inclusive language

Key concepts

- Understanding why is more important than knowing what.

- Inclusive language comes from within communities as opposed to labels imposed from outside these communities.

- Language is fluid and contextual. Terminology is always evolving.

- Personal, not prescriptive: One size does not fit all.

- Be willing to learn. It's okay to make mistakes. It's okay not to know. It's okay to ask questions.

- The learning process is ongoing.

MODULE 8.12

Inclusive Language: Key Concepts

Now let's go over a few key concepts to help you be more inclusive with your language. First of all, understanding *why* is as important as understanding *what*. In other words, just memorizing a list of words isn't being inclusive. It's about understanding the assumptions and connotations that come with the words that helps us be sensitive to others' feelings.

Inclusive language comes from within the communities described by that language as opposed to labels put on communities from the outside. In other words, inclusive language is about the empowerment of groups and individuals to define themselves in society.

However, you have to remember that what was commonly acceptable yesterday may not be so today—and may change again tomorrow. Also, not everyone who identifies within a particular group is going to have the same preferred label. In other words, there is not always one right answer. We have to learn what labels individuals prefer. To do that, we have to be willing to learn, to make mistakes, admit we don't know, do some homework, and ask respectful questions. And, because language changes, we have to be willing to keep learning, keep changing, and keep trying. There is an Inclusive Language Resource Sheet in the resource section of this module to get you started!

Building Blocks for Inclusion

Putting these building blocks for inclusion into action every day benefits everyone in the organization. Inclusive attitudes can enhance our relationships, collaborations, and creative endeavors. Inclusive practices can help us transform the policies and practices of our institutional infrastructure. And inclusive language helps us demonstrate our willingness to learn and uphold the dignity of our colleagues.

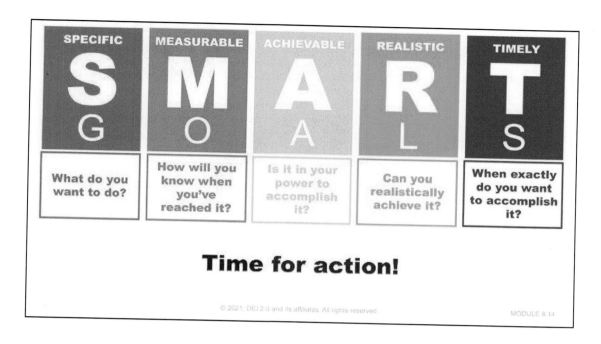

Time for Action!

At this point, you may be feeling a little overwhelmed by all the different things to learn and do. It is important that you don't let this feeling get in the way of action. Creating an action plan using S.M.A.R.T. goals will help you integrate these building blocks into your already busy schedules.

To this end, you are asked to create an action plan with three goals based on what you have learned in this module or in this course. The resource section provides you with some resources and ideas.

I'm asking you to commit to three goals as a starting point. This is lifelong learning and effort, but it gets much easier and more natural as we move forward.

Please remember that each step you take not only benefits you and those with whom you come in direct contact but directly contributes to the overall health of our organizations and society.

The Foundation for Inclusive Excellence

Now think about everything that we've covered in this module and how it relates to our goal of inclusive excellence. For example, consider how inclusive language relates to the success of students, faculty, and staff: When people feel respected and valued, they can bring their best to working and learning. Inclusive attitudes can enhance our education and scholarship. Looking at things through an inclusive lens can help us transform the policies and practices of our institutional infrastructure. And, of course, all of this helps ensure that we build and maintain a healthy climate and relationships with others in our learning communities. As you think about your action plan, remember that not only does each step benefit you or those with whom you come in direct contact but your actions directly contribute to the overall inclusive excellence of our universities. Thank you for doing this work!

Module 8 Activity: Action Planning

This module provides learners with an opportunity to think about and commit to next steps in their learning journey. It is important to provide participants with ideas and resources for planning concrete, achievable action steps.

Activity Instructions: Sample Text

Action Planning

Now it's time to think about your next steps, things that you can do right in your own sphere of influence. It is easy to get overwhelmed, which can lead to inaction. What you are asked to do in the final part of the course is commit to three or four things that you can reasonably achieve within the next 90 days. If you feel inspired to aim for more, please do so, but do try to be realistic with what you can do. Also, keep in mind that everything we've covered over the past few weeks gets easier the more we do it. It still requires work and effort, but we get better at it. One of your action items might be to review the course materials again and take a deeper dive into some of the additional resources provided.

The resource sheets posted in the module provide you with some ideas about how to use inclusive language, engage in inclusive practices, and expand your cultural awareness, but you are encouraged to think beyond these lists. On this week's discussion board, you'll be asked to share your action plans with your peer learners. Not only does this promote accountability, but you might give and/or get some new ideas.

Module 8 Discussion Forum

This discussion asks participants to share their ongoing commitment to diversity and inclusion work beyond the course duration. Sharing their action plans helps solidify that commitment and a sense of accountability. Below are a few examples of participant reactions to creating an action plan as well as some specific steps they plan to take.

Discussion Prompt

How was this activity for you? Please share your three (or more) action steps that you have committed to doing within the next 90 days. Explain why you chose these steps and the impact you hope they will have. Remember that we need to be able to hold ourselves and others accountable, so perhaps you might wish to team up with someone who is doing a similar action step such as forming a book club, going to lunch at an ethnic restaurant you haven't tried, or even doing a community project together. The potential impact of this learning community is magnified by multitudes if you continue this learning journey together.

Examples of Participant Discussion Forum Posts

[Kelly, 35 years old, White, female faculty member] I love the idea of creating action plans around this sort of work. I think it can be easy to say we want to change or be better, but creating an action plan makes it something in which we actually participate.

[Amanda, 25 years old, White, female staff member] I am a big fan of making action plans to actually make change happen, so I love that we were asked to do that for this module. I was a part of an informal discussion group focusing on diversity on campus for a short period of time, and my constant question was, what is one thing you can do over the next month to make a difference? So this was a good exercise for me.

[Greg, 57 years old, White, male faculty member] I chose these steps because they demonstrate my openness to learning and curiosity about others, which will hopefully lead to making others feel more valued and included by me.

1. Read a book about a different person, culture, country, and/or experience. This is actually something I do already because I love reading and I love reading about people from different cultures/countries. It's a good way to use something that I already do to help promote inclusiveness.
2. Talk with people from different backgrounds, cultures, etc. Because I work in the ESOL department, I am surrounded by people who are different from me, and it's important for me to get to know them so that I can make them feel valued and respected. This may be a little difficult for me because I'm not very outgoing, and I will have to push myself to speak with others that I don't know well.
3. Address accessibility issues when planning events. Part of my job is planning social activities for our students. This is an important step to take to make sure all of our students are able to participate in activities.

[Bruce, 42 years old, White, male faculty member] I plan to do the following:
1. Read an additional book written by someone with different background than myself about a major social issue in our country.

2. Be mindful in my interactions with others and really focus on being a good listener and modelling inclusive language in my conversations.

3. Reflect (in writing) on similarities and differences in my working style from others in my department and how that might affect my interactions with them.

I chose these steps because they are both attainable and measurable, and I will be able to hold myself accountable for their completion.

Discussion Forum Feedback: Sample Text

I enjoyed reading your action plans and am happy to see that you have some solid next steps ahead of you. I want to conclude this module with a few additional thoughts about inclusion.

Thinking More about Inclusion

At the most basic level, diversity is about differences. As we've discussed throughout this course, there are all kinds of differences among people. There are things you can see, such as race, gender, and physical ability—plus, a host of other things that you cannot see, such as learning style, sexual orientation, mental health, religious beliefs, and personal values. All of these things form parts of who we are, how we see the world, and how the world sees us. Given this understanding, it's safe to say that diversity is just a natural part of our organizational lives. But diversity is only half the equation to inclusive excellence. The other half is inclusion.

The truth is that building an inclusive workplace and campus takes time and effort. It's not often convenient or easy. And, unfortunately, we can't just check a box and be done. Being inclusive is an ongoing work in progress. It requires a willingness to take a look at the way things have always been done, things that have seemed perfectly fine for a long time, and to start asking some important questions about why we might wish to change them.

And, just as in everything else we try to do or learn, we have to be willing to make mistakes and to admit we don't know. People in dominant identity groups have to be particularly mindful when they have the good intention to be inclusive of marginalized identity groups. Sometimes, people decide to do things in the name of inclusion without having taken the time to find out what the people they are trying to include actually want or need. Or, worse, they may use information based on broad generalizations or stereotypes to inform their attempt at inclusion, rather than accurate information. This type of good intention can easily have the opposite impact.

So, just remember, it's not always easy, but it is always worth it in the end to try.

Take Heart, Take Action

If you reflect on the content we've covered in these past weeks, I think we have gotten a lot of ideas about how one might put the values considered into action. Speaking of action, I know that much of the content we have covered may have been overwhelming, but I urge you not to let that feeling immobilize you.

One way to avoid immobility is to make a reasonable action plan, which is why I included the activity in this module. We all have a lot to do, and it can be demotivating if we take on more than we can actually achieve. And while I do think that there is a sense of urgency to changing our campus culture, we also have to remember that every little bit helps. As the old saying goes, the ocean is made up of little drops of rain.

That said, you can amplify your inclusion efforts by joining forces with other people from this course, around campus, and in your department.

This is the last content module of the course. Participants are often cognitively tired or overloaded by this point. It is helpful to acknowledge and affirm these feelings, while also encouraging them to keep up the momentum.

Module 8 Conclusion: Sample Text

Congratulations! You have made it to the end of the final content module of the course! It has been a long and challenging journey for many of you. You learned many important concepts along the way, and now you have a toolkit full of inclusive practices to take with you moving forward. But don't go away yet! Our final module provides an opportunity to reflect on this journey we've taken together.

Module 8 References

Bandura, A. (1994). *Self-efficacy*. Wiley Online Library.

Combs, G. M., & Luthans, F. (2007). Diversity training: Analysis of the impact of self-efficacy. *Human Resource Development Quarterly, 18*(1), 91–120.

Cranton, P., & King, K. P. (2003). Transformative learning as a professional development goal. *New Directions for Adult and Continuing Education, 2003*(98), 31–38.

Module 9

LOOKING BACK AND MOVING FORWARD

The last module of the course provides no new content. The final discussion serves as the wrap-up to the course and gives participants an opportunity to reflect on their learning and experiences throughout. In this module, you will also want to include a course evaluation to garner feedback from participants about the course. You might also consider using the post-test survey instrument provided in the online resources.

Module 9 Overview: Sample Text

There is no new content presented in this module. Its purpose is to give you a chance to reflect on and share your thoughts about the course.

Essential Questions

- What will you take away from this learning experience?
- What did you learn about yourself by taking this course?
- What is your hope for moving forward?
- What are you grateful for in terms of our learning community: the input, feedback, sharing, and dialogue with your peers?

Tasks and Assignments

In this module, you will need to complete the following tasks:

Post and reply to the closing module discussion forum by _____ .

Complete the course evaluation by _____ .

Module 9 Discussion Forum

Although you have followed participants' progress throughout the course, the closing module discussion is always heartening to read because here is where you get a chance to see how the participants feel about what they learned and what they appreciated about their learning community. We often find ourselves inspired by the final comments of course participants, which is partly what makes this challenging work so fulfilling—as well as helps bolster our commitment to continuing this journey. In what follows, we provide a few examples of the inspirational responses that we have garnered from students, faculty, and staff through teaching Diversity 101.

Discussion Prompt

In thinking about the time we've spent together over the past several weeks, please feel free to say some parting (for now) words to your peer learners about what you will take way from your time together, what your hopes are for moving forward, and anything else you'd like to say as we close out this learning journey.

Examples of Participant Discussion Forum Posts

[John, 33 years old, White, male staff member] This course has helped provide a new perspective on my actions and views of others. I've appreciated reading the perspectives of others in the course and the openness that they have expressed. The specific strategies for inclusion have been beneficial. However, the items that impacted me the most were reading through the various lists of privileges that exist from those who have particular backgrounds. I hope that I can see my interactions and the interactions that others have through this new lens so that I can better support an inclusive environment.

[Jackie, 27 years old, Asian American, female staff member] This course has shown me a new perspective on diversity. I've learned more about myself and the privileges that I have and do not have. I have my goals I'll work on as I continue to learn about diversity. This was all valuable information. My hopes moving forward are to teach other coworkers, friends, and family what I've learned about diversity and hope I make a difference. It was nice meeting everyone and getting to know you.

[Leslie, 28 years old, White, female faculty member] I have really enjoyed this course and it has been very insightful. My biggest takeaway from this course was how it made me be more aware of diversity issues happening around me. I constantly found myself being reminded of this course throughout the day. It helped me shape my reaction to things and be more mindful about how my actions could be perceived by others. But it also helped me look at other people's reactions with a more open mind. Especially when their opinion or reaction differs from mine . . . instead of just wanting to shut them down or shut them out, I try to see the issue through their eyes. Chances are, they have had some sort of life experiences that helped shape their opinion.

[Freddie, 38 years old, White, male faculty member] I have learned a lot about many things. As I have said before, I have loved the opportunity to engage in honest conversations about difficult subjects with colleagues. I have enjoyed applying the lessons of this course to my family life, my work life, and my social life, and have been exploring new ways to write e-mails, to ask questions, to make suggestions in all aspects of my life. I have become, or rather I have tried to become, more mindful of my TONE and am making a concerted effort to adjust how I interact with family, friends, and coworkers with a view to being someone who actively improves the climate (as best I can). I have been adjusting my syllabi to reflect what I have learned about tone in the past couple of months; and I will do my utmost to chat with students and colleagues about different ways of thinking about diversity, about microaggressions and "invisible bias," and about strategies for responding to disparities in perception and experience when it comes to inclusion.

[Candy, 53 years old, White, female faculty member] I have thoroughly enjoyed learning alongside all of you as we dove deep into diversity, inclusion, privilege, microaggressions, our own institutions, and our own lives. I had a lot of self-reflection and tried to be open and vulnerable as I self-reflected on my own understandings, behaviors, reactions, and actions. I learned so much from each of you as well. I felt everyone was open and reflective as well as responsive. I appreciated that everyone respected each other's vulnerabilities. I hope we can all embark from this course with more tools and resources to continue learning and be activists for change.

[Tiffany, 42 years old, White, female staff member] This course is one that I would definitely recommend to colleagues. I was able to expand my understanding of others and myself through the lectures, videos, discussions, and introspection. The discussion guidelines that were established at the beginning of the course are transferrable to my work at the university and in my personal life. Respecting differences, assuming good intentions, being patient, and being generous can also work in our interactions with others. I know that I will utilize much of what was taught in this course when working with my students. I want to show that I am committed to creating an environment that is inclusive of everyone and that I will put action behind my words. I also plan to write a statement in my student group's expectations so that they know to do the same. It has been great getting to "meet" everyone and learn about different perspectives, struggles, and successes. Best of luck . . . and keep fighting the good fight!

[Sofia, 44 years old, Latina, female faculty member] I so appreciate being able to write openly and honestly about these issues. I want to thank each and every one of you for sharing. I learned volumes while devouring your posts. I will continue on in this endeavor to do my absolute best to make a difference in those I work with daily and those around me, both in my circle and those outside of that circle. I wish I could express in writing how much this class has meant and how I hope it is a required course for all who work on campuses.

Discussion Forum Feedback: Sample Text

Dear All,

Let me say once again what an honor and a pleasure it has been to spend these past few weeks with you. Your honesty, openness, and willingness to share your time, your stories, and your insights are an inspiration to me. It gives me hope that we can indeed come together and build a better campus culture and community for everyone.

I thank you all for taking the time out of your busy schedules to think about and explore these issues. Hopefully, these discussions have given you some renewed energy and ideas for putting these concepts into practice, whether it be in your workplace, your community group, your neighborhood, or your home.

PART 4

Conclusion

CONCLUSION

FINAL WORDS OF WISDOM FROM THE AUTHORS

To close our book, we wanted to provide some personal reflections on doing this work over the past few years, along with some thoughts about where to go next.

A Few Words from Dr. Goldstein Hode

I speak for both of us when I say that this book has been a labor of love. Our main driver was our shared goal of enhancing the capacity of our colleagues in higher education to do this critical work on their respective campuses. We freely admit that it is not easy to guide people through transformative learning processes intended to shake up, challenge, and expand their frames of reference for understanding themselves and others within socially structured relationships of power. That said, based on our research (Goldstein Hode et al., 2017; Hutchins & Goldstein Hode, 2021) and the great feedback from students, faculty, and staff over the years, we feel confident that we've tapped into an effective way to present content and facilitate the type of discussions and reflections that lead to transformative learning. We hope that sharing our work with you in this book will inspire and encourage you to develop your own course, taking as much or as little from this book as you feel appropriate for your context.

Although the Diversity 101 curriculum is *foundational* (meaning that it consists of basic concepts that are necessary building blocks for advancing this work) and *classic* (meaning that the concepts are general enough that it will not likely go out of circulation any time soon), it is also necessary to respond to changing contexts. For example, as explained in the preface of this book, the Diversity 101 curriculum and online course was first developed in 2012. At that time, the importance of diversity and inclusion was acknowledged in the corporate world and higher education. However, the imperative to grapple with making the cultural and structural changes long needed in predominantly White educational institutions was not widely felt or acknowledged.

Then, in 2015, our campus erupted in student protests sparked by the killing of Michael Brown in Ferguson, Missouri, just two hours east of campus. These protests not only shook our campus out of its complacency, they also lit a fire in student activism on campuses across the country. These students demanded change and accountability. They demanded that faculty and staff learn to understand and improve students' experiences on campus. They demanded a reckoning with structural racism and inequality. And thus, the demand for Diversity 101 quadrupled as faculty and staff scrambled to find some direction, some steps to take, something to do!

To meet this increased demand, I enlisted the help of previous Diversity 101 participants, who also had teaching or training experience, to facilitate small discussion groups. This allowed me to manage very large cohorts of 80–100 people by dividing them into smaller discussion groups of 15–20 with a facilitator who monitored and provided feedback to their discussions. This model of having a lead facilitator who sends weekly announcements framing and summarizing the modules and cofacilitators who engage with the discussions turned out to be an effective way to manage the large demand. Given where we are now in our current social context, I can only assume that demand will continue to grow, so this model may soon be the norm. This was just one example of changes that must be made to the course design, structure, or content to respond to changes on campus or in the broader social context.

We are now in the middle of both a global pandemic and ongoing protests against police violence and structural racism. I believe that both of these converging forces will greatly impact the curriculum of this course moving forward. There is a loud and clear call for White people to learn about and grapple with racism (and antiblack racism in particular), Whiteness, and antiracism. Some might argue that the curriculum offered in this book is not enough, and I would agree. Still, I also would argue that a foundational curriculum like the one we offer in this book is a necessary first step in the journey for everyone, not just White people. Remember, People of Color are not immune to being influenced by unconscious bias, making microaggressions, and embodying forms of privilege, so we all have our work to do. Diversity 101 provides an opportunity for everyone to engage in this work together, no matter their identity or personal experience.

While we must be careful not to minimize the urgent need to face the crisis of racial inequality in all its forms, we also must not forget about or overshadow other oppressed identity groups' experiences. As facilitators, we should strive to take an approach that both centralizes race and maintains a focus on other forms of oppression. It's tricky business, particularly with so many strong emotions at play. Acknowledging and normalizing these challenges will help your participants manage their reactions and engage in online discussions more effectively.

Moving forward with the foundational knowledge of Diversity 101 in place, there are many directions for continued professional development. Here I offer a few ideas for future course development:

- A course delving into the complexities of understanding how race, identity, privilege, economics, and history are all intertwined to perpetuate systems of racial inequality.
- A course focusing on intersectionality and applying an intersectional framework to analyze one's own experiences and social issues. This course would explore how race, gender, gender identity, sexual orientation, and social class converge to forge structural oppression and privilege in people's lived experiences.
- A course that helps participants develop a racial equity lens that can be applied to the analysis of policies, social problems, workplace and classroom practices, and norms.
- A skills development course focusing on facilitating and engaging in difficult dialogues.

All this is to say that there is so much more that needs to be done and that Diversity 101 is only a starting place. That said, it's a really good starting place, and I hope that our efforts make your efforts both less daunting and more effective. To this end, we have made all of our course materials (for both professional development and the for-credit course) available for download on our website. Now, I'll turn it over to my friend, cofacilitator, and coauthor to share his parting words of wisdom.

A Few Words from Dr. Hutchins

The opportunity to coauthor this book has been an exciting and deeply reflective process. I began my journey in diversity work in 2015 while pursuing my master's degree in Communication Studies at Marquette University. At the time, I was interested in whether the language of diversity and inclusion adopted by higher education institutions was actually living and breathing within the organizational culture. I had spent most of my academic and professional career in predominantly White spaces, where I felt that my organizational experiences were unequal, due primarily to my Black racial identity. Several of my students of color shared similar sentiments, which sparked my interest in diversity and inclusion work. I have since worked as a graduate assistant in the Division of Inclusion, Diversity, and Equity at the University of Missouri System, served as the instructor of record for a senior-level undergraduate diversity course there, published research on diversity, and served on diversity and inclusion committees and campus initiatives—all while being a graduate student. All this to say, my passion for inclusivity and valuing differences lies at the center of my work as a teacher, scholar, and practitioner, and I am deeply committed to this call.

I had no idea, when I first began diversity work nearly six years ago, of the emotional work and risk of asking learners to recall and reflect on their biases, privileges, and experiences of microaggressions. Especially in predominantly White institutions where I have taught, feelings of guilt, discomfort, and defensiveness were obstacles to transformative learning as they seemed to limit participants' desired change (Pope & Mueller, 2017). Grappling with guilt or shame is part of the transformative learning process (Mezirow, 1991); therefore, I hope that the rich content and the lessons shared in this book leave you feeling confident in your ability to help learners to process these feelings as motivators for change, just as we have had to and continue to do.

Importantly, the emotional work is not limited to the course participants' experiences but can be burdensome for you as the instructor or facilitator. Participants' stories will require that you closely monitor the virtual discussions for heated incidents, so you may at times find yourself, as I did, struggling to figure out how best to respond to a participant's lived experiences—especially those with which you do not identify. If you are like me, you may even find yourself frustrated at the injustices experienced by participants, and it will be vital that you practice self-care (whatever that looks like for you) and to suggest supportive resources to all participants in the learning community.

This book provides a foundation for implementing diversity education within higher education institutions, and I hope that you will take away from it an understanding that knowledge of different cultural groups does not automatically lead to transformative learning or the development of cultural competence (Cuyjet & Duncan, 2013). Specifically, the development of cultural competence requires that participants take actions outside of the course, such as thinking more carefully about the impact of their comments before speaking, incorporating inclusive practices into their everyday work, and advocating for others who do not share the same privileges. For this reason, all diversity and inclusion education should allow participants sufficient time and space to reflect on their fears, cultural experiences, and insights with their family, friends, and peers (Cooper et al., 2011), as well as an opportunity to revisit the conversation having had adequate time to process their learning. Our own research has shown that this off-line communication with family, friends, and coworkers is a key factor to transformative learning (Hutchins & Goldstein Hode, 2019). As an instructor or facilitator of diversity learning, you will also need to take the time to reflect, as you will always find yourself in the seat of the learner as well as instructor.

After having spent years engaging students in this critical and productive dialogue and having had the chance to reflect on my learning and experience in coauthoring this book, I hope to find ways to more directly address the oppressive systemic conditions that sparked my initial interest in diversity and inclusion work. I argue that while "diversity work" is indeed timely and essential, its ambiguous focus on all human differences can overlook institutional challenges that are specific to certain identity groups, such as my Black community, who have a unique, oppressive history in the United States. As a scholar and practitioner, I am now narrowing my work in diversity to explore the organizational experiences of marginalized and stigmatized identity groups. I hope that, wherever your diversity and inclusion journey takes you, you find fulfillment and joy in being a part of the fight for equality that we all hope to achieve someday.

CONCLUSION REFERENCES

Cooper, D. L., Howard-Hamilton, M. F., & Cuyjet, M. J. (2011). Achieving cultural competence as a practitioner, student, or faculty member: Theory to practice. In M. J. Cuyjet, M. F. Howard-Hamilton, & D. L. Cooper (Eds.), *Multiculturalism on campus: Theory, models, and practices for understanding diversity and creating inclusion* (pp. 401–420). Stylus.

Cuyjet, M. J., & Duncan, A. D. (2013). The impact of cultural competence on the moral development of student affairs professionals. *Journal of College and Character, 14*(4), 301–310. doi:10.1515/jcc-2013-0039

Goldstein Hode, M., Behm-Morawitz, E., & Hays, A. (2017). Testing the effectiveness of an online diversity course for faculty and staff. *Journal of Diversity in Higher Education, 11*(3). https://doi.org/10.1037/dhe0000063

Hutchins, D., & Goldstein Hode, M. (2021). Exploring faculty and staff development of cultural competence through communicative learning in an online diversity course. *Journal of Diversity in Higher Education, 14*(4), 468–479. https://doi.org/10.1037/dhe0000162

Mezirow, J. (1991). *Transformative dimensions of adult learning.* Jossey-Bass.

Pope, R. L., & Mueller, J. A. (2017). Multicultural competence and change on campus. In J. H. Schuh, S. R. Jones, and V. Torres (Eds.), *Student services: A handbook for the profession* (6th ed., pp. 392–407). Jossey-Bass.

DEI 2.0
DIVERSITY 101

PARTICIPANT WORKBOOK

COURSE NAME:

INSTRUCTOR:

WEBSITE: https://www.dei360consulting.com

PASSWORD: deitoolkit

Contents

GROWING A LEARNING COMMUNITY

Community is about a sense of belonging. It involves a conscious commitment to uphold and contribute to the needs and interests of the group. In the context of this course, it is assumed that we have a shared interest in our own personal growth and learning, as well as a commitment to making our communities more inclusive, equitable, and enjoyable for all. By participating in this course, you are a member of a learning community committed to supporting each other's learning through active participation and thoughtful engagement.

Learning communities are like gardens. We must first prepare the soil before we start planting seeds of knowledge. That's what this module is about!

Essential Questions

In this module, we'll explore the following essential questions designed to build the foundation for this course:

- What is a learning community?
- What does it mean to be part of a learning community whose purpose it is to explore difficult issues in order to create more welcoming and inclusive campuses and society?
- Who are the members of our Diversity 101 learning community?
- What are our responsibilities to each other to ensure this is a safe, supportive place for conversation and differences of perspective?

The following is a basic set of Community Norms and Guidelines for online learning communities, particularly regarding sensitive or challenging topics. These are offered as a starting point. If you want to change or add guidelines, please share that in our discussion. Guidelines such as these can be used in various contexts, so you may want to consider them further:

Community Norms and Guidelines

Participating in this course means being part of a learning community. The only way that this learning process will be effective is if you take responsibility for both your own learning and that of the group. Here are a few norms and guidelines for you to consider and discuss with your peers in the course. Consider how these might help make this a productive and worthwhile experience for everyone.

Respect deadlines. In order to simulate a full group discussion on the discussion boards, it is imperative that you post no later than the weekly deadlines as listed in each module.

Demonstrate respect for differences. We all come to the table with differing experiences and viewpoints, which means that we have so much to learn from each other! In order to get the most out of this opportunity, it is important that we don't shy away from differences. Rather, we should show respect for differences by seeking to understand, asking questions, clarifying our understanding, and/or respectfully explaining our own perspective. This allows everybody to come away with a new way of seeing the issue.

Respect confidentiality. Some of the topics/issues we discuss may be sensitive and/or personal. While it is totally okay to talk about the things you are learning with your colleagues, please do not share what other participants post without their explicit permission.

Assume good intentions. If someone says something that bothers you for any reason, assume that they did not mean to be offensive. Instead you might ask them to clarify what they meant, then explain the impact it had on you. If someone tells you that something you wrote bothered them, assume that they are not attacking you but rather that they are sharing something that might be important for you to know.

Be generous. Your weekly posts are not simply requirements for participation; they are your contributions to group learning. Please be generous to your peers by being thoughtful, open, and honest.

Be inclusive. It's important to be intentional about making sure we "see" each other in an online community by making sure that everyone has at least two responses and replying to people who ask us questions. If you are unsure who to respond to, try looking for posts that have not yet received a reply.

Be substantive. Your peers will get more out of a reply that goes beyond "I agree" or "I like your post." Explain why their post resonates with you. Conversely, try NOT to avoid responding to posts with which you disagree or that you do not understand. Ask questions, seek clarification, explain your differing view. This is how we all learn.

Be organized. Although this is a voluntary course, your timely participation is required to make it work. Past participants have suggested making reminders in your calendar to help keep up with posting deadlines. I highly recommend this strategy. However, I will send a "friendly reminder" as the deadline approaches. I will send another if you miss a deadline. If you get such messages from me, I hope you will forgive my "nagging" and remember that I'm just trying to keep us all moving along together so that we all get the most out of it. And if you need an extension, just let me know.

Be patient. Be patient with yourselves . . . expect some discomfort in this learning process. Be patient with each other . . . understand that we all come to this from different starting points and perspectives. Try to meet people where they are.

Module 1: Reflection Questions

What? What was the purpose of the module?	

What ideas, information, or concept stood out to you?	
So what? What does the content in this module have to do with your everyday life?	
Now what? What changes or action steps can you take to apply what you learned in this module to your everyday life?	

Module 1 References

Cox, M. D. (2004). Introduction to faculty learning communities. *New Directions for Teaching and Learning, 2004*(97), 5–23.

Hord, S. M. (2009). Professional learning communities. *Journal of Staff Development, 30*(1), 40–43.

Sherer, P. D., Shea, T. P., & Kristensen, E. (2003). Online communities of practice: A catalyst for faculty development. *Innovative Higher Education, 27*(3), 183–194.

Module 2

INTRODUCTION TO DIVERSITY

We all should know that diversity makes for a rich tapestry, and we must understand that all the threads of the tapestry are equal in value no matter what their color.
—Maya Angelou

Most people come to a diversity training or course with preconceived notions about what diversity means and why it matters. The purpose of this module is to deepen your perspectives about the concept of diversity and increase your understanding and ability to articulate why diversity, equity, and inclusion (DEI) are important concepts for individuals, groups, organizations, and society.

Essential Questions

- What is diversity?
- Why is diversity important to where we work and live?
- What does diversity have to do with me?

Part 1: What is Diversity?

This part of the module explores four dominant approaches to diversity in the workplace and higher education: *Diversity as demographics* (recruiting, hiring, and promoting previously excluded groups), *diversity as cultural differences* (managing diversity), *diversity as good for business* (harnessing diversity for educational or business goals), and *diversity as social justice* (addressing discrimination, harassment, and exclusion). The purpose of explaining approaches to diversity rather than definitions of diversity is to provide a more complex understanding of how diversity relates to workplace practices so that we can be more precise with our usage of the term and its implied meanings.

To understand the value of diversity, we need to know how a culture that is welcoming and inclusive of individual and group differences can impact our lives at various levels. After watching the video, brainstorm the potential positive impact of diversity and inclusion at each of the levels discussed. You can refer to the ones mentioned in the video, but it is more helpful to develop additional ideas.

What is Diversity? Activity Takeaway

Talking about diversity...

Demographics

Managing differences

Business case

Equity & inclusion

STOP RACISM

© 2021, DEI 2.0 and its affiliates. All rights reserved   MODULE 2A.3

The module activity asked you to ask a set of colleagues, friends, peers, and/or family members what diversity means. You then shared the experience of asking people to define diversity with your peers on the discussion board, and you read about their experiences. What is your takeaway from that activity?

Part 2: Why Should I Care about Diversity

To understand the value of diversity, we need to know how a culture that is welcoming and inclusive of individual and group differences can impact our lives at various levels. This part of the module is intended to build your capacity to articulate why diver- sity and inclusion are important, not just for some people but for everyone. This video presents a multilevel model of the importance and impact of diversity that provides a framework for understanding the interrelated relationship between individuals, groups, organizations, institutions, society, and the global context. After watching the video, brainstorm the potential positive impact of diversity and inclusion at each of the levels discussed. You can refer to the ones mentioned in the video, but it is more helpful to develop additional ideas.

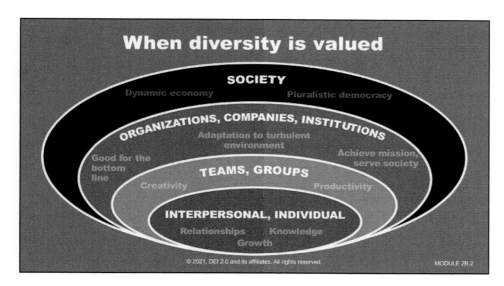

Module 2: Reflection Questions

How do individuals benefit when diversity and inclusion are valued in an organization?	

What are some of the benefits to the work of groups and teams when diversity and inclusion are valued?	
In what ways does the overall organization benefit when diversity and inclusion are valued?	
How does society benefit when its organizations and institutions value diversity and inclusion?	

Module 2 References

Alba, R. (2018). What majority-minority society? A critical analysis of the census bureau's projections of America's demographic future. *Socius: Sociological Research for a Dynamic World, 4*, 1–10.

Astin, A. W. (1993). Diversity and multiculturalism on the campus: How are students affected? *Change: The Magazine of Higher Learning, 25*(2), 44–49.

Centers for Disease Control and Prevention. (2020). *Disability impacts all of us.* National Center on Birth Defects and Developmental Disabilities. https://www.cdc.gov/ncbddd/disabilityandhealth/infographic-disability-impacts-all.html

Freeman, R. B., & Huang, W. (2015). Collaborating with people like me: Ethnic coauthorship within the United States. *Journal of Labor Economics, 33*(1), 289–318.

Gill, F., & Shaeye, A. (2021). Relative wages of immigrant men and the Great Recession. *Journal of Economics, Race, and Policy, 5*(1), 1–12.

Gurin, P., Dey, E. L., Hurtado, S., & Gurin, G. (2002). Diversity and higher education: Theory and impact on educational outcomes. *Harvard Educational Review, 72*(3), 330–367.

Henderson, L., & Herring, C. (2013). Does critical diversity pay in higher education? Race, gender, and departmental rankings in research universities. *Politics, Groups, and Identities, 1*(3), 299–310.

Hunt, V., Layton, D., & Prince, S. (2015, January 1). Why diversity matters. *McKinsey & Company.*

Jones, J. (2021, February 24). LGBT Identification Rises to 5.6% in Latest U.S. Estimate. *Gallup.* https://news.gallup.com/poll/329708/lgbt-identification-rises-latest-estimate.aspx

Knight, R. (2014). Managing people from 5 generations. *Harvard Business Review, 25*(9), 1–7.

Litvin, D. R. (1997). The discourse of diversity: From biology to management. *Organization, 4*(2), 187.

Milem, J. F. (2003). The educational benefits of diversity: Evidence from multiple sectors. In M. J. Chang, D. Witt, J. Jones, & K. Hakuta (Eds.), *Compelling Interest: Examining the Evidence on Racial Dynamics in Colleges and Universities* (pp. 126–169). Stanford Education.

Prasad, A. (2001). Understanding workplace empowerment as inclusion: A historical investigation of the discourse of difference in the United States. *The Journal of Applied Behavioral Science, 37*(1), 51–69.

Schmidt, S. (2021, February 24). 1 in 6 Gen Z adults are LGBT. And this number could continue to grow. *Washington Post,* 1–5.

Soares, R., Cobb, B., Lebow, E., Regis, A., & Wojnas, V. (2011, December 13). *2011 Catalyst Census: Fortune 500 women board directors (report).* Catalyst. Retrieved October 17, 2021, https://www.catalyst.org/research/2011-catalyst-census-fortune-500-women-board-directors/

Tadmor, C. T., Satterstrom, P., Jang, S., & Polzer, J. T. (2012). Beyond individual creativity: The superadditive benefits of multicultural experience for collective creativity in culturally diverse teams. *Journal of Cross-Cultural Psychology, 43*(3), 384–392.

U.S. Bureau of Labor Statistics. (2020, May 29). *TED: The Economics Daily.* Retrieved October 7, 2021, https://www.bls.gov/opub/ted/2020/foreign-born-workers-made-up-17-point-4-percent-of-labor-force-in-2019.htm

DIVERSITY AT THE INTERPERSONAL LEVEL

Strength lies in differences, not in similarities.
—Stephen Covey

The module builds self-awareness, complicates the notions of diversity and identity, and starts the conversation about the way we approach people who are different from ourselves. The module video, *Diversity and Identities*, includes an identity mapping activity designed to increase your level of self-awareness and awareness of others, a critical starting point for any conversation on diversity or cross-cultural competence.

Essential Questions

- What is identity?
- Why do our identities matter in the workplace?
- How do other people's ideas about our identities impact the way we see ourselves and lead our lives?
- How can our lack of knowledge about other people impact the way we perceive their identities?
- How can we try to see someone as they see themselves?

Identity Mapping Activity

My identity map

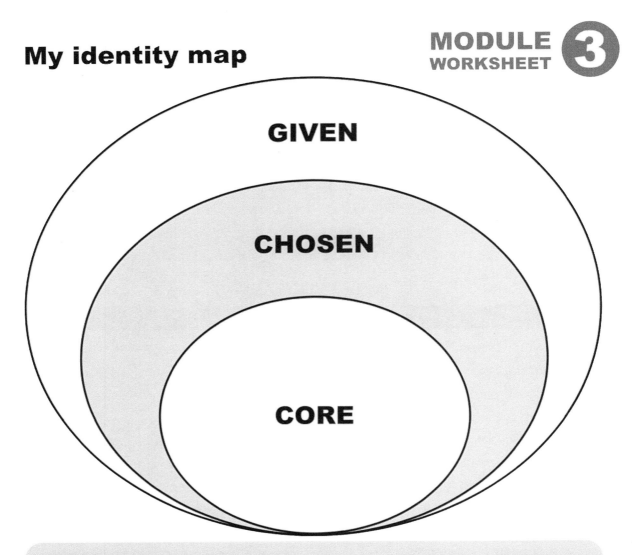

When we talk about our identities we're really answering the question "Who am I?" This is a complex question that deserves a complex answer. Our identities are made up of core, chosen and given aspects about ourselves. Core aspects are specific traits and characteristics that describe our unique selves. There are also chosen aspects of our identities such as groups and activities that we've chosen to be a part of. Given identities are the groups or characteristics that we are born into. Here are some examples to help you map your multiple levels of identities.

CORE: Personality traits (introvert/extrovert, spontaneous, organized), learning style, values, etc.

CHOSEN: profession, job, religious organization, political affiliation, volunteer groups, local community, activity groups, sports team, hobbies, family role (i.e., choosing to have children or to get married), education, etc.

GIVEN: race, ethnicity, nationality, religion, gender, gender identity, sexual orientation, disability, health, age/generation, physical characteristics (tall, short, thin, hefty), family role (i.e., your role as youngest, middle, oldest, or only child), socio-economic status, etc.

Module 3: Reflection Questions

What? What was the purpose of this module? What ideas, information, or concepts stood out to you?	
So what? What does the content in this module have to do with your everday life?	
Now what? What changes or actions can you take to apply what you learned in this module to your everday life?	

Example action items.	**Get to know people beyond visible identities.** Try out a few of these conversation starter questions with a colleague over coffee or with your students during office hours as a warm-up: https://coversationstarterworld.com/questions-to-get-to-know-someone /. **Write a diversity statement.** A diversity statement is a personal essay that depicts your past experiences and explains how they have contributed to your personal and professional growth. It is often asked for on job or educational program applications. Do an internet search for the term "personal diversity statements" to find examples and helpful resources.

Module 3 References

Allen, B. J. (2011). *Difference matters: Communicating social identity.* Waveland Press.

Ashforth, B. E., & Mael, F. (1989). Social identity theory and the organization. *Academy of Management Review, 14*(1), 20–39.

Eisenberg, E. M. (2001). Building a mystery: Toward a new theory of communication and identity. *Journal of Communication, 51*(3), 534–552.

Tajfel, H. (1978). Social categorization, social identity and social comparison. In H. Tajfel (Ed.), *Differentiation between social groups: Studies in the social psychology of intergroup relations* (pp. 61–76). Academic Press.

Module 4

INTRODUCTION TO UNCONSCIOUS BIAS

All of us have implicit biases to some degree. This does not necessarily mean we will act in an inappropriate or discriminatory manner, only that our first "blink" sends us certain information.

Acknowledging and understanding this implicit response and its value and role is critical to informed decision-making and is particularly critical to those whose decisions must embody fairness and justice.

—Malcolm Gladwell, *Blink*

Unconscious (or implicit) bias is a hot topic in diversity, equity, and inclusion education as well as a thriving area of research in such fields as healthcare, education, media representation, employment, and law enforcement. The concept of unconscious bias really began to enter the public discourse in the wake of a consistent stream of police shootings of African American boys and men. The concept of unconscious bias has been used to explain how White police officers could so frequently make fatal errors when assessing the threat in encounters with Black people. Unfortunately, in some of these discussions, the concept of *unconscious bias* was used as if it were synonymous with *racism*. For example, after one of the 2016 presidential debates in which Hillary Clinton stated that "I think implicit bias is a problem for everyone, not just police," a *Washington Times* headline trumpeted, "Hillary Clinton Calls the Entire Nation Racist" (Riddell, 2016). This headline represents a common and unfortunate misperception about what unconscious bias is and what it means.

To counter the idea that unconscious bias is an insult or character flaw, this module draws upon neuroscience research to explain that unconscious bias actually is a product of our natural brain function. The module video is largely based on the book *Thinking, Fast and Slow* by Daniel Kahneman, a Nobel Prize-winning behavioral economist. The content is also informed by social science research into the effects of unconscious biases to help us understand the systemic impact of individual instances of unconscious bias.

Essential Questions

- What is unconscious bias, and why does it matter?
- How do unconscious biases (positive or negative) play out in your daily life?
- How does unconscious bias affect you, others, and society as a whole?
- What can we do about unconscious biases?

For this activity, your task is to associate each one of the people pictured with one of the jobs on the worksheet. There are an equal number of people and jobs, so it's a one-to-one match-up. You don't have much to go on, so you'll have to rely on ideas, images, experiences, and even stereotypes stored in your brain. Please don't overthink it; just go with your gut impulse. When you are done, please reflect on these questions and post your reaction to the activity to the discussion forum.

- What information did you use to match people to certain jobs?
- Who was it easy for you to match with a particular job? Why?
- Who was it harder for you to match to a job? Why?
- Who did you put into the "professional" class jobs?
- Who did you put in the lower-wage jobs?
- What cognitive shortcuts did this reveal?

Who does what?

Associate each person with one of the jobs listed.

Marta   Bob   Amara   Kelly

Jennifer   Amber   Larry   Dan

Damion   Sasha   Steve   David

Who looks like the **chemist?**	Who looks like the **web designer?**	Who looks like the **flight attendant?**	Who looks like the **CEO?**
Who looks like the **soldier?**	Who looks like the **stockbrocker?**	Who looks like the **community activist?**	Who looks like the **hair stylist?**
Who looks like the **math teacher?**	Who looks like the **doctor?**	Who looks like the **minister?**	Who looks like the **hotel desk clerk?**

Module 4: Reflection Questions

What? What ideas, information, or concepts stood out to you?	
So what? What does the information about unconscious bias have to do with everyday life?	
Now what? What changes or actions can you take to mitigate unconscious bias?	

Example action items.	**Learn more about your biases.** Take a few of the Harvard Implicit Association Tests to discover implicit biases that may be impacting your decisions and actions: http://implicit.harvard.edu/implicit/takeatest.html **Do a bias self-audit.** Look through your social media contacts and connections. Who are the people you know, follow, read about? If most of the people are similar to you, try expanding your circles!

Module 4 References

Argyris, C. (1992). Overcoming organizational defenses. *The Journal for Quality and Participation, 15*(2), 26.

Banaji, M. R., & Greenwald, A. G. (2016). *Blindspot: Hidden biases of good people.* Bantam.

Blair, I. V., Ma, J. E., & Lenton, A. P. (2001). Imagining stereotypes away: The moderation of implicit stereotypes through mental imagery. *Journal of Personality and Social Psychology, 81*(5), 828–841.

Gowin, J. (2012). The neuroscience of racial bias. *Psychology Today.* https://www.psychologytoday.com/blog/you-illuminated/201208/the-neuro science-racial-bias

Kahneman, D. (2011). *Thinking, fast and slow.* Farrar, Straus, and Giroux.

Moreland, R. L., & Zajonc, R. B. (1982). Exposure effects in person perception: Familiarity, similarity, and attraction. *Journal of Experimental Social Psychology, 18*(5), 395–415.

Nickerson, R. S. (1998). Confirmation bias: A ubiquitous phenomenon in many guises. *Review of General Psychology, 2*(2), 175–220.

Nisbett, R. E., & Wilson, T. D. (1977). The halo effect: Evidence for unconscious alteration of judgments. *Journal of Personality and Social Psychology, 35*(4), 250.

Oyler, D. L., Price-Blackshear, M. A., Pratscher, S. D., & Bettencourt, B. A. (2021). Mindfulness and intergroup bias: A systematic review. *Group Processes & Intergroup Relations*, 1368430220978694. https://doi.org/10.1177/1368430220978694.

Riddell, K. (2016, September 26). Hillary Clinton calls U.S. racist in debate. *Washington Times.* https://www.washingtontimes.com/news/2016/sep/26/hillary-clinton-calls-us-racist-debate/

Rudman, L. A., Ashmore, R. D., & Gary, M. L. (2001). "Unlearning" automatic biases: The malleability of implicit prejudice and stereotypes. *Journal of Personality and Social Psychology, 81*(5), 856.

Staats, C. (2013). State of the science implicit bias review (p. 104). *The Kirwan Institute for the Study of Race and Ethnicity.* http://kirwaninstitute.osu.edu/?my-product=state-of-the-science-implicit-bias-review

Module 5

INTRODUCTION TO MICROAGGRESSIONS

On campuses and in workplaces, there are several types of communication and behavior that are damaging to individuals and organizations. In this module, we're going to explore the concept of microaggressions. Microaggressions come in the form of things like subtle slights, backhanded compliments, well-intentioned comments, and unintentional insults that are actually based on harmful stereotypes and unconscious biases related to race, sex, gender, sexual orientation, age, nationality, weight, disabilities, and so on. Microaggressions are harmful to individuals and organizations. Therefore, this module will raise your awareness about microaggressions and provide you with some strategies for addressing them.

Essential Questions

- What are microaggressions, and why do they matter?
- Do intentions matter?
- Why are microaggressions an obstacle to inclusion?
- What can we do about microaggressions?

Videos

The module video, "The Little Things We Say," a conceptual framework for understanding what microaggressions are, why they can have such a damaging impact, and what we can do about them.

Recognizing Microaggressions

Here are some typical examples of microaggressions. These statements can be hurtful because they communicate an underlying assumption, low expectations, or a stereotypical idea about someone. Why do you think these might hurt/insult/offend the person being addressed? Try to identify the negative and unspoken aspects of the following statements.

Microaggression	The underlying assumption, low expectations, or stereotypical idea
"Your English is really good, Yuan. Not like other Chinese employees I've had."	
"Really? You have a master's degree?" (said to administrative assistant)	
"You'll definitely get that grant. . . . They are always trying to support minorities."	
"I'm fine with gay people, but do they have to be so public about it?"	
"You can translate this into Spanish for me, can't you, Roberto?"	
BONUS: Now that you better understand microaggressions, think of at least one example of a microaggression you unintentionally said. Then, identify the underlying assumptions and messages your words imparted.	

Responding to Microaggression

To help build a culture of inclusion, we all need to be advocates in trying to put a stop to microaggressions. To do so, we must not only work on confronting and educating others, but we have to make sure we are aware of our values, biases, and assumptions. Because microaggressions are often unconscious and unintentional, it may be helpful to develop some expertise on microaggression theory and research, so you might help people understand the broader nature of the problem.

If you are a witness, rather than a target, of a microaggression, you are in an excellent position to call out the microaggression and explain to the person who committed it that intent does not equal impact. In some situations, you may not want or be able to call out the person who committed the microaggression because of power dynamics or safety concerns or because the offending person has left. However, you can still show support to the targeted person by validating their experience, letting them know that you witnessed it and that you do not think that what was said is okay.

The Do-Over

Think of one specific time when you experienced (aimed at you) or witnessed (aimed at someone else) a microaggression but did not respond to it at all, or at least not as well as you now wish you would have.

1. Below, tell the story of what happened, how you responded, or why you failed to do so, and the result. Include how you may feel about it now.

2. Then, take what you learned from this module and use it to craft a more effective response. When choosing your example, remember that not everything hurtful or offensive is a microaggression. Microaggressions are based on race/ethnicity/national origin, gender/gender identity/sexual orientation, disability, body size, and religion.

3. Write out the new do-over response as if you were talking back in the moment to the person who said the microaggression. Feel free to make up fictitious names.

A microaggression that I witnessed or experienced:	The Do-Over

Module 5: Reflection Questions

What? What ideas, information, or concepts about microaggressions stood out to you?	
So what? What does the content in this module have to do with everyday life?	
Now what? What changes or actions can you take to apply what you learned in this module to everyday life?	

Example action items.	**Prepare to respond to microaggressions.** Although it can be challenging to speak up effectively in the moment, it will be easier if you do your homework ahead of time by familiarizing yourself with common microaggressions and thinking about strategies for speaking up that might work for you. In addition to the resources provided in this module, this resource from Teaching Tolerance provides several examples and strategies for you to consider: https://www.tolerance.org/magazine/publications/ speak-up/six-steps-to-speak-up. **Start implementing the power of micro-affirmations.** Learn more about this evidence-based practice for counteracting the cumulative negative impact of microaggressions. https://www.gse.harvard.edu/news/uk/16/12/ accentuate-positive https://everfi.com/insights/blog/micro-affirmations- microaggressions-and-unconscious-bias/.

Module 5 References

Chait, J. (2015, January 27). Not a very P.C. thing to say: How the language police are perverting liberalism. *New York Magazine*. http://nymag.com/daily/intelli gencer/2015/01/not-a-very-pc-thing-to-say.html

Clark, R., Anderson, N. B., Clark, V. R., & Williams, D. R. (1999). Racism as a stressor for African Americans: A biopsychosocial model. *American Psychologist*, *54*(10), 805.

Dovidio, J. F. (2001). On the nature of contemporary prejudice: The third wave. *Journal of Social Issues*, *57*(4), 829–849.

Goldberg, M. (2015, March 16). The Laura Kipnis melodrama. *The Nation*. https:// www.thenation.com/article/laura-kipnis-melodrama/

Jay, M. (2009). Race-ing through the school day: African American educators' experiences with race and racism in schools. *International Journal of Qualitative Studies in Education, 22*(6), 671–685.

Lukianoff, G., & Haidt, J. (2015, September). The coddling of the American mind. *The Atlantic.* https://www.theatlantic.com/magazine/archive/2015/09/the-coddling-of-the-american-mind/399356/

Purdie-Vaughns, V., Steele, C. M., Davies, P. G., Ditlmann, R., & Crosby, J. R. (2008). Social identity contingencies: How diversity cues signal threat or safety for African Americans in mainstream institutions. *Journal of Personality and Social Psychology, 94*(4), 615.

Salvatore, J., & Shelton, J. N. (2007). Cognitive costs of exposure to racial prejudice. *Psychological Science, 18*(9), 810–815.

Solórzano, D., Ceja, M., & Yosso, T. (2000). Critical race theory, racial microaggressions, and campus racial climate: The experiences of African American college students. *The Journal of Negro Education, 69*(1/2), 60–73.

Sue, D. W. (2010). *Microaggressions and marginality: Manifestation, dynamics, and impact.* Wiley.

Sue, D. W., Capodilupo, C. M., & Holder, A. (2008). Racial microaggressions in the life experience of Black Americans. *Professional Psychology: Research and Practice, 39*(3), 329.

Yosso, T., Smith, W., Ceja, M., & Solórzano, D. (2009). Critical race theory, racial microaggressions, and campus racial climate for Latina/o undergraduates. *Harvard Educational Review, 79*(4), 659–691.

Module 6

INTRODUCTION TO PRIVILEGE

The more privilege you have, the more opportunity you have. The more opportunity you have, the more responsibility you have.

—Noam Chomsky

In this module, you are asked to critically examine aspects of your daily lives that you may consider normal or natural yet in fact are aspects of *unearned privilege*. Unearned privilege refers to the advantages that an individual receives by identifying with or being born into a specific group. For example, if you are Christian, your important holidays are broadly recognized in U.S. society and affirmed with time off from work. This is not always the case for people of other religious backgrounds. Please note as we go through this module that it is normal and appropriate if the content makes you feel a bit uncomfortable. As we grow in our self-awareness, we learn to see things in new ways—and we may not always like what we see. The good news is that by becoming more aware of ourselves and others, we are taking the first important step toward being more inclusive!

Essential Questions

- What is privilege, and why does it matter?
- Why is it so hard for some people to talk about privilege?
- How does privilege play out in our daily lives?
- What is the effect of privilege on individuals and society as a whole?
- How does privilege create obstacles to inclusion?
- What can we do about privilege, our own and other people's?

Key Points about Privilege

- Everyone has some forms of privilege; some have more than others.
- It's easy to recognize the privileges we do NOT have, but it can be quite difficult to see the ones we do have because they are often invisible to us.
- No blame, no shame. It's not your fault; all of us have been born into a system based on privilege that we did not create.
- Guilt is not productive. Taking action is!

- Privilege is NOT a zero-sum game. We can spread it around without losing anything.
- Conversations about privilege are often difficult but necessary.

Privilege is like being right-handed

Allen, B. J. (2010). *Difference matters: Communicating social identity.* Waveland Press.

© 2021, DEI 2.0 and its affiliates. All rights reserved.   MODULE 6.2

Privilege Self-Audit

First, make a list of your given identities, those you were born into. Then, write a + by those aspects of your identity that:

- + have little impact on daily life
- + do not cause you to feel unsafe in most circumstances
- + you have in common with the majority of people you work with
- + you have in common with people in the upper levels of our organization chart

	Write out your "given" identities.	Identities that get a +
nationality/country of citizenship		
age/generation		

socioeconomic status/social class		
ethnicity or race		
physical characteristics/ stature		
physical or mental disabilities		
religious or spiritual affiliation		
biological sex		
gender identity		
sexual orientation		
other aspects of your identity		

Privilege Checklists

You may want to read through all of these checklists, but as a starting point, read about the identities you identified with a + in the previous activity. For example, if you marked your physical ability status with a + because you do not have any physical disabilities that impact your life, read the "Able-Bodied Privilege Checklist."

Middle-Upper-Class Privilege Checklist: Socioeconomic class is a topic that often gets glossed over but has a significant impact on people's experience in society and in the university where middle-class norms are dominant. If you are a member of the middle-class or upper-class economic group (or, in some cases, perceived to be) listed below are benefits that may be granted to you based on your group membership—benefits not granted to folks in the lower classes.

The goal of the list is to help folks who have access to these privileges be more cognizant of their privilege, in an effort to foster a better understanding of class-based difference in our society.

1. Politicians pay attention to your class and fight for your vote in election seasons.
2. You can advocate for your class to politicians and not have to worry about being seen as looking for a handout.
3. You can readily find accurate (or noncaricatured) examples of members your class depicted in films, television, and other media.
4. New products are designed and marketed with your social class in mind.
5. If you see something advertised that you really want, you will buy it.
6. You can swear (or commit a crime) without people attributing it to the low morals of your class as a whole.
7. If you find yourself in a legally perilous situation, you can hire an attorney to ensure your case is heard justly.
8. You can talk with your mouth full and not have people attribute this to the uncivilized nature of your social class.
9. You can attend a "fancy" dinner without apprehension of doing something wrong or embarrassing the hosts.
10. You understand the difference between healthy and unhealthy food and can choose to eat healthy food if you wish.
11. You can walk around your neighborhood at night without legitimate concern for your safety.
12. In the case of medical emergency, you won't have to decide against visiting a doctor or the hospital due to economic reasons.
13. You have visited a doctor for a checkup.
14. Your eyesight, smile, and general health aren't inhibited by your income.
15. If you become sick, you can seek medical care immediately and not just "hope it goes away."
16. If you choose to wear hand-me-down or secondhand clothing, doing so won't be attributed to your social class and may actually be considered stylish.
17. You can update your wardrobe with new clothes to match current styles and trends.
18. As a kid, you were able to participate in sports and other extracurricular activities (field trips, clubs, etc.) with school friends.

19. As a kid, your friends' parents allowed your friends to play and sleep over at your house.

20. You don't have to worry that teachers or employers will treat you poorly or have negative expectations of you because of your class.

21. The schools you went to as a kid had updated textbooks, computers, and a solid faculty.

22. Growing up, college was an expectation of you (whether you chose to go or not), not a lofty dream.

23. Your decision to go or not to go to college wasn't based entirely on financial determinants.

24. People aren't surprised if they realize you are intelligent, hardworking, or honest.

25. An annual raise in pay at your job is measured in dollars, not cents.

26. You've likely never looked into a paycheck advance business (e.g., "Check Into Cash") and have definitely never used one.

27. You are never asked to speak for all members of your class.

28. When you've moved out of your home it has been voluntary and you had another home to move into.

29. It's your choice to own a reliable car or to choose other means of transportation.

30. Regardless of the season, you can count on being able to fall asleep in a room with a comfortable temperature.

31. When you flip a light switch in your house, you don't have to wonder if the light will come on (or if your utilities have been terminated).

32. People don't assume you've made an active choice to be in your social class but instead assume you're working to improve it.

33. The "dream" of a house, a healthy family, and a solid career isn't a dream at all but simply a plan.

34. People do not assume based on the dialect you grew up speaking that you are unintelligent or lazy.

35. When you choose to use variants of language (e.g., slang terms) people chalk them up to plasticity in the language (rather than assuming your particular dialectical variants deserve ridicule and punishment).

Killerman, S. (2020) *30+ Examples of middle-to-upper class privileges*. It's pronounced metrosexual. http://itspronouncedmetrosexual.com/2012/10/list-of-upperclass-privilege/

Christian Privilege Checklist: If you practice mainstream forms of Christianity, this list will help you understand how non-Christians may feel. It's not about shame. It's about understanding.

1. You can expect to have time off work to celebrate religious holidays.
2. Music and television programs pertaining to your religion's holidays are readily accessible.
3. It is easy to find stores that carry items that enable you to practice your faith and celebrate religious holidays.
4. You aren't pressured to celebrate holidays from another faith that may conflict with your religious values.
5. Holidays celebrating your faith are so widely supported you can often forget they are limited to your faith (e.g., wish someone a "Merry Christmas" or "Happy Easter" without considering their faith).
6. You can worship freely, without fear of violence or threats.
7. A bumper sticker supporting your religion won't likely lead to your car being vandalized.
8. You can practice your religious customs without being questioned, mocked, or inhibited.
9. If you are being tried in court, you can assume that the jury of "your peers" will share your faith and not hold that against you in weighing decisions.
10. When swearing an oath, you will place your hand on a religious scripture pertaining to your faith.
11. Positive references to your faith are seen dozens of times a day by everyone, regardless of their faith.
12. Politicians responsible for your governance are probably members of your faith.
13. Politicians can make decisions citing your faith without being labeled as heretics or extremists.
14. It is easy for you to find your faith accurately depicted in television, movies, books, and other media.
15. You can reasonably assume that anyone you encounter will have a decent understanding of your beliefs.
16. You will not be penalized (socially or otherwise) for not knowing other people's religious customs.

17. Your faith is accepted/supported at your workplace.

18. You can go into any career you want without it being associated with or explained by your faith.

19. You can travel to any part of the country and know your religion will be accepted and safe and that you will have access to religious spaces to practice your faith.

20. Your faith can be an aspect of your identity without being a defining aspect (e.g., people won't think of you as their "Christian" friend).

21. You can be polite, gentle, or peaceful and not be considered an "exception" to those practicing your faith.

22. Fundraising to support congregations of your faith will not be investigated as potentially threatening or terrorist behavior.

23. Construction of spaces of worship will not likely be halted due to your faith.

24. You are never asked to speak on behalf of all the members of your faith.

25. You can go anywhere and assume you will be surrounded by members of your faith.

26. Without special effort, your children will have a multitude of teachers who share your faith.

27. Without special effort, your children will have a multitude of friends who share your faith.

28. It is easily accessible for you or your children to be educated from kindergarten through post-grad at institutions of your faith.

29. Disclosing your faith to an adoption agency will not likely prevent you from being able to adopt children.

30. In the event of a divorce, the judge won't immediately grant custody of your children to your ex because of your faith.

Killerman, S. (2020) *30+ Examples of Christian privileges*. It's pronounced metrosexual. http://itspronouncedmetrosexual.com/2012/05/list-of-examples-of-christian-privileg/

White Privilege Checklist: Peggy McIntosh was one of the first social justice educators to publish a White Privilege Checklist back in 1989. Her original list is still one of the most widely cited and utilized lists. However, McIntosh specifies that her list was based on the context of her experience, and she encourages White people to do their own self-reflection and create their own lists. The following list was created in 2021 by Dr. Marlo Goldstein Hode, another White woman and social justice educator.

1. I am rarely (if ever) the only person of my race in a meeting, event, or restaurant.
2. Most of the people in my organization are the same race as me.
3. If a sales associate asks me if I need help in a store, I know that they are not asking because they are suspicious of me because of my race.
4. If I am denied a loan, I am sure that it is not due to my race.
5. If I want to buy a house, I am confident that the sellers will not deny my offer because of my race.
6. I can easily find a place to live in a neighborhood where many people of my race live and that has easy access to grocery stores, banks, and a variety of shops.
7. If I am asked for ID when I write a check or use a credit card, I am confident that I am not being singled out because of my race.
8. If I call the police for assistance, I do not fear that I will be beaten or shot.
9. If I get pulled over by the police, I do not fear that I will be beaten or shot.
10. I do not have to teach my children how to make themselves small when they talk to police.
11. If I go to the doctor in pain, I am confident that the medication and care that I receive will not be impacted by my race.
12. If I make a mistake, do not perform well, or am late to meeting, I do not worry that my actions will be attributed to my race.
13. The historic figures that I have been taught to admire are mostly of my race.
14. When I watch a television or awards show, people of my race are widely represented among the nominees and winners.
15. I can buy a wide variety of books and toys for children that are representative of children of their race.
16. No matter where I am in the country, I never have trouble finding hair care products or hair salons that are suitable for my hair.
17. I do not have to straighten or cut my hair short to be viewed as professional.
18. I do not have to alter the way I talk to be viewed as professional.
19. If I get pulled aside by TSA for extra screening, I am sure that I am not being racially profiled.

20. I have never been told that I am exceptional for someone of my race.

21. I can speak up about injustice or racism without being told that I am overacting.

22. I can take a job with an affirmative action employer without my coworkers suspecting that I was hired because of my race.

23. When I drive through rural America, I do not fear stopping at a gas station or hotel because the people might be hostile to people of my race.

24. When I read about racial disparities related to income, healthcare, criminal justice, my race is doing better than the others.

Able-Bodied Privilege Checklist: This list is meant to generate awareness of "ableism" (along the lines of sexism, and racism). If you do not have a physical or visible disability, then the following is a list of privileges that you may enjoy without being aware that people with disabilities often do not have these same benefits.

1. I can, if I wish, arrange to attend social events without worrying if they are physically accessible to me.

2. If I am in the company of people that make me uncomfortable, I can easily choose to move elsewhere.

3. I can easily find housing that is accessible to me, with no barriers to my mobility.

4. I can go shopping alone most of the time and be able to reach and obtain all of the items without assistance, know that cashiers will notice I am there, and can easily see and use the credit card machines. I also don't have to worry about finding a dressing room I can use, or that the one that is accessible to me is being used as a storage room.

5. I can turn on the television and see people of my ability level widely and accurately represented.

6. I am not called upon to speak as the token person for people of my mobility level.

7. I can advocate for my children in their schools without my ability level being blamed for my children's performance or behavior.

8. I can do well in a challenging situation without being told what an inspiration I am.

9. If I ask to speak to someone "in charge," I can be relatively assured that the person will speak directly to me and treat me like I know what I'm talking about.

10. I can belong to an organization/class/workplace and not feel that others resent my membership because of my ability level.

11. I do not have to fear being assaulted because of my ability level. If am abused by a partner I will have a safe place to go if I wish to leave.

12. I can be reasonably assured that I won't be late for meetings due to mobility barriers.

13. As I grow up from childhood I will not feel that my body is inferior or undesirable, and that it should be "fixed," allowing me to feel confident in my current and future relationships.

14. When speaking with medical professionals, I can expect them to understand how my body works, to answer my questions, and respect my decisions.

15. My neighborhood allows me to move about on sidewalks, into stores, and into friends' homes without difficulty.

16. People do not tell me that my ability level means I should not have children. They will be happy for me when I become pregnant, and I can easily find supportive medical professionals and parents like me.

17. I can be reasonably sure that my ability level will not discourage employers from hiring me.

18. I know that my income can increase based on my performance, and I can seek new and better employment if I choose; I do not have to face a court battle to get an increase in my income.

19. I can choose to share my life with someone without it being seen as a disadvantage to them.

20. If people like me have been discriminated against in history, I can expect to learn about it in school, and how that discrimination was overcome.

21. All people like me are seen as living lives that are worth living.

Graham, M. (2009) *The invisible backpack of able-bodied privilege checklist*. Sit down, fight back. https://melissagraham.ca/2009/10/12/the-invisible-back pack-of-able-bodied-privilege-checklist/

Male Privilege Checklist: If you identify as a man, there are a bunch of unearned benefits you get that folks with other genders do not. And there's a good chance you've never thought about these things. Try to be more cognizant of these privileges in your daily life, and you'll understand how much work we have to do in order to make a society that is equitable to all people, of all genders.

1. If you have a bad day or are in a bad mood, people aren't going to blame it on your gender.
2. You can be careless with your money and not have people blame it on your gender.
3. You can be a careless driver and not have people blame it on your gender.
4. You can be confident that your coworkers won't assume you were hired because of your gender.
5. If you are never promoted, it isn't because of your gender.
6. You can expect to be paid equitably for the work you do and not paid less because of your gender.
7. If you are unable to succeed in your career, that won't be seen as evidence against your gender in the workplace.
8. A decision to hire you won't be based on whether the employer assumes you will be having children in the near future.
9. You can generally work comfortably (or walk down a public street) without the fear of sexual harassment.
10. You can generally walk alone at night without the fear of being raped or otherwise harmed.
11. You can go on a date with a stranger without the fear of being raped.
12. You can dress how you want and not worry it will be used as a defense if you are raped.
13. If you are straight, you are not likely to be abused by your partner nor be told to continue living in an abusive household for your children.
14. You can decide not to have children and not have your masculinity questioned.
15. If you stay at home, society will praise you for caring for your children instead of expecting you to be the full-time caretaker.
16. You can balance a career and a family without being called selfish for not staying at home (or being constantly pressured to stay at home).
17. If you are straight and decide to have children with your partner, you can assume this will not affect your career.
18. If you rise to prominence in an organization/role, no one will assume it is because you slept your way to the top.

19. You can seek political office without having your gender be a part of your platform.
20. You can seek political office without fear of your relationship with your children, or whom you hire to take care of them, being scrutinized by the press.
21. Most political representatives share your gender, particularly the higher-ups.
22. Your political officials fight for issues that pertain to your gender, or at least don't dismiss your issues as "special interest."
23. You can ask for the "person in charge" and will more likely be greeted by a member of your gender.
24. As a child, you were able to find plenty of non-limiting, non-gender-role-stereotyped media to view.
25. You can disregard your appearance without worrying about being criticized at work or in social situations.
26. You can spend time on your appearance without being criticized for upholding unhealthy gender norms.
27. If you're not conventionally attractive (or in shape), you don't have to worry as much about it negatively affecting your social or career potential.
28. You're not expected to spend excessive amounts of money on grooming, style, and appearance to fit in, while making less money.
29. You can have promiscuous sex and be viewed positively for it.
30. You can go to a car dealership or mechanic and assume you'll get a fair deal and not be taken advantage of.
31. Colloquial phrases and conventional language reflect your gender (e.g., mailman, "all men are created equal").
32. Every major religion in the world is led by individuals of your gender.
33. You can practice religion without subjugating yourself or thinking of yourself as less because of your gender.
34. You are unlikely to be interrupted in conversations because of your gender.

Killerman, S. (2020) *30+ Examples of male privileges*. It's pronounced metrosexual. http://itspronouncedmetrosexual.com/2012/11/30-examples-of-male-privilege/

Heterosexual (aka Straight) Privilege Checklist: If you do not know any people who identify as gay or lesbian, then many of these "privileges" might be new to you. If you are straight, these are unearned benefits you receive as a result of the sexuality you were born with. If you are straight (or in some cases, perceived to be), you can live without ever having to think twice, face, confront, engage, or cope with anything listed below. These privileges are granted to you, and many of them are things you've likely taken for granted.

1. Receiving public recognition and support for an intimate relationship.
2. Expressing affection in most social situations and not expecting hostile or violent reactions from others.
3. Living with your partner openly.
4. Expressing pain when a relationship ends from death or separation and receiving support from others.
5. Receiving social acceptance from neighbors, colleagues, and good friends.
6. Learning about romance and relationships from fictional movies and television shows.
7. Having role models of your gender and sexual orientation.
8. Having positive and accurate media images of people with whom you can identify.
9. Expecting to be around others of your sexuality most of the time. Not worrying about being the only one of your sexuality in a class, on a job, or in a social situation.
10. Talking openly about your relationship, vacations, and family planning you and your lover/partner are doing.
11. Easily finding a neighborhood in which residents will accept how you have constituted your household.
12. Raising, adopting, and teaching children without people believing that you will molest them or force them into your sexuality.
13. Working in a job dominated by people of your gender, but not feeling as though you are a representative/spokesperson for your sexuality.
14. Receiving paid leave from employment when grieving the death of your spouse.
15. Assuming strangers won't ask, "How does sex work for you?" or other too-personal questions.
16. Sharing health, auto, and homeowners' insurance policies at reduced rates.
17. Not having to hide or lie about women- or men-only social activities.

18. Acting, dressing, or talking as you choose without it being a reflection on people of your sexuality.

19. Freely teaching about lesbians, gay men, and bisexuals without being seen as having a bias because of your sexuality or forcing your "homosexual agenda" on students.

20. Having property laws work in your favor, filing joint tax returns, and automatically inheriting from your spouse under probate laws.

21. Sharing joint child custody.

22. Going wherever you wish knowing that you will not be harassed, beaten, or killed because of your sexuality.

23. Not worrying about being mistreated by the police nor victimized by the criminal justice system because of your sexuality.

24. Being granted immediate access to your loved one in case of accident or emergency.

25. Knowing that your basic civil rights will not be denied or outlawed because some people disapprove of your sexuality.

26. Expecting that your children will be given texts in school that support your kind of family unit and will not be taught that your sexuality is a "perversion."

27. Freely expressing your sexuality without fear of being prosecuted for breaking the law.

28. Belonging to the religious denomination of your choice and knowing that your sexuality will not be denounced by its religious leaders.

29. Knowing that you will not be fired from a job nor denied a promotion based on your sexuality.

30. Not being asked by your child's school to only send one parent to back-to-school night so as not to upset the other parents by having same-sex partners in the class together.

31. Playing a professional sport and not worrying that your athletic ability will be overshadowed by your sexuality and the fact that you share a locker room with the same gender.

32. Not having to worry about being evicted if your landlord finds out about your sexuality.

33. Not having to "come out" (explain to people that you're straight, as they will most likely assume it).

34. Knowing that people aren't going to mutter about your sexuality behind your back.

35. Knowing that being open with your sexuality isn't going to change how people view you.

36. Being able to live anywhere in the world and find people like yourself, unlike gay people, who are limited geographically. (Even if the people in more rural areas aren't homophobic, living in a low-density population means increased social isolation, and a smaller dating pool, for queer folks. Even among urban areas, there are only a few cities in the world, relatively speaking, where gay people can live openly and without too much fear.)

37. Being able to have your partner from a different country obtain citizenship in your country through marriage.

38. Not having people think your sexuality is a mental health problem.

39. Not having to think about whether your kid's friend's parents will flip out when they pick their kid up from a play date and are greeted by you and your partner.

40. Not having to worry that people won't let their children play with your children because of your sexuality.

41. Not having to worry about where you can move, alone or with your spouse, and have equal job opportunities abroad.

42. Being able to move abroad with your children without sudden changes of your legal status and the possibly of even losing your children.

Killerman, S. (2020) *30+ Examples of heterosexual privileges*. It's pronounced metrosexual. http://itspronouncedmetrosexual.com/2012/01/29-examples -of-heterosexual-privilege/

Cisgender Privilege Checklist: This list provides some insights into the daily experience of transgender individuals. If you are cisgender, listed below are benefits that result from your alignment of identity and perceived identity. If you are cisgender, there's a good chance you've never thought about these things (or even your cisgender identity). Try to be more cognizant, and you'll start to realize how much work we cisgender persons have to do in order to make things better for the transgender folks, who don't have access to these privileges. It might be helpful to learn or enhance your understanding of some of the terminology before proceeding. This website provides an excellent summary of this complex topic: http://itspronouncedmetrosexual.com/2011/11/break ing-through-the-binary-gender-explained-using-continuums/.

1. You can use public restrooms without fear of verbal abuse, physical intimidation, or arrest.

2. You can use public facilities such as gym locker rooms and store changing rooms without stares, fear, or anxiety.

3. Strangers don't assume they can ask you what your genitals look like and how you have sex.

4. Your validity as a man/woman/human is not based on how much surgery you've had or how well you "pass" as non-transgender.

5. You can walk through the world and generally blend in, not being constantly stared or gawked at, whispered about, pointed at, or laughed at because of your gender expression.

6. You can access gender-exclusive spaces (e.g., a space or activity for women), and not be excluded due to your trans status.

7. Strangers call you by the name you provide and don't ask what your "real name" (birth name) is and then assume that they have a right to call you by that name.

8. You can reasonably assume that your ability to acquire a job, rent an apartment, or secure a loan will not be denied on the basis of your gender identity/expression.

9. You can flirt, engage in courtship, or form a relationship and not fear that your biological status may be cause for rejection or attack, nor will it cause your partner to question their sexual orientation.

10. If you end up in the emergency room, you do not have to worry that your gender will keep you from receiving appropriate treatment or that all of your medical issues will be seen as a result of your gender.

11. Your identity was not formally (until 2013) considered a mental pathology ("gender identity disorder" in the DSM IV) by the psychological and medical establishments, and still pathologized by the public.

12. You don't need to worry about being placed in a sex-segregated detention center, holding facility, jail, or prison that is incongruent with your identity.

13. You don't have to worry about being profiled on the street as a sex worker because of your gender expression.

14. You are not required to undergo an extensive psychological evaluation in order to receive basic medical care.

15. You do not have to defend your right to be a part of "queer" (or the queer community), and gays and lesbians will not try to exclude you from "their" equal

rights movement because of your gender identity (or any equality movement, including feminist rights).

16. If you are murdered (or have any crime committed against you), your gender expression will not be used as a justification for your murder ("gay panic"), nor as a reason to coddle the perpetrators.

17. You can easily find role models and mentors to emulate who share your identity.

18. Hollywood accurately depicts people of your gender in films and television, without tokenizing your identity as the focus of a dramatic storyline or the punchline of a joke.

19. You can assume that everyone you encounter will understand your identity and will not think you're confused, misled, or hell-bound when you reveal it to them.

20. You can purchase clothes that match your gender identity without being refused service, mocked by staff, or questioned about your genitals.

21. You can purchase shoes that fit your gender expression without having to order them in special sizes or asking someone to custom-make them.

22. No stranger checking your identification or driver's license will ever insult or glare at you because your name or sex does not match the sex they believed you to be based on your gender expression.

23. You can reasonably assume that you will not be denied services at a hospital, bank, or other institution because the staff does not believe the gender marker on your ID card matches your gender identity.

24. Your gender is one of the options listed on a form you are asked to complete.

25. You can tick a box on a form without someone disagreeing and telling you not to lie.

26. You don't have to fear interactions with police officers due to your gender identity.

27. You can go places with friends on a whim knowing there will be bathrooms at your destination that you can use without a hassle, or worse.

28. You don't have to convince your parents of your true gender and/or have to earn their and the rest of your family's members' love and respect all over again because of your gender identity.

29. You don't have to remind your extended family over and over to use your correct gender pronouns (e.g., after transitioning).

30. You don't have to deal with old photographs that do not reflect who you truly are.

31. If you're intimate with someone, you know they aren't just looking to satisfy a curiosity or kink pertaining to your gender identity (e.g., the "novelty" of having sex with a trans person).

32. You can pretend that anatomy and gender are irrevocably entwined when having the "boy parts and girl parts" talk with children, instead of having to explain the actual complexity of the issue.

Killerman, S. (2020) *30+ Examples of cis-gender privileges*. It's pronounced metro sexual. http://itspronouncedmetrosexual.com/2011/11/list-of-cisgender-privileges/

U.S. Citizenship Privilege Checklist: This is something that most of us do not have to think about but that impacts many of our neighbors, clients, coworkers, and students. These privileges may resonate with you to various degrees depending on your identities, life experiences, and where you hold societal power.

1. Most if not all of the time I am able to surround myself with people who share a common or collective history, who understand the norms of U.S. society, who speak the same language that I do, and who understand my culture.

2. I am not worried on a daily basis about being "discovered" and deported along with, or away from, my family.

3. I don't have to worry that a small misstep could lead to my deportation, even if I currently have legal papers to be in the U.S.

4. I can apply for a passport that will allow me to travel back and forth to most other countries in the world.

5. I can think nothing of crossing the border to visit Tijuana, Mexico, for a day of shopping and sightseeing, while Mexican citizens must qualify economically to obtain even a tourist visa to enter the United States, and there are a great many who do not qualify.

6. If I want to get a driver's license, it's a simple matter of bringing along my birth certificate, social security card, insurance card, and taking the test. There's no need to worry about whether I have the proper documents required to get a driver's license.

7. If I apply for a job, I do not have to worry about what to write under "Social Security Number."

8. When Social Security and Medicare are taken out of my paycheck, I have a reasonable hope that someday either my dependents or I will receive the benefit of those taxes.

9. I can go into any bank and set up a checking account without fear of discrimination, thus knowing my money is safer than it would be on my person or elsewhere.

10. If a police officer pulls me over, I can be sure I haven't been singled out because of my perceived immigration status.

11. I can be reasonably sure that if I need legal, medical advice, or other kinds of professional assistance, my citizenship status will not be a possible hindrance to me receiving the service.

12. I can vote in any election on propositions and referenda and or for people who will make laws affecting my way of life and my community.

13. I may consider running for political office to serve my community.

14. I, or a member of my family, can apply for scholarship aid to the institutions of higher education that are supported by my family's tax dollars.

15. I have not been forced to ask myself what would compel me to risk my life to enter the United States Whether by crossing a barren desert for days without food or water, traveling over seas in the hull of an unsafe and ill-provisioned ship, or any other dangerous form of transport, I have not been forced to leave my family, my home, and my roots behind me to enter a country that not only feels hostile to me, but is also difficult to understand at times.

16. If am treated violently or inappropriately by a federal entity, I have some hope of legal recourse.

17. I can choose whether or not to take part in discussions surrounding how my lifestyle or the actions of my government have impacted the lives of those in other countries.

18. If I decide to organize politically or speak out about my country's unjust policies, I am likely to be addressing systems that I was raised around and understand. Also, those in power are more likely to listen to me and credit my arguments than those of a noncitizen.

Coloradans for Immigrant Rights (n.d.). *Citizenship privilege.* https://collective-liberation.org/wp-content/uploads/2013/01/Citizenship_Privilege_Ally_Basics_CFIR.pdf

Youth Privilege: Although young people (women in particular, perhaps) face biases and stereotypes in the workplace, older workers (also particularly women) face another set of issues related to age. This list provides some insight into privileges that younger people might not be aware of.

1. Others don't see you as a sexless being.
2. When speaking to you, others don't assume you are hard of hearing and raise their voice.
3. Your age demographic is proportionately represented in TV shows and movies.
4. You're not assumed to be technologically illiterate.
5. You're not the punch line for jokes because of how old you are.
6. You're not ascribed negative stereotypes like "geezer," "old fart," and Boomer.
7. You're not ascribed positive stereotypes like "grandmotherly" and "golden oldie," which can still be still hurtful even though they also have positive meanings.
8. People don't automatically assume you're slow or dim-witted.
9. People don't overlook you for job opportunities or advancement because they assume you won't be able to "keep up" or "get with the times."
10. People don't assume you're closed-minded and set in your ways.
11. Others don't think that everyone your age is exactly alike and shares the same interests.
12. Others don't automatically dismiss what you have to say as boring or outdated.
13. If you wear stylish clothing, people don't think it's weird or abnormal.
14. If you are outgoing, funny, like to dance, speak your mind, or basically do anything besides golf or play cards, others don't view it as strange or atypical for your age—and say, "Good for you!"
15. You're not seen as physically weak or feeble.
16. Others don't talk down to you, as if they're admonishing a disobedient child.
17. You don't have to worry about being the victim of elder abuse—the exploitation and mistreatment of older people by someone they trust or who cares for them.
18. Your consumer needs and purchasing power is not mostly ignored by advertisers.

19. Your overall appearance is considered culturally acceptable and is not ignored by the beauty/fashion/health industry.
20. You're not automatically assigned to one of two classes: the poor retiree relying on government funds or the rich, well-traveled, independent, and gracefully aging citizen.

Ridgway, S. (2013). *20+ examples of age privilege*. Everyday feminism. http://every dayfeminism.com/2013/01/20-examples-of-age-privilege/

Thin Privilege: Under the broader umbrella of "lookism," which is preferential treatment for those who embody the culturally dominant ideas about "ideal" body (weight, height, and attractiveness), this privilege checklist provides insight for people who are never judged or mistreated because of their body size. The following are examples of thin privilege that people who are seen by society as being physically "too big" experience regularly in their lives.

1. You're not assumed to be unhealthy just because of your size.
2. Your size is probably not the first thing people notice about you.
3. When you're at the grocery store, people don't comment on the food selection in your cart in the name of "trying to be helpful."
4. Your health insurance rates are not higher than everyone else's.
5. You can expect to pay reasonable prices for your clothing.
6. You can expect to find your clothing size sold locally.
7. You can expect to find clothing in the latest styles and colors instead of colorless, shapeless, and outdated styles meant to hide your body.
8. You don't receive suggestions from your friends and family to join Weight Watchers or any other weight-loss program.
9. When you go to the doctor, they don't suspect diabetes (or high blood pressure, high cholesterol, or other "weight-related" diagnoses) as the first/most likely diagnosis.
10. You don't get told, "You have such a pretty/handsome face" (implying: if only you'd lose weight you could be even more attractive).
11. People do not assume that you are lazy, based solely on your size.
12. You're not the brunt of jokes for countless numbers of comedians.
13. Airlines won't charge you extra to fly.

14. You are not perceived as looking sloppy or unprofessional based on your size.

15. You can eat what you want and when you want in public and not have others judge you for it or make assumptions about your eating habits.

16. You can walk out of a gas station with a box of doughnuts and not have people yell at you to "Better lay off them doughnuts!" or "Grab a salad."

17. People don't ask your partners what it's like to have sex with you because of your size.

18. Your body type isn't sexually fetishized.

19. You're more likely to get a raise or promotion at work than someone who is overweight.

20. Friends don't describe you to others using a qualifier, e.g., "But he's REALLY nice."

21. The media doesn't describe your body shape as part of a "national health crisis."

22. You can choose to not be preoccupied with your size and shape because you have other priorities, and don't fear being judged.

Ridgway, S. (2012). *22 examples of thin privilege*. Everyday feminism. https://everydayfeminism.com/2012/11/20-examples-of-thin-privilege/

Module 4: Reflection Questions	
What? What ideas, information, or concepts stood out to you?	

So what? What does the content in this module have to do with your everyday life?	
Now what? What changes or actions can you take to apply what you learned in this module to your everyday life?	
Example Action Items.	**Start the 21-Day Racial Equity Challenge**: You'll find many resources and ideas for staying engaged with these topics. https://debbyirving.com/21-day-challenge/

Module 6 References

Case, K. A., & Cole, E. (2013). Deconstructing privilege when students resist: The journey back into the community of engaged learners. In K. Case (Ed.), *Deconstructing privilege: Teaching and learning as allies in the classroom* (pp. 34–48). Rutledge.

Case, K. A., & Wise, T. (2013). Pedagogy for the privileged: Addressing inequality without shame or blame. In K. Case (Ed.), *Deconstructing privilege: Teaching and learning as allies in the classroom* (pp. 17–33). Rutledge.

McIntosh, P. (1989). *"White privilege: Unpacking the invisible knapsack" and "Some notes for facilitators."* National SEED Project. https://nationalseedproject. org/Key-SEED-Texts/white-privilege-unpacking-the-invisible-knapsack

Module 7

INCLUSIVE EXCELLENCE

A school that prepares students for academic and life success has a democratic, inclusive spirit. The spirit, or climate, of a school is greater than the sum of its parts.
—Maurice Elias, Psychology Professor

This module introduces an Inclusive Excellence framework (Smith, 2020), which is being implemented on many campuses to guide institutional efforts at integrating diversity and inclusion into all aspects of operations and functioning. In order for such a framework to be implemented, it is important that organizational members understand what it is and why it is important. To that end, the purpose of this module is to introduce the framework and allow you to explore how it relates to daily life on campus.

Essential Questions

- What does a diverse and inclusive campus environment have to do with institutional excellence?
- How does the work you do relate to inclusive excellence?
- What do diversity and inclusion currently look like on your campus and in your department?

Videos

"Diversity on Campus"

Tasks and Assignments

Diversity Audit Activity (3 parts)

Post and reply to Module 7 discussion by _____ .

Inclusive Excellence Framework

Access and Success — Policies, offices, and programs designed to increase underrepresented students and faculty access and success.

Education and Scholarship — Programs, classes, and training that engage students, faculty, and staff in varied perspectives of domestic and global diversity, inclusion, and social justice.

Climate and Intergroup Relations — Resources, offices, and programs that celebrate and educate about diversity and inclusion.

Institutional Infrastructure — Policies, departments, and programs designed to garner resources and manage information about diversity and inclusion.

Community Engagement — Programs and resources designed to provide leadership in inclusion, diversity, and equity in local communities, including increased outreach to historically underserved/diverse populations.

© 2021, DEI 2.0 and its affiliates. All rights reserved.   MODULE 7.1

Diversity Audit Part 1: Department/Unit Questions

1. As far as you know, what types of diversity do and don't exist among the people in your office, department, lab, or work unit?

2. In what ways does or doesn't the physical environment reflect inclusion? Who would likely feel most comfortable and welcome there? Who might feel less comfortable and welcome there?

3. Who is pictured, or most often pictured, in promotional or educational materials (electronic or paper)?

4. Are entrances, exits, water fountains, vending machines, classrooms, and bathrooms accessible for people with physical disabilities?

5. Do transgender people have access to bathrooms they can use without any concerns over harassment or safety?

6. Is there a designated place in where babies can be nursed?

7. Does your department celebrate holidays? If so, which ones, and how are they celebrated?

8. Are any non-Christian holidays celebrated or acknowledged? If so, how?

9. How often do you and your colleagues have discussions that center on diversity and inclusion (either formally or informally)?

10. How often do you hear comments or jokes that are potentially offensive to others, even if they were not intended to be?

11. How comfortable do you and your peers/colleagues feel voicing a different opinion or perspective than that of the majority in a meeting or class?

Diversity Audit Part 2: Campus Website

For this part of the audit, you are asked to do a keyword search on your university's homepage to discover the types of programs, offices, and resources that exist to support the different areas of inclusive excellence.

Start by typing the word *diversity* into the search box. This should yield several pages of results. As you review the listings, try to figure out to which of the five Inclusive Excellence areas each result relates. Keep track of your findings in the spaces below. You may find that certain results might fit into more than one area, which is expected because the areas are so closely interrelated that sometimes it can be hard to distinguish clearly one from another.

Areas of Inclusive Excellence	Diversity Audit Findings (list names or weblinks to office, programs, information)
Access & Success HINT: Try additional keyword searches such as "access AND underrepresented" or "programs for minority students" or "student success."	
Education & Scholarship HINT: Try keyword searches (diversity, multicultural, cultural, social justice) in your campus course catalog, research areas of faculty, and/or professional programs for faculty, staff, and students.	

Campus Climate & Intergroup Relations HINT: Try keyword searches related to specific identity groups (i.e., LGBTQ, international students, African American students) or programming designed to increase knowledge and awareness.	
Institutional Infrastructure HINT: Try searching for "diversity AND policy" or "diversity AND scholarship" or "diversity AND funding" or instead of "diversity" use specific identity groups.	

| **Community Engagement**

HINT: Try a search for "local communities" or "economic outreach." | |

Diversity Audit Part 3: Institutional Mission Statement

For the final part of this activity, you are asked to read your institution's mission statement. Often such statements include vision and values statements as well. As you read these guiding principles, think about how diversity and inclusion are integral to meeting your institution's mission, vision, and goals. You might also look at the strategic goals of your department. Write down keywords or phrases from the mission statement (as well as vision, values, and goals statements, if available) related to diversity and inclusion in general and the areas of inclusive excellence.

Notes:

Module 7: Reflection Questions

What?

What was the purpose of the module? What ideas, information, or concepts stood out to you?

So what?

How did your findings impact you or your understanding of diversity in relation to higher education?

Now what?	
What can you do to apply what you learned in this module?	
Example action items.	Consider implementing one or both of these action items to continue your learning from this module: **Start filling in the knowledge gaps.** It is likely that during the diversity audit activities, you encountered a topic or two with which you were not very knowledgeable. Choose one and start learning more about it! **Familiarize yourself with campus resources.** Take the time to visit and get information from some of the places you found in your diversity audit searches.

Module 7 References

Knowles, M. S., Holton, E., & Swanson, R. A. (2015). *The adult learner: The definitive classic in adult education and human resource development.* Butterworth-Heinemann.

Smith, D. G. (2020). *Diversity's promise for higher education: Making it work.* JHU Press.

INCLUSION IN ACTION

Inclusion is not a matter of political correctness. It is the key to growth.
—Reverend Jesse Jackson

Building a culture of inclusion involves our attitudes, our daily practices, and our language. The truth is that building an inclusive workplace and campus takes time and effort. It's not convenient or easy. Unfortunately, we can't just check a box and be done. Being inclusive is an ongoing work in progress. It requires a willingness to take a look at the way things have always been done, things that have seemed perfectly fine for a long time, and asking some important questions about why we might wish to change them.

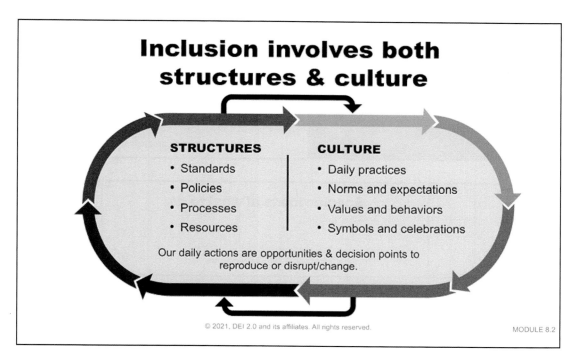

Inclusion involves both structures & culture

STRUCTURES
- Standards
- Policies
- Processes
- Resources

CULTURE
- Daily practices
- Norms and expectations
- Values and behaviors
- Symbols and celebrations

Our daily actions are opportunities & decision points to reproduce or disrupt/change.

© 2021, DEI 2.0 and its affiliates. All rights reserved.

MODULE 8.2

In this module, we'll explore three concepts for building a culture of inclusion: inclusive attitudes, inclusive practices, and inclusive language. And then you will be asked to create a personal action plan for inclusion, because this course is only beneficial if you apply what you've learned!

Learn more about and start using inclusive language. Which areas of inclusive language are less familiar to you? Start there!		

Module 8 References

Bandura, A. (1994). *Self-efficacy*. Wiley Online Library.

Combs, G. M., & Luthans, F. (2007). Diversity training: Analysis of the impact of self-efficacy. *Human Resource Development Quarterly, 18*(1), 91–120.

Cranton, P., & King, K. P. (2003). Transformative learning as a professional development goal. *New Directions for Adult and Continuing Education, 2003*(98), 31–38.

TOOLKIT RESOURCES

The following resources are available for download on the companion website: www.dei360consulting.com. The passcode to download the materials is **deitoolkit**.

Book Section	Downloadable Resource
	Participant Workbook
Building and Facilitating Diversity 101 for Faculty and Staff	Pre/post Test Surveys Annotated Diversity 101 Example Syllabus Example Course Calendar Summer Session Example Course Calendar Full Semester Discussion Forum Rubric (Summative Assessment) Group Project Description and Instructions for Students Organizational Changes Strategies (For Final Project) Final Project Description, Instructions to Students and Grading Rubric
Module 1	Example of Community Norms & Guidelines
Module 2	What is diversity? PowerPoint Slide Deck Why should I care about diversity? PowerPoint Slide Deck

Book Section	Downloadable Resource
Module 3	Diversity and Identities PowerPoint Slide Deck Identity Mapping Activity Worksheet
Module 4	Fast and Slow Thinking PowerPoint Slide Deck Who Does What? Worksheet
Module 5	The Little Things We Say PowerPoint Slide Deck
Module 6	Margins and Mainstreams PowerPoint Slide Deck Privilege Self-Audit and Check Lists
Module 7	Inclusive Excellence PowerPoint
Module 8	Building a Culture of Inclusion PowerPoint Slide Deck Action Planning Resources

ACKNOWLEDGMENTS

This is Marlo writing the acknowledgments, but I speak for both Darvelle and myself when I say how grateful we are to the entire publishing team of the University of Missouri Press for their enthusiasm and ongoing support for this *untraditional* project. We recognize and appreciate the leap of faith and creative spirit it took for an academic press to be open to a project that is completely different from their typical offerings. This would not have been made possible were it not for the leadership of the UM Press director, David Rosenbaum, who opened the door for this project after hearing a presentation I gave to campus leadership about the research findings of my DEI course. I happened to mention that I planned to turn the course content into a book, and David gave me his card and connected me to the editor in chief, Andrew Davidson.

Andrew has been a friend, a cheerleader, and an above-the-call-of-duty editor. His first step to tackling this unusual project was to sign up for the course himself. By participating in the course, he gained personal insights as well as a first-hand understanding of what we were trying to accomplish with our course and this book. The entire UM Press team has been phenomenally supportive and helpful with every step of this process.

I took a hiatus from working on the book when I took a new job with the Association for College and University Educators (ACUE). This slight break turned out to be great for the book because, under the brilliant tutelage of their chief academic officer, Dr. Penny MacCormack, I honed my online inclusive teaching knowledge and skills. The guidance for online course design and teaching provided in this book is founded on evidence-based best practices I learned while working with Penny and the amazing team at ACUE.

Darvelle and I are both extremely grateful to the Communication Department at the University of Missouri-Columbia, where we both earned our doctorates in the field of Organizational Communication. The theories we learned about social identities, raced and gendered power structures, privilege, stigma, sense-making, and so much more provided the backbone of the curriculum in this book. By undertaking this work as critical scholars, we were able to provide a nuanced and thoughtful approach to these important and complex topics. We also thank Dr. Pat Parker, a fellow Organizational Communication scholar, who offered insightful feedback on both early and later drafts.

The amazing graphics and design work of our PowerPoints, worksheets, website, and other resources are all credited to the multitalented artist and designer Rebecca Calvin. She took our vision and turned it into a reality of licensed images and customized graphics that you are now able to use in your own version of this course.

And, last but not least, I want to thank Darvelle, who graciously agreed to partner with me when I had completely run out of juice. His insights, enthusiasm, and hard work reignited my passion for the project and together we created this resource that will allow you to build a very effective and engaging learning journey. Our blood, sweat, tears, and love are embedded in every page of this book, and we hope you take it and make it your own.

About the Authors

Marlo Goldstein Hode, PhD, serves as the Senior Manager of Strategic Diversity Initiatives for the Office of Diversity, Equity, and Inclusion at the University of Missouri–St. Louis. She developed the first-of-its-kind online diversity course for faculty and staff at all four campuses of the University of Missouri System and holds a courtesy faculty position in the Department of Communications at UM–Columbia. She is the author of many peer-reviewed journal articles and book chapters and serves on the editorial board of the *Journal of Diversity in Higher Education.*

Darvelle Hutchins, PhD, serves as the Senior Director of Culture, Diversity, and Inclusion with the New Orleans Saints and New Orleans Pelicans. His research focuses on diversity, power, and stigmatized identities in organizational contexts and has been featured in multiple journals, books, and digital outlets, including the *Journal of Diversity in Higher Education, Organizing Inclusion: Moving Diversity from Demographics to Communication Processes* (Routledge), and the Association of College and University Educators' (ACUE's) inclusive teaching toolkit. Darvelle has designed and taught courses on organizational culture, communication, and diversity in academic settings, corporate workplaces, and the United States Armed Forces.